Designing Virtual Learning for Application & Impact

50 TECHNIQUES TO ENSURE RESULTS

CINDY HUGGETT, JACK J. PHILLIPS
PATRICIA PULLIAM PHILLIPS & EMMA WEBER

PRESS

Alexandria, VA

ATD Press is an internationally renowned source of insightful and practical information on talent development, training, and professional development.

ATD Press
1640 King Street
Alexandria, VA 22314 USA

Ordering information: Books published by ATD Press can be purchased by visiting ATD's website at td.org/books or by calling 800.628.2783 or 703.683.8100.

Library of Congress Control Number: 2022949750

ISBN-10: 1-953946-77-1
ISBN-13: 978-1-953946-77-5
e-ISBN: 978-1-953946-88-1

ATD Press Editorial Staff
Director: Sarah Halgas
Manager: Melissa Jones
Community Manager, Learning Technology: Alexandria Clapp
Text Designer: Shirley E.M. Raybuck
Cover Designers: Shirley E.M. Raybuck and Brandon Rush

Printed by BR Printers, San Jose, CA

Contents

Preface

There are many books on virtual learning and the design of virtual learning, and there are (probably too many) books on measurement and evaluation. So, what's different about this one? It's about designing virtual learning to deliver the ultimate accountability: impact and ROI.

The Need

We're sure you are familiar with the five levels of outcomes from any type of learning program. The first two levels, *reaction* and *learning*, are important to most organizations and are collected for almost every program. The third level is *application*, which reflects the use of the learning. This is where many organizations fall short with virtual learning. Application checks to see if the participants use the information they've learned, which is harder to do when participants are remote. The fourth level is *impact*, which is the consequence of application. The application is needed for a purpose and that purpose is to deliver an impact. Virtual learning is rarely measured at this level. The fifth level, *ROI*, asks, "Is it worth it?" Did the program provide more value to the organization than it cost? Again, virtual learning is rarely measured at this level, but sometimes it should be.

This book argues that a learning program needs to deliver impact, whether you measure it or not. Impact should be the focus and the desired success level. If you think impact isn't important, just ask the person who funds your program, "Would you like virtual learning to have an impact in the organization?" We're estimating that 95 percent will say yes. And, if you ask, "Would you like it to deliver more monetary benefits than it costs?" we think 80 percent or more will say yes. Monetary benefits come from the impact data. And if you want to end up with impact, you should begin with impact. Therefore, you're not just designing for learning—you're designing your virtual learning programs for application and impact. That is the focus of this book.

The Author Team

Our author team—Cindy Huggett, Emma Weber, and Jack and Patti Phillips—is perfect for this challenge. Cindy is a well-known expert and leading author in virtual learning, with more than 20 years' experience helping global organizations create effective and engaging virtual programs. She upskills instructional designers and facilitators on how to use virtual technologies. Emma is an international expert on the transfer of learning to the workplace, which is the critical focus of this book. She has created many tools, publications, and resources focused on learning transfer. Patti and Jack Phillips are leaders in the measurement field and have devoted nearly three decades to showing others how to evaluate programs to impact and ROI levels.

The Flow of the Book

This book is divided into three parts.

Part 1 sets the stage for success and introduces the entire concept of the book:

- **Chapter 1** presents the challenges and opportunities to delivering impact and ROI and provides some details about why this approach is necessary and actions you must take now.
- **Chapter 2** starts with why—a business need. It shows you how to make the business connection with your program. If you want to end with the impact, you start with the impact, which is the critical message in this chapter.
- **Chapter 3** involves making sure you have the right solution. Sometimes learning is not the right solution, or virtual learning is not the right way to do it. This chapter helps you determine whether learning is the solution and if virtual learning is the way to go.

Part 2 focuses on designing for results. This is the heart of this book, with six chapters focusing on designing for application and impact:

- **Chapter 4** focuses on how to bring the proper focus to the entire team, particularly with the use of objectives at different levels. We discuss how to create objectives for reaction, learning, application, and impact before the program is designed, developed, or implemented. Smart objectives make everyone's job much easier because you know where you are going, what participants are supposed to do, and when success will be achieved.
- **Chapter 5** focuses on steps you can take before the actual learning program (or module) is conducted. This is important because it sets expectations for participants and obtains commitment.

- **Chapter 6** presents actions to take during the program that will stimulate the participants' activities after the program. The participants must see the connection between what they are learning and what they need to do.
- **Chapter 7** examines the actions you can take after the learning module is completed. This chapter provides enabling processes that can make a big difference. These actions are designed in advance and implemented to support application—an important level of accountability.
- **Chapter 8** shows how you can use technology to enable the use of the content. This is a growing part of the transfer of learning literature.
- **Chapter 9** helps you sort through the techniques, selecting those techniques that work best for you. With more than 50 techniques to choose from and even more that you may have collected along the way, many options exist. Which ones are the best for you? This chapter helps you sort out an optimal approach.

Part 3 discusses the methodology to evaluate impact and ROI. These chapters show you how to collect and analyze the data and present and leverage the results.

- **Chapter 10** outlines how to collect data with the focus on application and impact. A variety of methods are available and explored in this chapter.
- **Chapter 11** is the most important from an organizational leader's perspective because it shows how the impact data is analyzed and ultimately prepared for the ROI calculation. It details how to isolate the effects of the program on the impact, convert data to money, capture the cost, and calculate the ROI.
- **Chapter 12** focuses on telling the story, which involves presenting the data to key stakeholders and leveraging results to help make the program better, enhancing funding for future programs, building more support and commitment, and satisfying all the stakeholders that made it happen.

Throughout this book the author team uses the terms *learning and development* and *talent development* interchangeably to reflect the continued evolution of the training field. You'll learn from their expertise and experience to gain a complete blueprint you can use to design virtual learning for application and impact.

PART 1
Setting the Stage for Success

Introduction:
The Challenges and
Opportunities

Despite the recent rise in popularity and mass adoption of virtual learning by global organizations, it isn't new. As early as the 1970s, a precursor to what we know today as virtual learning took place at Lockheed Georgia (now part of Lockheed Martin). Lockheed had a large team of about 15,000 engineers at that location and offered a master's degree in engineering for continuing professional development. The Georgia Institute of Technology conducted the program on campus in Atlanta, some 25 miles away. The program used telephone landlines and a special writing instrument that visually displayed the professor's writing on a screen at Lockheed. The professor was live, virtually conducting the session at Georgia Tech, and the participants could have a dialogue with the professor in a classroom at their facility.

In the early 2000s, virtual learning became more mainstream, and by 2019, about 14 percent of all formal learning took place in a virtual classroom.[1] Of course, in 2020, the COVID-19 pandemic brought virtual learning to the forefront of everyone's mind as organizations rapidly shifted facilitator-led learning to the online classroom. With this almost overnight change came new experiences, new technologies, and new expectations.

Showing the value of learning has also become increasingly important as leaders look for ways to trim budgets and increase productivity. While emphasizing the value and business results of organizational learning initiatives has always been important, it has risen to a crescendo thanks to the rapid growth of virtual learning, the rising expectations of top executives, and the increased availability of technology tools.

This book provides the master blueprint for designing virtual learning to deliver application and impact. It's based on our combined 125 years of experience and the proven methods we have used with clients around the globe. We'll walk you through, step-by-step, how to design your virtual learning programs to show value and demonstrate impact.

This book outlines a design process that focuses on delivering on-the-job application of learning and a positive impact on business results. In turn, this impact allows for return on investment (ROI) calculations, which are also important to many leaders. In this opening chapter, we'll describe the current situation, what caused it, and how we correct it. Then, the remaining chapters will explore tools and techniques you can implement immediately. The ability to design virtual learning for application and impact is an essential skill for all training professionals. This book will show you how.

Defining Virtual Learning

If you ask 20 people to define virtual learning, you will likely hear 20 different responses. Virtual learning could refer to any type of online training, including participating in a stand-alone e-learning program or watching educational videos posted to a website. Virtual learning could also be any type of online class, with or without interaction.

For the purposes of this book, we'll define *virtual learning* as:

> A synchronous, live online, facilitator-led training program with distinct learning objectives and a geographically dispersed audience. Each participant joins the online classroom individually, and once there they can connect, communicate, and collaborate.

Virtual learning may be a single online class, but it's often part of an overall training curriculum with multiple components. For example, participants start the program by meeting with a facilitator in a virtual classroom; then they complete a self-directed assignment before meeting again the next day or the next week. Our definition of virtual learning encompasses any facilitated live online training, with or without ancillary activities.

To be successful, virtual learning needs to be intentionally designed with interactions that lead to learning results, application, and impact. It needs a skilled facilitator who can engage a remote audience. And it needs seamless technology along with prepared participants. When done well, these items can create a powerful learning experience that delivers on business results. Unfortunately, many virtual learning programs have fallen short of these standards.

The Value Chain of Learning Outcomes

Virtual learning at its core is still learning. Therefore, it is helpful to think about a successful learning experience as a logical flow of data and understand that it occurs at different levels. And, depending on whose perspective you are concerned about, success can vary. Although there are many stakeholders, it is essential to understand the perceptions of those who *fund* virtual learning, *support* virtual learning, and *sponsor* virtual learning. What they need and want for virtual learning often differs from those who design it, create it, implement it, or use it.

So, let's take a closer look at the fundamental levels of learning outcomes.

Level 0: Input

It's easy to confuse input with outcomes. For example, when someone registers for a program, logs in to a virtual classroom, and participates in group activities, we capture these statistics and use them to show that the program was successful. We will call these individuals "participants" or "learners" throughout this book. The individuals were there, they participated, and they completed the program. However, this is data and it does not speak to outcomes—it just indicates that participants were present. It's a check-the-box mentality.

Measuring input is essential because you have to involve the right people, at the right time, with the right amount of content. Input measures can be placed into three main categories: volume, time, and costs (for example, the number of people, how long they were connected to the virtual platform, and the program cost). Knowing who is in attendance and how long they participate is important because it can affect the ultimate results. However, this still isn't outcome data—it is only input.

Level 1: Reaction

For years, we have used smile sheets to focus on how people react to our learning programs. We want participants to be happy, because when they are happy we believe that they make a program successful. Conversely, if participants are not happy, they will not participate.

But reaction alone does not get us to where we need to be, and some reactions are more critical than others. It may not be enough to simply ensure participants are happy and find the program to be enjoyable, entertaining, helpful, and engaging. You want their reactions to be powerful and predictive of use. For example, measures such as "this is relevant to my work," "this is important to my success," "this is something I will use," and "this is something I will recommend" are powerful reactions. But they are still only reactions. We need to measure learning, which influences reaction.

Level 2: Learning

At the heart of any learning program is whether participants acquired the necessary knowledge, skills, or both. After all, if learning doesn't occur, the program won't be successful. The amount of knowledge acquired influences the participants' reactions—the more they know, the more they will be able to do, and the better they will feel about their experience.

We often measure learning right after the participants have learned the material, which allows us to determine immediate knowledge gain. When creating virtual learning content, it's even more critical to capture knowledge gain, and perhaps even recheck it, to make sure that participants are able to retain the information. We want to capture the results, document them, and report them as soon as possible after the session ends.

Level 3: Application and Implementation

When people transfer and apply the knowledge gained from a learning program into their day-to-day role, it leads to behavior change. However, if participants don't use what they learn, the program is probably a waste of the organization's time and resources. Therefore, for programs the organization deems important, it is essential to track the data surrounding the use of the knowledge.

Use of content includes actions, activities, and behaviors, such as when participants use the technology, follow a process, or properly apply a procedure. Typical measures include extent of use, frequency of use, and success with use. We also want to capture the barriers to and enablers of use, which will help improve the program in the future. If barriers are removed or minimized, and the enablers are encouraged and embraced, participants will be more likely to use what they learn.

While this is important, application without impact is just being busy. It's also a concern for some organizational leaders, who often respond with "So what?" when our focus is solely trained on what people are doing. This leads us to the next level, impact.

Level 4: Impact

Impact is the consequence of application. Impact measures are the important organizational measures that are already established in the system, such as productivity, quality, and time. These measures cover so many areas; for example, quality includes mistakes, rework, waste, failures, incidents, accidents, unplanned absences, and regrettable turnover. There may be hundreds of these measures in an organization's system.

One faulty assumption of virtual learning is that it's not as effective as in-person programs. Yet virtual learning can connect to impact measures. Even a decade ago, Chad Udell suggested that mobile learning should be connected to many types of measures. Virtual learning can affect these measures as well:

- Decreased product returns and customer complaints
- Increased productivity and accuracy
- Fewer mistakes and incidents

- Increased sales
- Less waste
- Fewer compliance discrepancies and accidents
- Decreased defects
- Increased and on-time shipments
- Decreased cycle time and downtime
- Reduced operating cost
- Reduced response time to customers[2]

These measures generate the most important data set for the organizational leaders—as well as donors, supporters, and sponsors—who fund and support virtual learning. In 2009, some important research sponsored by ATD created a wake-up call for chief learning officers. This research involved data collected directly from Fortune 500 CEOs, and with a tremendous amount of data collection effort, 96 CEOs provided data. This research clearly showed that the data we are providing to CEOs is not something that they necessarily want, and we are not providing what they actually want. For example, 53 percent said that they see reaction data now, but only 22 percent said that they wanted it. The number 1 measure of importance was impact, and 96 percent said that they would like to see that, but only 8 percent see that now. ROI was the second most important measure, with 74 percent saying they would like to see it, but only 4 percent saying they receive it. This research sparked much focus and attention on changing the type of data that is collected and reported to senior executives.

A follow-up study conducted by *Chief Learning Officer* magazine six years later showed that 35.6 percent of learning and development organizations use business data to demonstrate the impact of learning and development on the broader enterprise, while 21.6 percent use ROI for that same purpose. More important, 71.2 percent said that they either were using ROI or planned to use ROI in the near future. It was surprising to see this turnaround.

Training magazine has been promoting the same concept with its audience, and it reports significant improvement. Each year when *Training* magazine selects its Training Top 125 Organizations, one of the main criteria is the extent to which the organization is showing results at the impact level; the ROI is a plus. This reinforces to its audience that the connection to the business is important. Each year *Training* magazine examines what is called the Top 10 Hall of Fame. These are the organizations that seem to always make that list, and it does a study to see what makes them so special. Its reports are permeated with comments about their value. For example, a recent report began with this statement: "Ultimately, the success of any program is based on whether it improves business results." Another more recent report contained three ROI studies, where one was a forecasted ROI in advance of the program. The professional field is making progress, but there is still much room for improvement. Being able to show the impact of virtual learning is critical in today's uncertain economy and challenging environment.

When taken together, application and impact measures can show that virtual learning makes a difference. But because of their reliance on technology, many virtual learning programs require significant investments. So even if you can show that participants are using the knowledge and making an impact, some stakeholders will want to know if the program is worth it. This is a major concern for expensive problems and costly learning solutions in particular. Executives want to know—does the program produce enough benefits to pay for its costs? The next level, return on investment, provides this answer.

Level 5: Return on Investment (ROI)

Showing that the learning program's monetary benefits exceed its cost is necessary if anyone questions the worth of a program. Organizational leaders may wonder if there are other, less expensive ways to correct the problem. Determining a program's ROI allows the training department to show the efficient use of funds. This concept has been around for centuries, and we suggest calculating it two ways:

- Benefit-cost ratio
- Return on investment expressed as a percent

The ability to see the monetary benefits of a learning program presents the ultimate accountability for the use of the funds. Stakeholders need to see ROI when allocating budgets, considering costs, or funding new learning projects. Although showing ROI is not necessary for every organizational learning program, it's an essential level for some, especially virtual learning programs.

The Classic Logic Model

When these evaluation levels are arranged in a chain of value, we have what is depicted in Figure 1-1. This classic logic model forms the basis of most evaluation systems in the world. Originally developed in the 1800s, this evaluation framework was brought to the learning space by Raymond Katzell in the 1950s, and then popularized by Don Kirkpatrick in 1959 and 1960. The concept of ROI was introduced to the learning and development space in the 1970s, and the first book devoted to these levels, *Handbook of Training, Evaluation, and Measurement Methods*, was published in 1983.[3]

Figure 1-1. The Value Chain

	Level	Issue	Measures	Targets
This Is Easy Always measured	0	Inputs	Volume, Hours, Convenience, Cost	100%
This Is Easy Almost always measured	1	Reaction	*Relevance, Engaging, *Important, Useful, *New Content, *Intent to Use, *Recommend to Others	100%
Not Difficult Usually measured	2	Learning	Concepts, Trends, Facts, Contacts, Skills, Competencies	98%
Possible Often measured	3	Application	Use of Content, Frequency of Use, Success With Use, Barriers, Enablers	30%
Not So Difficult to Connect Sometimes measured	4	Impact	Productivity, Time, Quality, Costs, Image, Reputation, Engagement, Compliance	10%
Possible for Many Programs Rarely measured	5	ROI	Benefit-Cost Ratio or Return on Investment (expressed as a percent)	5%

*Can Predict

Executives Prefer

Must take a step to isolate the effects

*Best practice: Percent of programs evaluated at this level each year.

Few, if any, would dispute the rationale and logic behind this model. It presents a logical flow of data with each step acting as a prerequisite for the next. This framework is essential for understanding success in all learning programs.

What Stakeholders Value

It is helpful to remember that different people have different concerns about what makes a learning program successful. Facilitators often care about participant reaction scores. Managers want to know that their employees learned something new and can apply it on the job. Learners want to know that their time was spent well, especially when participating in virtual learning programs. Other stakeholders want to see impact; still others want to see ROI. All these perspectives are important.

Further, senior administrators and leaders want to see how the learning is connected to the impact. While reactions and learning are important, application and impact matter most. The impact shows why you are implementing the program. Therefore, this book focuses specifically on how to design virtual learning for application and impact.

The Current Status of Learning and Development Success

The COVID-19 pandemic forced organizations around the globe to convert in-person classes to virtual ones, requiring an accelerated design process. In many cases, programs that were in the physical classroom one week were in the virtual classroom the next.

Trainers were tossed into virtual classrooms without preparation, and learners were expected to keep up with the changes. While organizations with already established virtual learning programs fared better than those that were new to the modality, nearly all struggled with the sudden shift. And as a result, evaluation metrics and measures were often left by the wayside.

This abrupt movement highlighted an already challenging issue in learning and development: taking accountability for showing value. Despite some improvements in recent years, it's still a challenge. In an article celebrating 70 years of *TD* magazine, Paula Ketter wrote: "As we examined magazine issues published in the 1940s, we saw some of the same topics discussed then that are as relevant today. Proving training's worth has been a constant pain point for industry professionals and, seven decades later, we are finally seeing training gaining steam in organizations."[4] The issue is that while many learning and development professionals want to prove the value of their training programs, they lack progress in their ability to move up the value chain to Levels 3, 4, and 5.

In addition, surveys by ROI Institute show that this continues to be a huge problem. We typically survey our audiences of L&D professionals at the beginning of conference presentations and webinars by asking them for levels of agreement to five critical questions. They have provided some very candid answers, particularly when they knew the data was anonymous. Let's examine our research into these five perennially sticky issues, and how they create challenges to showing application and impact in virtual learning.

Learning Waste

The term *scrap learning* is used frequently in the L&D community to define the amount of learning that participants do not use. Someone has paid to provide learning content, and if participants don't use the information, then that money and time investment is wasted. What is surprising is the extent of the problem.

In response to our true/false survey question about learning waste over the years, we've continued to see a disappointing response:

> Most learning is wasted (not used) after the program is conducted.
> 78 percent of respondents said this is true.

This is very revealing—L&D professionals know that most participants are not using the knowledge they learn. Prior to the COVID-19 pandemic, we were slowly seeing responses to this question improve (more false than true). Unfortunately, once classroom programs switched to virtual learning, the number began to decline again.

Individuals working in the transfer of learning field address this issue all the time. As a profession, we must continue to explore ways to accelerate the needed improvement, particularly in the virtual learning space.

Are We Measuring the Right Thing?

When we ask practitioners how far up the value chain they measure success, we usually find that they are infrequently measuring in-person learning programs at Level 3, and rarely measuring virtual programs at that level. In addition, measuring to Level 4 is rare for the in-person programs and extremely rare for virtual learning.

However, as we have already noted, program sponsors, supporters, funders, and leaders want to see results measured at the impact level. This leads us to the next true/false question we ask L&D professionals:

> The learning outcome desired by executives is rarely measured in organizations.
> 89 percent of respondents said this was true.

This response is insightful and suggests that while practitioners know what should be measured for organizational leaders, they still don't do it. Is this because they don't know how to measure or connect to impact? Or is it because the impact is not something under their control? Or does it happen after the program, once participants are back in the job environment, where they don't have access to the data? Or maybe the learners simply aren't applying the new knowledge or skills.

There are many issues here, but the reality is that we are missing the mark with our stakeholders. Funders need to see the connection that learning and virtual learning programs have to business measures, and perhaps even the connection to ROI—showing the monetary benefits compared with the cost.

Do We Make a Difference?

Most people want to know that they are making a difference, and that their work matters. In the learning context, we make a difference in the organization by providing application and impact. This leads us to the next true/false question for L&D professionals:

> Most learning providers do not have data that shows they make a difference in the organization.
> 81 percent of respondents said this was true.

Again, this is very telling information—it appears that little or no data is being collected for application and impact. The critical point is that L&D professionals are essentially admitting that they don't have the data to show that they're making a difference in the organization. And if they can't show that they're making a difference, L&D could be perceived as irrelevant to the organization. The challenge is clear; more data is needed for application and impact. It could be that virtual teams are making a difference, but just don't have the data. The challenge is to measure along the value chain more frequently and make improvements along the way. If virtual learning is not perceived as making a difference, funding and support could be in jeopardy. This lack of information is risky in today's economic situation.

Are We a Cost or an Investment?

Here's a classic question often raised about any activity in an organization: "Is this activity a cost to the organization or an investment that yields a return on investment?"

The answer is vital because organizational leaders will support, protect, enhance, and fund activities they believe represent an investment. However, if they don't see your program as an investment and instead see it as a cost, they will control, reduce, minimize, freeze, or pause it—all the bad things that we all have experienced. When we explored this issue with L&D leaders, we asked them to indicate if the following was mostly true or mostly false:

> Most executives see learning as a cost and not an investment.
> 93 percent of respondents said this was true.

This number has always been high, and while it was improving prior to the COVID-19 pandemic, the switch to virtual learning has contributed to its rise again.

However, it is easy to see the remedy. L&D needs to be able to show organizational leaders that major programs are important to organizations and represent a significant investment by proving that the programs also have a good return on investment. This is possible by using the same formula a CFO would use to show the ROI for a building or other capital expenditure. We have to make more progress with this issue and change the perception.

Sometimes when executives talk about their L&D budget, they'll boast about the investment they are making in people. But privately, when it comes to funding the essentials, learning and development is often one of the first budgets to get cut. Companies do this because they don't clearly see that L&D is an investment. This dilemma can be solved by designing for application and impact.

Hard Skills vs. Soft Skills

Another interesting issue surfaces when comparing hard skills with soft skills. Hard skills programs deal with training around IT, technical training, job tasks, procedures, and other areas in STEM (science, technology, engineering, and mathematics). These hard skills are often perceived as critical to the organization and its forward progress.

Soft skills, on the other hand, are more interpersonal in nature, such as communication, team building, leadership, empathy, and empowerment. The mere fact that these skills are labeled "soft" shows the perception that they may be inferior, causing some to question their value. The last question we ask the L&D leaders shows how their top executives view this perception:

> Most executives see hard skills as more valuable than soft skills.
> 87 percent of respondents said this true.

When organizational leaders perceive soft skills as inferior, they are less likely to support training to enhance them. At the same time, leaders are the first to acknowledge that the best organizations in the world—the most admired, the most sustainable, the most innovative, and the great places to work—all excel in soft skills. And as advances and technology speed up, soft skills will become even more important for differentiating an organization's competitiveness and performance.

How does this affect virtual learning? At first, it was assumed that virtual learning would be best suited for learning hard skills. Many of the earliest virtual training programs were created to teach software and other IT-related skills. These topics were appropriate for the virtual classroom because much of the learning could be done on the job and was related to the work being done. In many organizations, soft skills programs were less likely to be in a virtual format.

However, when everything switched to virtual learning because of the pandemic, soft skills had to go virtual too. If organizational leaders begin to perceive these virtual soft skills programs as a cost, they will quickly cut them. So, it is vital to address this issue in two ways: Convince leaders that soft skills make a difference. And then convince them that virtual learning can deliver soft skills results.

So, there you have it. These are some of the biggest challenges for the learning and development industry. Now let's examine how these challenges are magnified with the virtual learning format.

Measuring Success in Virtual Learning (Why Virtual Learning Often Fails)

As we've seen in our survey results, along with additional anecdotal evidence, attempting to measure the success of virtual learning has not been as effective as measuring the success of in-person learning. There are four main reasons virtual learning seems to break down compared with in-person learning:

- Many training programs are designed for learning, not impact.
- Participants tend to multitask in virtual training.
- Manager support for virtual learning is missing.
- Virtual learning faces massive technology challenges.

Many Training Programs Are Designed for Learning, Not Impact

Developers and designers usually think their work is complete once learning occurs. In other words, their focus is on making sure that the participants have learned the knowledge and skills necessary to be successful. After all, when a participant leaves the program, they go back to their workspace, and that's where L&D's involvement with them ends—or so it seems.

Learning is needed—without it, the program fails. But it's not enough. Just because there is learning does not mean that there will be application.

> Designing virtual learning to deliver learning is a good strategy.
> Designing virtual learning to only deliver learning is a bad strategy.

In parallel studies of virtual learning and traditional classroom training, we found that in-person learning was more likely to be designed for application and impact. We're not entirely sure why this is, but we have come to some conclusions based on conversations with designers of both kinds of training:

- With in-person learning, the designer realizes the program will take participants away from their work for an extended period of time. In the designer's mind, this pushes the learning program into something of more importance. It has to be successful, and something participants will use. So, the designer is more likely to step up to the challenge and make sure the program delivers the results needed back on the job. When it comes to virtual learning, we've found that many designers get caught up in designing a slick online presentation and forget about the need to focus on application and impact.
- L&D professionals have been improving their ability to transfer learning to the job thanks to the continued presence of books and important references published by thought leaders and practitioners in the field. However, virtual design books and

resources tend to focus more heavily on the interaction and engagement side of virtual learning programs, and lack content on incorporating application and impact. (This is why we are writing this book.) If virtual designers only consult training references focused only on engagement, they'll miss out on this important aspect of creating a training program.

- Some virtual designers may think that participants will automatically be able to use their new knowledge back on the job. However, this logic fails to consider the many barriers that inhibit the use of the content. If virtual designers don't build in design elements that help participants overcome these obstacles, it will be harder for the learners to be successful.

- Some virtual instructional designers have also indicated that they might simply ignore application and impact if their client doesn't appear to want to spend time, effort, and resources on the issue. This is what happens when we fall prey to the misperception that virtual learning doesn't need the same design rigor required for in-person learning.

- Some virtual designers believe that application and impact are out of their control. With this mindset, they choose to focus on what they can control (what happens in the virtual learning program), and don't pay attention to what they can't (what happens on the job).

As W. Edwards Deming, a renowned quality guru, said, "Every system is perfectly designed to get the results it gets." If you design for learning, that is what you will get. If you design for application, you will get that. If you design for application and impact, you will get that. Therefore, the key is to design for impact, which then forces you to incorporate learning and application to reach the impact. After all, impact is the most desired measure of learning for organizational leaders, who want to see business results.

This book is an attempt to focus on just that issue—designing for application and impact—recognizing that many L&D professionals are already good at designing for learning.

Multitasking During Virtual Training

The most commonly cited virtual learning challenge is when participants don't pay attention.[5] The virtual environment allows them to hide behind their screens, only half paying attention to the program. Although learning providers, expert designers, and skilled facilitators continue to feverishly tackle this issue, rampant multitasking remains a huge challenge. We know from the research that multitasking inhibits learning. In fact, it is challenging to have serious learning in any kind of multitasking format.[6]

Remember, everything is connected. The chain of value (Figure 1-1) clearly shows how application is inhibited when learning is inhibited. And if application is inhibited, impact is inhibited. Finally, if impact is inhibited, the ROI will be negative.

The good news is, between the providers, designers, and facilitators, this is a problem that can be solved. There are many creative ways to enhance engagement and involvement while also enhancing learning. However, if this is not done well, the time it takes to ensure that people are having fun, being active, and staying engaged can also significantly reduce the amount of content that participants can learn. And while also true for an in-person program, this reduction in learning time becomes even more exaggerated for virtual learners. It takes exactly the right balance of activity, engagement, and learning for virtual learning programs to be successful. In this book you'll find a path for designing virtual learning for application and impact, as well as proven techniques to ensure learning occurs and participants are engaged and able to apply what they've learned on the job to deliver impact to the organization.

Missing Manager Support

Much of the literature available in the learning transfer field cites that the participant's manager is the most critical influencer after they have completed a learning program. As a general rule, when the manager supports the participant's knowledge gain by spending time with them and actively working to apply the learning, it will drive results. Conversely, if the manager doesn't actively support the learning, it won't be applied. The participant's manager must be an active part of the learning mix. We'll discuss what options are available to combat this situation in Part 2.

For practical reasons, managers are more likely to be involved when their direct report is participating in an in-person training program. After all, the person has to leave the work area (sometimes traveling to a completely different location) to participate in the program. Their absence, in turn, brings attention to the manager, who will likely want to be involved in setting expectations for the person's participation and learning in the program. The manager may also be more likely to follow up with the participant after they've completed the program.

In virtual learning, on the other hand, this support is not as common. Because the virtual learning participant typically remains sitting at their desk (rather than moving to a different location), working at their laptop, and (in some cases) multitasking and responding to email, the manager may not even be aware that they are taking a virtual program. Again, we'll explore some solutions for this issue in later chapters.

Massive Technology Challenges

Obviously, virtual learning breaks down when technology fails or gets in the way. A participant cannot effectively learn if they have to spend most of the class attempting to reconnect to the virtual platform. Choppy facilitator audio is distracting, as are virtual classroom tools that don't function as planned. These challenges can be a result of user error or lack of sufficient comfort with technology. Or they might stem from systemic issues, such as regional rolling power outages and poor internet connections that affect many parts of the globe.

The good news is that designers, developers, technology providers, and internet companies are working on these issues to make the situation better. More focus is still needed, but that is beyond the scope of what we will cover in this book.

What We Can Do About It

Here's a quick summary of what can we do to improve the current situation. How do we address the issues surrounding a learning program's ability to deliver results, which are exacerbated by the difficulties of virtual learning? There are four things we can and must do.

Create Support Systems Leading to Success

Many of us in the measurement and evaluation profession have suggested, encouraged, and supported the use of more measurement and evaluation. We have tackled this in many different ways and in many different media. But for many reasons, we have not been completely successful in helping L&D teams overcome obstacles that get in the way of measurement and evaluation. Although our premise was that when people measure at the business level, they also make adjustments and improve programs, we recognize that the challenge to accomplish this was too much.

Therefore, we now promote the addition of support systems to help. We are proposing to fix this system by tweaking what's been done and bringing in key concepts from other fields, with these important elements:

- A focus on designing for results throughout the process
- A logical, nine-step process flow
- Shared responsibilities along the way
- Tools, templates, and support throughout

Use Your Village

Virtual learning success, more so than other training modalities, relies on a village of enthusiastic supporters. Think about the different stakeholders involved in a program or project—Figure 1-2 represents those engaged in a virtual learning program. Although the job titles listed in the figure may not match every organization exactly, they each represent the key staff responsibilities involved in creating, designing, developing, implementing, delivering, and evaluating virtual learning.

Figure 1-2. Stakeholders Engaged in Virtual Learning Programs

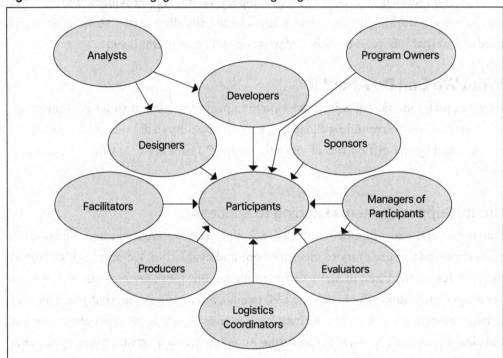

Remember, what's considered a success can vary, depending on each stakeholder's perspective. The designers and developers may define success when learning has occurred. The program owner may define success once the learning has occurred *and* the participants use the knowledge. Those who sponsor, support, or fund the program may want to see an impact on the organization before they determine it to be a success. Top executives, including the CFO, might like to know if the program is worth it and delivers more value than it costs. Even participants have different definitions of success—while some want the learning program to be interactive, exciting, challenging, and fun, more are asking, "Why am I here?" and "What am I supposed to do?" These questions suggest that a participant's idea of success is moving beyond the keyboard or smartphone.

The entire team—not just the evaluator—must be involved when determining the outcomes that define success. Every individual listed in the roles and responsibilities in Figure 1-2 must understand their role in designing for impact, not just learning. Yes, this takes additional time and effort, but it is worth it. And the consequences of failing to do this are worse—the lack of results will continue to be a problem.

Start With the End in Mind

As Stephen Covey taught us so well in *The 7 Habits of Highly Effective People,* we should begin with the end in mind. We have to realize that the end is not learning—learning is simply a means to an end. And it's also not application—application is another means to an end. The end is impact, which, if necessary, can continue to be evaluated through to ROI. If we first identify the desired impact, we can start with that, allowing everyone to clearly see what is needed and what they must do to be successful.

The first step in designing a virtual learning solution must be to establish a clear focus on the outcome. We must specifically define the end result in terms of business needs and measures, so that the outcome—the actual improvement in the measures—and the resulting ROI are clear. This provides the necessary focus for every step in the process. Beginning with the end in mind also involves pinpointing all the details to ensure proper planning and successful execution.

Focus on Impact

To start with the end in mind, the focus must be on the program's impact. By setting this expectation, stakeholders know that the job is not done until they can show that impact has occurred. This allows them to create all tools, processes, templates, job aids, support, encouragement, and assistance to ensure that individuals use what they have learned to have that impact. We no longer have the luxury of assuming that measuring learning is our only focus.

The process of connecting learning to a business need, including a specific business measure, represents a change in the learning and talent development field. Although it seems logical to start with "why?" so many programs actually start with a solution, followed by an effort to find the reason for the solution. Consequently, adjusting to first focus on "why?" will require changing the way programs are initiated to ensure that the connection exists prior to making an investment. Some people will resist the change, but it is necessary to ensure the delivery of business value. It is difficult to have a business contribution without beginning with the business measure.

Enter Design Thinking and a New Approach

To make the process of designing virtual learning systematic, feasible, and successful, we'll need to adopt a new way of thinking about how to design, deliver, and measure results. The innovation technique design thinking is well positioned for delivering value from a project and capturing the impact data.

Design thinking works on the assumption that when success is clearly defined, the entire team will design for that definition of success. If you want higher graduation rates, everyone works on that. If you want low costs, everyone is focused on that issue. If you want to reduce crime rates, the focus is there for every stakeholder. Success is achieved when the impact—low costs, higher graduation rates, less crime—has occurred. With that success defined, the team works through a series of steps, using design thinking principles to reach the desired success.

Although design thinking was initially introduced in 1987, it really gained popularity in Tim Brown's 2009 book, *Change by Design*.[7] Four years later, Idris Mootee's book, *Design Thinking for Strategic Innovation*, broadened the scope and flexibility of the process.[8] Although the principles of design thinking often vary from author to author, there are 10 that seem to be universal:

1. A problem-solving approach to handle problems on a systems level
2. A mindset for curiosity and inquiry
3. A framework to balance needs and feasibility
4. A way to take on design challenges by applying empathy
5. A culture that fosters exploration and experimentation
6. A fixed process and a toolkit
7. A storytelling process to inspire senior executives
8. A new competitive logic of business strategy
9. A means to solve complex or wicked problems
10. A means to reduce risks[9]

We have taken the first eight principles from this list and adapted them to our ROI Process Model to create a framework that ensures L&D designs virtual learning for results, captures that data, and makes the case for more investment.[10] Each step is fully described in Figure 1-3, and the design thinking principle used is highlighted.

Figure 1-3. Designing for Results

1. Start With Why: Aligning Programs With the Business
  • Alignment is the key
  • Is it a problem or an opportunity?
  • Need specific business measure(s)
	Design Thinking Principle:
	A problem solving approach
	to handle problems on a
	systems level

2. Make It Feasible: Selecting the Right Solution
  • What are we doing (or not doing) that's influencing the impact
    measure?
  • How can we achieve this performance?
	Design Thinking Principle:
	A mindset for curiosity
	and inquiry

3. Expect Success: Designing for Results
  • Set objectives at multiple levels
  • Define success
  • Expand responsibilities
	Design Thinking Principle:
	A framework to balance
	needs and feasibility

4. Make It Matter: Designing for Input, Reaction, and Learning
  • Focus on the objectives
  • Think about ROI
  • Make it relevant
  • Make it important
  • Make it action-oriented
  • Capture attention and interest
  • Create inclusiveness and collaboration
  • Keep engagement levels high
	Design Thinking Principle:
	A way to take on design
	challenges by
	applying empathy

5. Make It Stick: Designing for Application and Impact
  • Focus on objectives
  • Ensure transfer of learning
  • Design application tools
  • Collect data
	Design Thinking Principle:
	A culture that fosters
	exploration and
	experimentation

6. Make It Credible: Measuring Results and Calculating ROI
  • Isolating the effects of projects
  • Converting data to money
  • Tabulating Costs
  • Calculating ROI
	Design Thinking Principle:
	A fixed process
	and a toolkit

7. Tell the Story: Communicating Results to Key Stakeholders
  • Define audience
  • Identify why they need it
  • Select method
  • Move quickly
  • Consider one-page summary
	Design Thinking Principle:
	A storytelling process to
	inspire senior executives

8. Optimize Results: Using Black Box Thinking to Increase Funding
  • Measure
  • Improve
  • Fund
	Design Thinking Principle:
	A new competitive logic of
	business strategy

Adapted from Phillips and Phillips (2017).

The Virtual Learning Impact and ROI Process Model

To design engaging virtual learning that also demonstrates impact and ROI, it is important to follow the ROI Process Model to ensure consistent, reliable results. The rest of this
book will explore each step in more detail, but let's first review a few highlights related
to the end goal: impact and ROI.

Plan the Evaluation

Planning your impact ROI evaluation is not only an important first phase in the design
process; it is also an important step in the selection and development of virtual solutions. Without a plan it will be difficult for you to know where you are going, much less
when you arrive. Your plan begins by clarifying the business needs for a program and
ensuring the most feasible solution has been identified. The next step is to develop specific, measurable objectives and design the program around those objectives. This
includes selecting the right virtual learning solution, mapping out the activities that
lead to learning, and ensuring the program is designed for impact. From there, you
develop your data collection plan. This includes defining the measures for each level of
evaluation, selecting the data collection instrument, identifying the data source, and
determining the timing of data collection. Any available baseline data for the measures
you are taking should also be collected during this time.

Next, develop the ROI analysis plan. This means selecting the most appropriate technique to isolate the effects of the virtual learning program on impact data and the most
credible method for converting data to money. Cost categories and communication targets are also determined. In addition, as you develop these planning documents, you will
identify how to seamlessly integrate the evaluation approach into the virtual
learning program.

Collect Data

When the planning phase is completed, data collection begins. Levels 1 and 2 data are
collected during the virtual learning program with common instruments, including end-
of-course surveys, written tests and exercises, and demonstrations. Follow-up data (Levels 3 and 4) is collected sometime after the virtual learning program has ended, when
application of the newly acquired knowledge and skills becomes routine and enough
time has passed to observe impact on key measures. A point to remember is that if you
identified the measures to improve through initial analysis, you will measure the change
in performance in those same measures during the evaluation. It is feasible to believe
that your data collection methods during the evaluation could be the same as those used

during the needs analysis. This is one area where virtual learning adds benefits. You're already using technology to connect with participants, and most virtual classroom platforms include tools to help you collect and analyze the data.

Analyze Data

Once the data is available, analysis begins using the approach chosen during the planning stage. Now it's a matter of execution. Isolating the effects of the program on impact data is the first step in data analysis, and it's taken while collecting data at Level 4. Often overlooked when evaluating the success of virtual programs, this step answers the critical question, "How do you know it was your program that improved the measures?" While some will say this is difficult, we argue (and have argued for years) that it doesn't have to be. Besides, without this step, the results you report will lack credibility.

The move from Level 4 to Level 5 begins with converting Level 4: Impact measures to monetary value. This step often instills the greatest fear in talent development professionals, but when they understand the data conversion techniques, along with the five steps of how to do it, the fear usually subsides.

Fully loaded costs are developed during the data analysis phase. These costs include needs assessment (when conducted), design, delivery, and evaluation costs. The intent is to leave no associated cost unreported. Intangible benefits are also identified. These are the Level 4 measures that are not converted to monetary value. They can also represent any unplanned program benefits.

The last step of the data analysis phase is the math. Using simple addition, subtraction, multiplication, and division, you can calculate the ROI.

Optimize Results

Optimizing results is the most important phase in the evaluation process. Evaluation without communication and communication without action are worthless endeavors. If you tell no one how the program is progressing, how can you improve the learning and talent development process, secure additional funding, justify programs, or market programs to future participants?

There are a variety of ways to report data. For example, micro reports include the complete ROI impact study, while macro reports can be done for all programs and include scorecards, dashboards, and other reporting tools.

But communication must lead to action—and that action requires stepping back and analyzing what can be learned from the data. Black box thinking, which we'll explore in chapter 8, is required if you want to get value from your program evaluation investments.

The job of talent development professionals is not to "train" people, but to drive improvement in output, quality, cost, time, customer satisfaction, job satisfaction, work habits, and innovation. Doing this well means assessing, measuring, and evaluating and then taking action based on the findings. Figure 1-4 offers something to remember about the evaluation process.

Figure 1-4. Evaluation Leads to Allocation

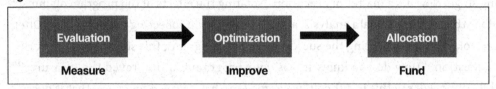

The ultimate use of data generated through the ROI Methodology is to show a virtual learning program's value, specifically its economic value. However, there are also a variety of other uses for the data, including to justify spending, improve the talent development process, and gain support.

Actions to Take to Design for Application and Impact

There are three main timeframes to consider when measuring transfer of learning to the workplace: things we do before the journey, things we do during the journey, and things we do after the journey is complete. When virtual learning is part of a series or blended curriculum, it may be harder to categorize a clear before, during, and after. If this is the case, we can think of it in three phases: the preparation phase (before), the learning phase (during), and the application phase (after).

Additionally, the transfer involves three main stakeholders: the manager of the participant, the participant, and the facilitator. Although all stakeholders—including designers, developers, producers, facilitators, logistics coordinators, program owners, sponsors, supporters, and analysts—have a role in the design of the program, these three will command the majority of our attention. Our approach is to involve all stakeholders to tackle the issue comprehensively.

Chapters 4–8 focus on designing for application and impact. These chapters comprise the heart of this book, first outlining how to design for impact and then branching out into specific actions you can take to effectively prepare for the learning program, engage virtual learners, and help learners apply the knowledge they've gained back on the job. We recognize that this is not a complete list, so we encourage you to explore, use, and share these techniques.

Why Is This Important . . . Now?

Before we wind down this chapter, it is helpful to remember the importance of designing virtual learning for application and impact. Virtual learning is at a tipping point, with improved technology and the expectation that it will continue to be a widely used format. But when budgets are slashed, showing that virtual learning is an investment rather than an expense is vital. Thus, we need a renewed sense of urgency to make sure virtual learning delivers results for those who support it, expect it, and even demand it. We need to be proactive in demonstrating value to the organization, and show that virtual learning is a viable solution.

Next Steps

This chapter highlighted the learning and development community's challenges in designing virtual learning to deliver application, impact, and even ROI. It also highlighted the opportunities that exist. When virtual learning is designed for application and impact, it helps L&D obtain support, respect, influence, and, yes, funding. With that backdrop, it is now time to start working through the ROI Process Model. The first step is to connect the virtual learning program to a business impact.

Start With Why: Align Virtual Learning With the Business

Financial services company Edward Jones was experiencing unusually high first-year turnover for branch office administrators. In total, the company had 16,000 branch office administrators whose training was largely self-directed and supported by a one-to-one relationship with a branch office administrator. However, some new hires indicated they felt isolated learning on their own and wanted more time to prepare for their new role before interacting with clients.

Based on this feedback, leadership was concerned that the new hire onboarding might be contributing to the high turnover rates. With this in mind, the company designed a new branch office onboarding process that consisted of a six-month online and virtual instructor-led training (VILT) program. The new process provided dedicated time for onboarding that incorporated flexibility to complement the branch office administrator's experience while meeting branch, region, and market needs. More than 60 experienced branch office administrators, as well as a few financial advisors and home office associates, co-created the content and participated in concept testing and piloting.[1] As a result of this program, first-year branch manager turnover decreased from 16.9 percent to 13.6 percent, the lowest ever for the branch office administrator attrition rate.

The key to the program's success lies in the fact that it started with the end in mind. The need for the new onboarding process focused on lowering the attrition rate. It is critical for new virtual programs to identify the business measure that needs to improve in the beginning. The new program provides the vehicle to make the improvement.

The First Step

Virtual learning programs have many origins. Some instructional designers will say the process begins with a request: Someone in the organization asks for a training program, and the designer responds by creating it. Other designers will say they have been tasked with converting an in-person classroom program to a virtual one because of changing organizational requirements. And still others will share their process for discovering needs and creating virtual learning solutions in response to what they find.

The genesis of each of these origin stories *should* be an organizational need for a virtual learning solution. Programs created on a whim, or simply at the request of someone who thinks training might help solve a problem, rarely lead to on-the-job application and impact. And programs that don't account for audience analysis or reasons to be virtual may simply be a waste of resources.

Sadly, many instructional designers assume that someone has already done an analysis when they receive a learning request, so they'll immediately start sketching out a desired design. That's like starting a presentation by crafting slides, instead of doing an audience analysis and determining the big idea. The better way to design a virtual learning program that ensures on-the-job application and business impact is to begin with the end in mind: to closely examine business needs and create corresponding solutions.

The need for designers to start with "why?" transcends all types of learning programs, yet it's especially important for virtual solutions. It's easy for virtual learning to be overlooked as a nice-to-have option instead of a business imperative. Virtual learning requires financial investments in technology that could be quickly pulled if it's not perceived as a value-add. When designers tie virtual learning solutions to business impact, they ensure contributions to the organization's bottom line. Therefore, the first design step is to align the program with impact.

Why Business Impact?

A fair question to ask is, "Why is success set at the impact level and not the lower levels?" In other words, why aren't we satisfied with measuring participant learning? After all, it's easy to assume that when learning occurs, success is achieved. Instructional designers focus on creating interactive and engaging virtual programs, which is important but not enough. There is more to virtual learning than that. Here are four specific reasons business impact is the desired level of success to be delivered with virtual learning.

It's Logical

As presented in chapter 1, the value chain represents a logical flow of the outcome data. It's reasonable to want to move down the value chain beyond reaction and learning. If there is no application after learning, then the program was pointless. Without application, there is no impact. And without impact, virtual learning is a total waste in terms of financial resources. So logically, it's important to push the success level beyond learning to ensure that application has occurred. Application without impact is just being busy.

It's the Ultimate "Why?" Question

When participants are invited to attend a virtual learning program, they have to pause their workday to log in to the online classroom. This can make the program seem like an interruption to their work, and participants may wonder why they are taking the program or where it fits among their many priorities. If participants aren't sure of the program's purpose, they are more likely to multitask throughout. However, if the program is well designed and focused on learning, application, and impact, participants will quickly realize that they are there for a purpose. It is not to just be entertained and enjoy the experience, and it's more than just learning for the sake of learning. They are there to do more: Whether it's to get better at a certain job task, to achieve efficiencies in their work, or to contribute to a key organizational goal, they have reason to place priority on the program.

When participants ask, "Why do I need to be doing this?" the answer leads to the consequence of doing something, and that's the impact. Thus the impact becomes the ultimate "Why?" question.

Organizational Leaders Want It

As presented in chapter 1, research continues to suggest that the top measure desired by organizational leaders from the learning and talent development area is business impact—the connection of programs to important business measures. The second most important measure is the financial ROI, which compares the monetary benefits of a particular program with its cost. The ATD-supported study provides the strongest evidence of executives' interest in these two measures.[2]

Supporters Want It

Finally, those who support the program want to see the business impact because they want to know that their work matters. For example, virtual facilitators, designers, and developers want to know that the time and effort they devoted to the learning program made a difference. The owners, who have a sense of responsibility for the program, want to see whether it made a difference. Remember, making a difference means you can show application and impact—not just knowledge gain. Because of this, those who support the process, even on the sidelines, want to see the program's impact. Without impact, there is not much of a story to tell.

Finally, the immediate managers of the participants need to see the impact because they are typically held accountable for their team's performance. Because the program's impact measures are often key performance indicators (KPIs) for the manager, it is in their best interest to see that impact. This fosters a sense of personal ownership and interest when the managers can see how the virtual learning program connects to something important to them.

Overall, there are many reasons business impact is the best measure for a virtual learning program, whether it occurs in a business or nonbusiness setting. Even nonprofit organizations, educational institutions, and government agencies have stakeholders who look for key performance indicators, financial stewardship, and organizational results. By ensuring programs are aligned to the business, L&D is more likely to be perceived as successful by all stakeholders.

Overcoming Objections

It's no secret achieving business impact requires investment of time and resources. In our experience, some organizations are more willing to make this investment. Others, however, assume a "just get it done" mentality, wanting to move quickly to get a learning solution out the door. They assume they know what's needed based on intuition or prior experience. Another common reaction is to resist change. Organizational leadership says, "It's not the way we've done it before, so why start now?" This may require a change in the way the training department accepts or responds to requests. Still other organizations and designers correctly recognize that not all learning solutions require an in-depth analysis. For example, required compliance programs and regulated safety training may be mandatory by law and therefore analysis is not as critical. But unfortunately, they apply that mentality to all programs.

Despite these objections, needs analysis does not have to be difficult. Simple techniques may uncover the cause of the problem or the need for a specific program. In most cases, it's worth the time and effort to design learning programs for application and impact.

The Alignment Framework

The first step in the virtual learning design process is to align with business needs. To understand alignment, it is helpful to review the framework shown in Figure 2-1.

Organization of the Alignment Framework

This chapter and the next explore the left side of the Alignment Model, beginning with payoff needs and business needs in this chapter. Performance needs, learning needs, and preferences are explored in chapter 3. The objectives derived directly from these needs are defined, making a strong case for having multiple levels of objectives that correspond with specific needs. Objectives are then covered in chapter 4. The right side of the model is essentially the measurement of success presented in chapters 9 and 10.

Figure 2-1. The Alignment Model

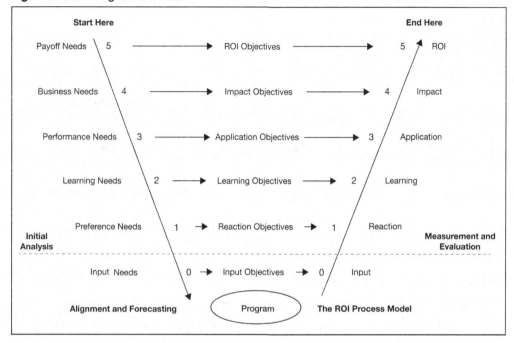

Payoff Needs

The Alignment Model begins in the upper left corner with payoff needs, which are opportunities for the organization to make money, save money, or do some greater good. Discovering these needs begins with the following questions:

- Is this program worth doing?
- Is this a problem or an issue worth addressing?
- Is this an opportunity worth pursuing?
- Is the program feasible?
- What is the likelihood of a positive ROI?

The answer is clear for virtual learning solutions that address significant problems
or opportunities with potentially high rewards. The questions may be more challenging
to answer for lower-profile programs or those for which the possible payoff is less apparent. For example, there's a clear payoff opportunity if the organization is rapidly expanding its remote workforce and needs to quickly onboard new employees. But the overall
payoff is more questionable for a popular but dated time management program that
focuses on use of paper planners, even if it may still have some use in certain parts of
the organization.

In any case, these initial questions present the first opportunity to ensure that a virtual learning program is in alignment with the needs of the organization. The analysis

can be simple or comprehensive and show the program's ultimate payoff in either profit or cost savings (Figure 2-2).

Figure 2-2. The Payoff Opportunity

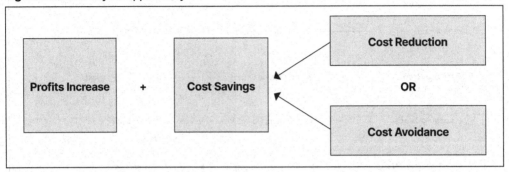

Virtual learning programs that improve sales, increase market share, introduce new products, open new markets, enhance customer service, or increase customer loyalty will generate improvements in profit by increasing sales revenue. Other revenue-generating measures include increasing memberships, increasing donations, obtaining grants, and generating tuition from new and returning students—all of which, after taking out the cost of doing business, should leave a profitable benefit.

Most virtual learning programs will pay off with cost savings that occur through cost reduction or cost avoidance. Examples of cost savings include improved quality, reduced cycle time, lowered downtime, decreased complaints, lower employee turnover, and minimized delays. When the goal is solving a problem, monetary value is often based on cost reduction.

Cost-avoidance programs aim to reduce risks, avoid problems, or prevent unwanted events. Some finance and accounting staff may view cost avoidance as an inappropriate measure for developing monetary benefits and calculating ROI. However, if the assumptions are correct, an avoided cost (for example, compliance fines) can be more rewarding than reducing an actual cost. Preventing a problem by providing a virtual learning solution is more cost-effective than waiting for it to occur and then having to correct it.

Determining the potential payoff (the first step in the needs analysis process) is closely related to the next step, determining the business need, because the potential payoff is often based on one or more business needs. Determining the payoff is a function of two factors: the potential monetary value of improving a business measure and the approximate program cost. Ascertaining these monetary values in detail usually yields a more credible forecast of a program's potential to add value. However, this step may be omitted if the issue (the business need) is an obviously high-payoff activity or must be resolved regardless of cost, such as a safety concern, regulatory compliance issue, or competitive matter. Being able to justify the investment for virtual learning programs, on the other hand, may be necessary, because of the costs of technology enhancements like upgraded software platforms and new equipment for facilitators and participants.

If the following statements are true, a detailed needs analysis showing business impact will be helpful:

❑ **There is minimal support for the proposed program.** The payoff analysis can provide an estimated value of the improvement (or cost avoidance) and the potential contribution to business goals.

❑ **The proposed program is going to be very expensive.** Estimating the potential payoff is important before spending major resources on a program.

❑ **When funding is needed for a program.** This is particularly true if the funding comes from external resources or there is serious competition for internal funding sources.

❑ **When a key sponsor wants more analysis before the program moves forward.** Although a sponsor may support the program enthusiastically, they may need to see more information before they can solidify their confidence and give final approval.

Knowledge of the potential payoff is not needed if most stakeholders agree that it will be high or if the problem in question must be resolved regardless of the cost.

Key Questions to Ask

Designers can begin their analysis with several potential questions:

- Why is this an issue?
- What happens if we do nothing?
- Is this issue critical?
- Is this issue linked to strategy?
- Is it possible to correct it?
- Is it feasible to improve it?
- How much is it costing us?
- Can we find a solution?
- Are there multiple solutions?
- Who will support the program?
- Who will not support the program?
- How much will the solution(s) cost?
- How can we fund the program?
- Are there some important intangible benefits involved?
- Is there a potential payoff (positive ROI)?
- Do we need to forecast outcomes, including ROI?

The answers will help make the case for proceeding with or without analysis. They may also indicate that the program isn't needed. Understanding the implications of moving forward (or not) can reveal the legitimacy of the proposed program.

The good news is that the answers to these questions may be readily available if the need was already realized and the consequences validated. For example, many organizations have calculated the standard value for the cost of employee turnover by reviewing existing data or similar studies. With this cost in hand, the problem's impact is known. The cost of the program can usually be estimated, even if the specifics are still under consideration. The proposed virtual learning program's cost can then be compared with the problem's cost to get a sense of added value.

Obvious vs. Not-So-Obvious Payoffs

The potential payoff is obvious for some programs but not so obvious for others. Opportunities with obvious payoffs are serious problems that executives, administrators, or officials need to address:

- The time to process a claim has increased 30 percent in two years.
- Sexual harassment complaints per 1,000 employees are the highest in the industry.
- System downtime is double last year's performance.
- Very low market share in a market with few players.
- Inadequate customer service: 3.89 on a 10-point customer satisfaction scale.
- This year's out-of-compliance fines total $1.2 million, up 82 percent from last year.
- Grievances are up 38 percent from last year.

For these situations, moving to the business needs level would be safe. Once you have determined which job performance needs will improve business needs if addressed, a forecast may be appropriate.

In other circumstances, the issues might be unclear, arising from intuition, political motives, or biases. In these cases, the payoff is more unclear and thus requires clarification. The opportunities listed here, for example, are common requests that can deliver value, but only if they are focused and clearly defined at the start:

- Implement a team-building project.
- Improve leadership competencies for all managers.
- Establish a project management office.
- Provide job training for unemployed workers.
- Train all team leaders on crucial conversations.
- Develop an "open-book" company.
- Implement the same work process that GE has used.
- Implement Lean training throughout the system.

- Implement a transformation program involving all employees.
- Create a wellness and fitness center.
- Create an engaged workforce.

Some requests are common, as executives and administrators suggest a different process to change a dysfunctional situation or to achieve vague or nonspecific goals. However, in Jack and Patti's work at ROI Institute, they have seen many of these vague and open-ended opportunities lead to valuable programs. Don't overlook a vague request—instead take the time to define, approve, and focus on the desired business impact of the programs.

What If It's a Program Conversion to Virtual Learning?

It's common for virtual learning programs to be created because an existing traditional in-person program needs to be facilitated in a new format. Organizations may want to expand the reach of a program and offer it to remote employees who wouldn't otherwise be able to participate. Other reasons exist as well, such as participant preferences for virtual learning solutions or the desire to create a spaced learning program with short modules offered over time.

Should the designer assume that they don't need to do an analysis for the virtual program because one was done on the in-person program? Can they skip ahead, past the business analysis, and start with a future step? Or do they need to start over again at the beginning? The answer is, "It depends."

Factors to consider include how long ago the program was created or last updated, along with current business conditions. Designers should find out whether a full analysis was done when the program was originally created, or if that part was skipped. If no analysis is available, or has been forgotten, we recommend a fresh start. The benefits gained from tying the virtual learning program to business impact are so important. Designers may be able to shortcut the process by validating the information as opposed to discovering it for the first time, but knowing and being able to articulate the connection to business impact is even more valuable than the time that would save.

Many years ago, one of Cindy's clients, a large global hotel chain, decided to move their new manager program from a multiweek in-person experience to a largely virtual one. Instead of participants coming together for several weeks of learning, they would complete a series of tasks, including attending daily facilitator-led virtual classes, from the comfort of their own hotel properties. The new program culminated in an in-person event where the participants got to meet one another, tour the organization's headquarters, and validate their learning accomplishments. Initially, the instructional designers set out to simply convert the existing classroom program to a virtual one, but they quickly realized the program was dated and needed a refresh. So they went back to the beginning, conducting a quick needs analysis to ensure alignment with current business needs. It was time and resources well spent.

Reasons for Virtual Learning Programs

As discussed in chapter 1, there are several reasons virtual learning programs are not successful. One key reason is not connecting to a business measure from the outset. If the program is designed only for learning and not for impact, it will not be perceived as adding value. A similar but slightly different reason for program failure is not generating enough monetary value to cover the cost of the program.

A lack of initial business alignment brings into question the reasons for new program or project implementation. Some of the main reasons organizations implement programs include the following:

- An analysis indicates a need exists.
- A regulation requires it.
- It appears to be a serious problem.
- Management requests it.
- Other organizations in the industry have implemented it.
- Staff members thought it was needed.
- It supports new equipment, procedures, or technology.
- It provides access to a necessary program that learners wouldn't otherwise be able to attend because of physical location.

Some of these appear to be legitimate reasons to move forward. If analysis supports a credible reason, then a program is probably needed. If a regulation requires it, then it must be implemented. Other reasons organizations might have for creating a new program may appear to be necessary, but only if the program is implemented efficiently. For example, a program that supports new policies and practices; new equipment, procedures, or technology; or existing processes would be a legitimate request only if support for implementation exists. If remote audiences need access to a program that they wouldn't otherwise be able to attend, then that's a legitimate reason to create a virtual learning program.

Suspect and misguided reasons for creating a new program also exist; for example, if other organizations have implemented a particular program or if the program is based on a fad. These are the types of programs that often fail to add adequate value. Unfortunately, leaders may still request these types of learning programs because of their continuous desire to find the right solutions or to pursue the next new idea.[3]

The Costs of the Problem

Problems are expensive and resolving them can have a tremendous impact. Determining the cost of a problem requires L&D to examine potential consequences and convert those consequences to monetary values. Potential business problems include:

- Inventory shortages
- Wasted time
- Mistakes
- Waste
- Delays
- Bottlenecks
- Productivity problems
- Inefficiencies
- Excessive direct costs
- Equipment damage
- Equipment underused
- Excessive program time
- Incidents
- Excessive employee turnover
- Employee withdrawal
- Accidents
- Excessive staffing
- Employee dissatisfaction
- Customer dissatisfaction
- Excessive conflicts
- Tarnished image
- Lack of coordination
- Excessive stress

Some measures that define these problems can easily be converted to money. Intangible measures, on the other hand, require data conversion techniques that are too costly or for which the results lack credibility. For example, inventory shortages often result in the direct cost of the inventory as well as the cost of carrying the inventory.

Time can easily be translated into money by calculating the fully loaded cost of the individual's time spent on unproductive tasks. Calculating time for completing a program, task, or cycle involves measures that can be converted to money. Mistakes, waste, delays, and bottlenecks can often be converted to money through their consequences. Productivity problems and inefficiencies, equipment damage, and equipment in use are other examples of easy conversions.

When examining costs, it is important to consider all costs and their implications. For example, the full costs of accidents include not only the cost of lost workdays and medical expenses, but also the effect on insurance premiums, the time required for investigations, the damage to equipment, and the time required for employees to address the accident. A customer complaint includes the cost of the time required to resolve the complaint as well as the value of the item or service that is adjusted because of it. However, the most important item to account for in a complaint is the cost of lost future business and goodwill from both the complaining customer and potential customers who learn about the issue.

The Value of Opportunity

Just as it is usually possible to tabulate the cost of a problem, it is also possible to determine the value of an opportunity. Examples of opportunities include:

- Implementing innovation and creativity for managers
- Developing an inclusive workforce
- Implementing a new process
- Installing new technology
- Upgrading the workforce for a more competitive environment

In these situations, a problem may not exist, but there is a tremendous opportunity to get ahead of the competition. Properly placing a value on this opportunity requires considering what may happen if the program is not pursued or taking into account the windfall that might be realized by seizing the opportunity. Monetary value is derived by following different scenarios to convert specific business impact measures to money. The difficulty in this situation is ensuring a credible analysis. Forecasting the value of an opportunity relies on many assumptions, whereas calculating the value of a known outcome is often grounded in a more credible analysis.

To Forecast or Not to Forecast

Seeking and placing value on an opportunity leads to an important decision for talent development leaders to make: to forecast or not to forecast business value and ROI. If the stakes are high, and support for the virtual learning program is not in place, a detailed forecast may be the only way to gain support and funding. If a forecast is pursued, the rigor of the analysis becomes an issue. In some cases, it's possible to provide an informal forecast that is based on certain assumptions about alternative outcome scenarios. In others, you will need to provide a detailed forecast that involves collecting data from a variety of experts, using previous studies from other programs, or perhaps a more sophisticated analysis.[4]

Business Needs

Returning to the Alignment Model (Figure 2-1), determining specific business needs is directly linked to developing the potential payoff. When determining the business needs, specific measures are pinpointed to clearly assess the situation. In this book we use the term *business* for governments, nonprofits, NGOs, and educational institutions, as well as private-sector organizations. Programs and projects in all types of organizations can lead to monetary value-add by improving productivity, quality, and efficiency as well as by saving time and reducing costs.

Determining the Opportunity

A business need is represented by a business measure. Any process, item, or perception can be measured, which is critical for this level of analysis. If the program focuses on solving a problem—something clearly established in the minds of program initiators—the measures are often obvious. They may also be obvious if the program prevents a problem or if it takes advantage of a potential opportunity. Otherwise, how will the opportunity be described? How will the value proposition be defined? The important point is that measures are in the system, ready to be captured for this level of analysis. The challenge is to identify the measures and to find them economically and swiftly.

Identifying the Business Measure—Hard Data

To help focus on the desired measures, we first need to clarify the difference between hard data and soft data: *Hard data* is the primary measure of improvement presented in rational, undisputed facts that exist somewhere in the organization's system. It is easy to measure and quantify and is relatively easy to convert to monetary values. The ultimate criteria for measuring the effectiveness of an organization rest on hard data items—such as revenue, productivity, profitability, cost control, and quality assurance.

Hard data is objectively based and represents common and credible measures of an organization's performance. The four categories of hard data—output, quality, cost, and time—along with examples of each, are shown in Figure 2-3.

Figure 2-3. Examples of Hard Data

Output		Time	
• Completion rate	• Inventory turnover	• Cycle time	• Learning time
• Units produced	• Patient visits	• Equipment downtime	• Meeting schedules
• Tons manufactured	• Applications	• Overtime	• Repair time
• Items assembled	processed	• On-time shipments	• Efficiency
• Money collected	• Students graduated	• Time to program	• Work stoppages
• Items sold	• Tasks completed	completion	• Order response
• New accounts	• Output per hour	• Processing time	• Late reporting
generated	• Productivity	• Supervisory time	• Lost time days
• Forms processed	• Work backlog	• Time to proficiency	
• Loans approved	• Incentive bonus		
	• Shipments		

Figure 2-3. *Cont.*

Costs		Quality	
• Budget variances	• Program costs	• Failure rates	• Deviations from
• Unit costs	• Sales expenses	• Dropout rates	standard
• Costs by account	• Shelter costs	• Scrap	• Inventory adjustments
• Variable costs	• Treatment costs	• Waste rejects	• Timecard corrections
• Fixed costs	• Participant costs	• Error rates	• Incidents
• Overhead costs		• Reworks required	• Compliance
• Operating costs		• Shortages	discrepancies
• Program cost savings		• Product defects	• Agency fines
• Accident costs		• Product failures	

Let's look closer at each type of hard data:

- **Output.** Every organization has basic, routinely monitored measurements of output, which makes it easy to compare outputs before and after a program is implemented. If the organization anticipates that a program will drive an output measure, those who are qualified to can usually estimate the output changes.

- **Quality.** If quality is a major concern for the organization, it likely has processes in place to measure and monitor quality. In addition, use of quality-improvement processes (such as total-quality management, continuous quality improvement, and Six Sigma) allows organizations to pinpoint the correct quality measures—and, in many cases, place a monetary value on them. If a program or project is designed to improve quality, the value of the results can be documented using the standard cost of quality.

- **Cost.** Many projects and programs are designed to lower, control, or eliminate the cost of a specific process or activity. Achieving these cost targets contributes immediately to the bottom line. Some organizations have an extreme focus on cost reduction. Consider Walmart, whose tagline is "Always low prices. Always." The entire organization focuses on lowering costs on all processes and products and passing the savings along to customers. When direct cost savings are used, no efforts are necessary to convert data to monetary value and there can be as many cost items as there are accounts in a cost accounting system. In addition, costs can be combined in any number of ways depending on the needs of a program or project.

- **Time.** Some organizations gauge their performance almost exclusively by time. For example, consider FedEx, whose tagline is "The world on time." When asked what business FedEx is in, the company's top executives say, "We engineer time." In fact, time is so critical that FedEx uses it to define success or failure. Time savings may mean that a program was completed faster than originally planned, a product was introduced earlier, or a network was restored faster. These savings can translate into lower costs.

Defining the Business Need—Soft Data

Hard data may take months to materialize once the changes have been made and programs implemented. Therefore, it can be useful to supplement hard data with soft data—such as attitude, motivation, and satisfaction (Figure 2-4). Although it's often more difficult to collect, analyze, and convert to monetary values, soft data frequently serves as proxy or a supplement to hard data. Soft data is often subjective and less credible as a performance measurement because it typically reflects behaviors rather than the consequence of those behaviors.

Figure 2-4. Examples of Soft Data

Work Habits	Customer Service
• Tardiness	• Customer complaints
• Violations of work rules	• Customer satisfaction
• Violations of safety rules	• Customer dissatisfaction
• Communication breakdowns	• Customer impressions
• Excessive time off	• Customer loyalty
• Remote work perceptions	• Customer retention
	• Customer value
	• Customers lost
Work Climate and Satisfaction	**Employee Development and Advancement**
• Grievances	• Promotions
• Discrimination charges	• Capability
• Employee complaints	• Intellectual capital
• Job satisfaction	• Programs completed
• Organization commitment	• Requests for transfer
• Employee engagement	• Performance appraisal ratings
• Employee loyalty	• Readiness
• Intent to leave	• Networking
• Stress	
Initiative and Innovation	**Image and Reputation**
• Creativity	• Brand awareness
• New ideas	• Reputation
• Suggestions	• Leadership
• New products and services	• Social responsibility
• Trademarks	• Environmental friendliness
• Copyrights and patents	• Social consciousness
• Process improvements	• Diversity
• Partnerships	• External awards
• Alliances	

Let's look closer at the different types of soft data:

- **Work habits.** Dysfunctional work habits can lead to an unproductive and ineffective work group, while productive habits can boost the group's output and morale. While some work habits can fall into the hard data category because they are easy to convert to monetary values, others are harder to quantify. With remote work now commonplace, work habits are not as easily seen and require better communication among virtual team members.

- **Work climate and satisfaction.** Complaints and grievances could be considered hard data because of their ease of conversion to money. However, these measures are typically considered soft data. Job satisfaction, organizational commitment, and employee engagement show how attitudes shape the organization. Stress is often a by-product of a fast-paced work climate, along with the additional pressures highlighted during the recent global events. These issues are becoming increasingly important.

- **Customer service.** Because increased global competition fosters a greater need to serve and satisfy customers, more organizations are putting customer service measures into place that show the levels of customer satisfaction, loyalty, and retention.

- **Employee development and advancement.** Employees are routinely developed, assigned new jobs, and promoted throughout organizations. Building capability, creating intellectual capital, enhancing readiness, and fostering networks are important processes. Many soft data measures are available to indicate the consequences of those activities and processes.

- **Initiative and innovation.** A variety of measures can be developed to show the creative spirit of employees and the related outcomes—such as ideas, suggestions, copyrights, patents, and products and services. While the collective creative spirit of employees may be considered a soft data item, the outcomes of creativity and innovation may be placed in the hard data category. Still, many executives consider innovation measurements to be soft data.

- **Image and reputation.** Perhaps some of the softest measures are in the image category. For example, organizational leaders may be attempting to increase brand awareness, particularly with sales and marketing programs or projects. Reputation is another key area, as more organizations seek to improve their standing as good employers, good citizens, and good stewards of investors' money. Leadership outcomes—probably the most sought-after measure—are influenced by the projects and programs designed to build leadership within the organization. This measure is also influenced by the organization's perception of how well a leader has navigated the massive workforce changes that have occurred in the past few years. Image, social responsibility, environmental friendliness, and social consciousness are key outputs of a variety of programs and projects aimed at making an organization well rounded. Diversity is important as well, with many new programs designed to improve the diversity of people, ideas, and products within the organization. Finally, external awards are the outcomes of many activities and programs that compare the organization to industry measures of success.

Using Tangible vs. Intangible Data—A Better Approach

Tangible data items can be converted to money credibly using minimum resources. These data points are reported as monetary values or placed in an ROI calculation. Soft data measures can become tangible if they can be converted to money, and this is possible for some of the measures listed in Figure 2-4. However, the critical issue with many soft data categories is the difficulty of converting them to monetary values.

Remember that an *intangible measure* (based on the standards of the ROI Methodology) is a measure that cannot be converted to money credibly or with minimum resources. If a data item cannot be converted to money credibly with minimum resources, it is listed as an intangible measure. And even when it can be converted, it's often still more practical and realistic to categorize it as soft data.

This book opts to use the terms *tangible* and *intangible* rather than hard or soft data. This is the best approach to use for virtual program evaluation, because the data classification is tied to the organizational setting. Each organization determines whether a measure is tangible or intangible. For example, in some organizations, a measure for customer satisfaction is easily available, costs little to obtain, and thus can easily be converted to money. Therefore, the measure is tangible. However, in other organizations where customer satisfaction is not easily converted to money, the measure is intangible.

Finding Sources of Impact Data

Hard and soft impact data sources often come from the organization's routine reporting systems. In many situations, these items revealed the need for the program or project. Here's just a sample of the vast array of possible documents, systems, databases, and reports that can be used to select the specific measure or measures to monitor throughout the program:

- Department records
- Human capital databases
- Quality reports
- Manufacturing reports
- Compliance reports
- Annual reports
- Benchmarking reports
- R&D status
- Cost statements
- Scorecards
- Productivity records
- Work unit reports
- Payroll records
- Test records
- Marketing reports
- Service records
- Safety and health reports
- Industry or trade association records
- Project management records
- Financial records
- Dashboards
- Employee engagement reports

If data isn't readily available to them or easy to find in a database, talent development team members may incorrectly believe that corporate data sources are scarce. However, the necessary data can usually be identified with a little determination and searching. In our experience, more than 90 percent of the measures that matter to a specific program or project are already developed and available in a database or system. It's rarely necessary to develop a new data collection system or process.

Identifying All the Measures

When searching for the proper measures to connect to a virtual learning program and pinpoint business needs, it's helpful to consider every measure that could be influenced. Sometimes, collateral measures move in harmony with the program. For example, efforts to improve safety may also improve productivity and increase job satisfaction. Thinking about the adverse impact on certain measures may also help. For example, when cycle times are reduced, quality may suffer, or when sales increase, customer satisfaction may deteriorate. Finally, talent development team members must prepare for unintended consequences that might be connected to or influenced by the program and capture them as other data items.

What Happens If You Do Nothing?

When settling on the precise business measures for the virtual learning program, it is also beneficial to think about what would happen if the organization did nothing. In these cases, asking the following questions may help you better understand the consequences of inaction:

- Will the situation deteriorate?
- Will operational problems surface?
- Will budgets be affected?
- Will we lose influence or support?
- Will we miss the opportunity?

Your answers can help the organization settle on a precise set of measures with a hint of the extent to which they may change or improve. When examining the full context of the situation, it's possible to identify other measures that may influence the program. This allows you to see the complete process and pinpoint each measure that may be connected to the project or program.

Next Steps

Start with "why?" is the first step in the eight-step results-based design process. The "why?" of virtual learning programs is the business need. This chapter illustrates the importance of connecting certain virtual learning programs to the business. At one extreme, some organizations do not pursue virtual learning programs unless there is a direct business connection. A more practical approach is to be selective, making the connection when the request seems to be expensive, critical to the organization, part of a strategy, or important to the management team.

It is then important to address the potential payoff needs, answering the fundamental two-part question: Is this a problem worth solving or an opportunity worth pursuing? We also need to pinpoint one or more business measures already in the system that need to improve as a result of the virtual learning program.

The next step is to make sure learning is the right solution to improve the business measure, and if so, if virtual learning is the proper way to deliver it. The next chapter explores the issue of ensuring that your solution is the right one.

Job Aid: A Checklist of Interview Questions to Ask to Determine Payoff Needs

Use this checklist in your next stakeholder interview.

- ❏ Why is this an issue?
- ❏ What happens if we do nothing?
- ❏ Is this issue critical?
- ❏ Is this issue linked to strategy?
- ❏ Is it possible to correct it?
- ❏ Is it feasible to improve it?
- ❏ How much is it costing us?
- ❏ Can we find a solution?
- ❏ Are there multiple solutions?
- ❏ Who will support the program?
- ❏ Who will not support the program?
- ❏ How much will the solution(s) cost?
- ❏ How can we fund the program?
- ❏ Are there some important intangible benefits involved?
- ❏ Is there a potential payoff (positive ROI)?
- ❏ Do we need to forecast outcomes, including ROI?

Make It Feasible: Selecting the Right Solution

Southeast Healthcare (SEH), a regional provider of a variety of healthcare services through a chain of hospitals, health management organizations (HMOs), and clinics, has grown steadily in the last few years. It has also earned a reputation as a robust and financially sound company, with an aggressive management team poised for additional growth.

However, SEH—like many other organizations throughout the US and healthcare industry—was also experiencing an increasing number of sexual harassment claims. This increase across the country was sparked in part by a growing public awareness of the issue and by the willingness of victims to report their harassment complaints. A significant number of the complaints at SEH were converting to charges and lawsuits and executives believed that this represented a persistent and irritating problem. In addition, they thought the organization's unusually high turnover levels may be linked to the increased reporting of sexual harassment.

Senior management, concerned about continued sexual harassment complaints and the increasing cost of defending the company, asked the HR vice president to take corrective and preventive action. The HR vice president suggested that the human resources development (HRD) staff develop a virtual workshop centered on workplace harassment for employees or managers or both, but only if a lack of understanding and knowledge of the issue existed.

In response to the request, the HRD staff conducted interviews with the entire equal employment opportunities (EEO) and affirmative action (AA) staff to explore why sexual harassment claims were increasing. They found that there was a significant lack of understanding of the company's policy on sexual harassment and what actually constituted inappropriate or illegal behavior. In addition, the HRD team examined complaints from the last year for issues and patterns, as well as exit interviews of terminating employees to see if there was a linkage to sexual harassment. They found that approximately 11 percent of terminating employees identified sexual harassment as a factor in their decision to leave the organization.

Based on this information, SEH executives asked the team to proceed with this program. Because the HRD staff did not conduct a full-scale needs assessment, they augmented the input from the EEO/AA staff with the exit interviews from 10 randomly selected first-level supervisors to explore the level of understanding of the policy, inappropriate and illegal behavior, and the perceived causes of the increased complaint activity.

Based on the analysis of the complaints, the typical person accused of sexual harassment was a supervisor and male, whereas the typical victim was nonsupervisory and female. The analysis also revealed that the type of sexual harassment typically experienced at SEH was "an individual making unwelcome sexual advances or other verbal or physical conduct of a sexual nature with the purpose of, or that creates the effect of, unreasonably interfering with an individual's work performance or creating an intimidating, hostile, or offensive working environment" (as defined by the EEOC). As part of SEH's policy, supervisors and managers were required to conduct a limited investigation of informal complaints and to discuss issues as they surfaced.

Armed with input from the interviews and detailed feedback from the EEO/AA staff, the HRD staff identified the major causes of the problem. The HRD staff found an apparent lack of understanding of both the company's sexual harassment policy and what constituted inappropriate and illegal behavior. In addition, there was an apparent insensitivity to the issue within the company.

The HRD staff believed that these issues could be minimized by developing a clear understanding of SEH's policy regarding harassment and by teaching managers to identify illegal and inappropriate activity. As a result, a comprehensive training solution was created, including an in-person workshop for managers, a virtual learning program for employees, and ancillary meetings on the topic.

First, they designed a one-day in-person sexual harassment prevention workshop for all first-level and second-level supervisors and managers. The program had several broad objectives:

- Recognize and administer the company's policy on sexual harassment.
- Identify inappropriate and illegal behavior related to sexual harassment.
- Investigate and discuss sexual harassment issues.
- Conduct a meeting with all direct reports to discuss policy and expected behavior.
- Ensure that the workplace is free from sexual harassment.
- Reduce the number of sexual harassment complaints.

Because of the serious implications of this issue, it was important for all employees to also have a thorough understanding of the policy, as well as how to identify and report inappropriate behavior. The HRD team designed a two-hour, facilitator-led virtual program for the many SEH employees scattered across the company's various locations. In addition to being able to ask questions and have conversations during the program, attendees would have the following learning objectives:

- Recognize the company's policy on sexual harassment.
- Identify inappropriate and illegal behavior related to sexual harassment.
- Report inappropriate behavior according to company procedures.

Once everyone had attended their respective learning events, each supervisor was then asked to conduct a meeting with their direct employees to discuss the topic.

The key to working through this problem at SEH was discovering that it was caused by a lack of knowledge and skill. Because the underlying issue was knowledge related, the needs could be met with a learning solution, specifically a combination of in-person and virtual programs.

Most designers are familiar with the challenge of finding the right solution for an issue. Unfortunately, they don't always get it right. Sometimes, even if the project generates excitement and the team is committed to getting it done, the follow-up data reveals that it didn't work because it was the wrong solution. Someone says, "The training didn't work," or someone else says, "We need even more training." When this happens, it's likely that the program was suggested, recommended, or even required by someone (often a senior executive) who did not have the proper dialogue or do an assessment or analysis.

Even if there is a clear business need and the program appears to be the right choice, without proper focus and analysis, your results can demonstrate a disconnect between need and solution. In the last chapter, we discussed the obvious and not-so-obvious payoff opportunities, along with the importance of uncovering the business need that defines those opportunities. Defining the potential payoff and specific business measures that need to improve are the first steps in clarifying "why" an organization needs a specific program. The next challenge is selecting the proper solution, and determining if that solution should be in-person, online, or a combination of both. That's the focus of this chapter.

Solution selection is a serious issue. The wrong solution will waste resources and tarnish the image of the talent development function. Even if a senior executive requests a program, it is necessary for the talent development team to clarify that the solution is appropriate and position that program for success. The team must also use proper analysis to carefully decide what type of learning solution is best: in-person? Online? Blended? Virtual? A combination? So, the first question is to determine if a learning solution will solve the problem, and if the answer is "yes," then the second question is to determine the best format for the learning design.

Let's first begin with determining if learning is the right solution, and then address the format selection.

Performance Needs

The previous chapter discussed payoff needs and business needs. With business needs in hand, the next step is determining how to improve the business measures. This step identifies the causes of problems or what's needed to take advantage of an opportunity—in other words, you have to determine what performance needs are influencing the business needs.

To uncover performance needs, an instructional designer must understand the problem or opportunity and identify the solution that will meet the business needs. In the past, the designer might have assessed learning needs and translated them into a learning program. This has now evolved into a performance consulting role where the performance consultant or analyst delves deeper into the analysis, looking for causes of problems and uncovering solutions. The skill set for the performance consultant is different from that of a typical analyst because it begins with the ability to have a dialogue with the stakeholder who requested the training (the requester).[1]

It's possible the requester won't want to have this conversation. After all, they are the customer and have already communicated their thoughts about the problem and its solution. Given that they think the learning and talent development function has the power to address their need, it's hard to turn them down. They may worry that asking too many questions may cause the requester to perceive the learning function as an unwilling partner and take their request elsewhere.

To combat this concern, we propose nine tips to help designers open the conversation with a requester and determine performance needs, resulting in more appropriate and effective virtual learning programs:

- **Examine the data and records.** Sometimes, a request is connected to a data set, such as call time, accidents, employee turnover, productivity, or sales. In these cases, start by reviewing the records and explore trends before speaking with the requester because the cause may be evident in the data. For example, if exit interviews show that employees are leaving for higher pay, and if the data is credible, then a learning solution will not correct the problem. A learning solution also won't help if inadequate personal protective equipment is resulting in employees having too many accidents. The more a designer can speak to existing, relevant data, the more credibility they will have, and the better the conversation will be.
- **Initiate the discussion.** Pinning down the details of a request is necessary for driving real results. The alignment model (recall Figure 2-1) is a perfect guide to

initiating this conversation. On the left side of the alignment model are the different levels of needs assessment. In the ideal world, the requester identifies the payoff and business needs and asks for help identifying the other levels of needs, which point to a solution. Reality, however, is different. The requester usually begins with a requested program—a perceived learning solution—and the conversation then moves up the left side of the model. In doing so, the performance consultant clarifies learning, performance, business, and payoff needs.

- **Use benchmarking from similar solutions.** Can you point to similar programs with business outcomes that can help you assess the situation? If the requester suggests a well-documented program but has no clear idea of the outcomes they seek in terms of business impact, refer to measures in a case study. In addition, case studies and benchmarking data are excellent tools to keep a conversation going.

- **Use evaluation as the hook.** If the discussion is going nowhere on the left side of the alignment model, maybe it's time to move to the right side. This leads to a simple question, "What levels of evaluation do you expect to achieve as a result of the program?" Then you can take the request through the different measures that can be captured at each of the five levels. The typical requester response is that they would like to see the impact, and some may be intrigued with the concept of ROI. If they indicate interest in these two levels, remind them that you don't see business needs. Provide examples of business needs and ask them to elaborate on the business measures that matter. Essentially, in this situation, the focus of the conversation is more on evaluation and less on analysis.

- **Involve others.** If the request is coming from a senior executive, there are probably other individuals who understand the issue in more detail. Engaging them in the conversation may lead to some interesting discussions regarding the cause of the problem and potential solutions, including the one requested by the senior executive. Sometimes, the people closest to the work being done will offer a solution that's completely different from those who observe a situation but lack the day-to-day context.

- **Discuss disasters in other places.** Sometimes it is helpful to bring out examples of programs that went astray in other organizations or even within the same organization. Disasters happen. Implementing programs for the wrong reasons and failing to deliver results is not a new concept. It may be helpful to discuss a suggested program's previous failings and what it would take to avoid those failings in the future.

- **Discuss the consequences.** In keeping with the discussion about disasters, it can be important to assess the risks and consequences of pursuing an inappropriate program. Have the requester consider the time, resources, and costs associated with implementation. That information may be enough to get them to consider alternatives.

- **Analysis techniques.** Another approach to assessing performance needs is to use diagnostic tools, such as statistical process control, brainstorming, problem analysis, cause-and-effect diagrams, force-field analysis, mind mapping, affinity diagrams, simulations, diagnostic instruments, focus groups, probing interviews, job satisfaction surveys, engagement surveys, exit interviews, exit surveys, and nominal group technique. Many of these analytical techniques use tools from problem solving, quality assurance, and performance improvement to search for multiple solutions. This is important because performance is often inhibited for several reasons. However, multiple solutions must be considered in terms of implementation—deciding whether to explore them in total or tackle them in priority order. Details of these techniques are contained in many references.[2]

- **Keep it sensible.** It's important to consider what resources are needed to examine records, research databases, and observe situations and individuals. Analysis takes time. Performance needs can vary considerably and may include ineffective behavior, dysfunctional work climate, inadequate systems, and disconnected process flows. Uncovering those needs through either conversation or analytical techniques may seem daunting, especially when considering the number of factors that could be causing business measures to perform at the right level. The risk of overanalyzing the situation is great. Take a sensible approach to assessing the performance gaps that need closing. Consider the value of improving the targeted business measures and balance the analysis investment with the benefits of solving the problem. For example, if you are losing remote employees at a rate of 25 percent per year, and the cost of that turnover is 150 percent of their annual salary (plus benefits), you would be wise to get to the cause of the problem and find a solution that can address several performance gaps at once. On the other hand, if the business measure is to increase sales, and the culture is one where salespeople have not fully engaged in conversations with customers, a deep analysis isn't necessary to know that piloting a simple, off-the-shelf interactive virtual selling skills program might be a good idea. Always bear in mind, when thinking about the level of investment in analysis, that there is a difference between statistical significance and practical significance. Sometimes, certainty in cause-and-effect relationships is based on what is practical, logical, and sensible.

Example in Action

A senior executive in a large nonprofit organization requests a team-building program for his team. The performance consultant asks, "What is occurring (or not occurring) in your team that leads you to conclude you need team building?" This harmless question receives the following response: "They are working in silos, especially now that almost everyone works remotely; they don't communicate very well; they don't seem to want to help one another; they won't share information; and they see others make mistakes without helping them." It is helpful to validate the learning need with another question, "Do they know how to work this way now?" And then a follow-on question of "Did they work this way before the move to remote work?" The quick response to both questions is "no," which can be validated with a few interviews. These are critical behaviors that point toward a solution that will embed better behaviors in the team. These are performance needs. But even more information is needed if the program is to contribute to the business. Performance asks, "How is this affecting your key performance indicators or other important measures?" The response is, "We don't really have a problem with our KPIs. I just don't want this behavior, so please implement the program." The performance consultant explains the situation using the Alignment Model as a guide. "We can implement the program, but there are no business needs for it, except maybe an intangible of teamwork. Is that OK with you?" This question requires the executive to think about the request, and possibly decide not to pursue it.

Learning and Preference Needs

As the designer continues moving through the Alignment Model to determine if a learning program will solve the business problem or take advantage of the business opportunity, the next phase is to determine the learning needs. If the performance needs, uncovered in the previous step, require new knowledge acquisition to ensure all parties know what they need to do and how to do it, then learning needs must be considered.

In some cases, learning itself could be the principal solution, as in competency development, major technology changes, capability development, and system installations. Learning programs must center on the knowledge and skill required for these tasks. For other programs, learning is a minor solution and often involves simply understanding the process, procedure, or policy. For example, when implementing a new work-from-home policy for an organization, the learning component requires understanding how the policy works and the participants' role in it. These items could be learned by reviewing a video demonstration or reading a job aid instead of attending a training class. In short, a learning solution is not always needed, but all solutions have a learning component.

A variety of approaches are available to measure specific learning needs, including interviewing subject matter experts (SMEs) and reviewing documentation. In some instances, it's appropriate to conduct a full job and task analysis. See the references section for our recommendations on how to discover and capture learning needs.[3] Later in this chapter, we will review how specific learning needs may contribute to the need for a virtual learning format.

The final level of needs analysis is based on preferences, which drive the program requirements and influence the format decision. The organization may have preferences for learning formats based upon available resources or historical precedence. In other words, an organization's go-to method for learning programs may be self-directed e-learning simply because its designer is comfortable creating it.

In addition, a thorough review of participant backgrounds, locations, experiences, and preferences will provide insight as to the best structure for the learning program. For example, if participants are co-located in the same office building, it is easier to hold an in-person training class, whereas a virtual learning solution may be preferable if participants are spread around the globe. Also, participants may have constraints, such as limited ability to travel to attend a learning program, or job requirements that make it difficult to participate in learning programs during the workday. This initial experience may lead to a fondness for that same type of learning program for subsequent topics. Overall, these preferences help define how the program will be implemented.

If the learning program is a solution to a problem, this step defines how the solution will be put into place. If the program addresses an opportunity, this step outlines how to do so, taking into consideration the preference needs of those involved in the program.

The typical preference needs from the participant's perspective represent statements that could define the parameters of the program in terms of value, necessity, and convenience. With virtual learning, the participant input also influences its overall structure. For example, will the program need to be a blended series with several short virtual classes, or do schedules allow for longer online learning sessions? And will participants prefer more time with their peers and the facilitator, or would they rather do more self-directed assignments? In general, most participants need the program to be:

- Relevant to their work
- Action-oriented
- Something they will recommend to others
- Easy to use
- Convenient
- A good investment
- Implemented without disruption of work

Implementation is based on the input of several key stakeholders. For example, participants involved in the program (those who must make it work) may have a particular preference, but it could exceed the available resources, time, and budget. The immediate manager's input may help minimize the amount of disruption and maximize resources. Those who support or own the program often place preferences around the program in terms of urgency and importance. A training department may have limited facilitator resources or lack a virtual platform for hands-on tasks. The organization may have technology restraints such as required use of a VPN or limited use of webcams. These factors could all potentially affect the program structure.

Matching Learning Solutions to Needs

The most difficult part of this stage of the design process may be to match the best learning solution or solutions to the needs or causes of the problem. This task is as much an art as it is a science. There are three principles to follow to ensure that the solution addresses all the needs or causes:

- Some learning solutions are obvious because the causes point directly to a solution. For example, when a new product is released, sales teams need to learn its features and benefits before they can sell it. The solution is clear.
- Solutions can come in different sizes. For example, new manager training could cover basic leadership skills in a short series of virtual classes, or it could encompass the full scope of management skills in a multimonth blended learning journey.
- Some problems take a long time to solve and will need a multifaceted solution. For example, if the root cause of high employee turnover stems from a tarnished public image of the organization (such as bad press or recent negative events), combined with frustration over poor communication skills among managers, it could take a long time to repair the situation. Multiple types of initiatives, including some learning solutions, could be needed to fix the issue.

Selecting Learning Solutions for Maximum Payoff

The next step is to make sure that the focus is only on solutions that have maximum payoff. Two major issues can affect that payoff: the cost of the solution and the monetary benefit from the implementation. To achieve maximum payoff, costs should be considered. The smaller the cost, the greater the potential payoff. From the benefits side, the greater the benefits, the greater the potential payoff.

Many organizations assume that virtual learning costs less than in-person learning. After all, there are no travel expenses or classroom catering expenses, material printing costs are reduced, and online programs tend to be more efficient because they are shorter in length. While these statements are true, it does not mean that virtual learning programs are without cost.

In fact, the initial investment in virtual learning can be significant, especially if it is new for an organization. A virtual classroom platform designed for training must be selected and implemented. (Note that there's a difference between an online meeting or videoconferencing platform and an online training platform; see the references for more detail.) Facilitators and participants may need updated equipment, such as noise-canceling headsets and devices with webcams. Designers and facilitators also need training on how to use the platforms and create an engaging virtual class that appeals to remote participants. There's also the investment in time and resources to convert in-person classes to online or to design them from scratch—and research shows it takes more time to develop effective virtual classes than their in-person counterparts.[4] Perhaps most surprising to some, the best virtual training classes have two leaders—either a facilitator and producer or two co-facilitators.

Once efficiencies are realized over time, and the initial investment costs decrease, it's likely that virtual learning will become a more cost-effective solution. However, lower costs should not be the only reason for recommending or selecting a virtual learning solution. Virtual learning should be selected because it is the best solution to solve the business problem or capitalize on the business opportunity.

Let's look at some other factors to consider.

Short-Term vs. Long-Term Costs

Some solutions, such as leadership development for all managers, may be expensive to implement on a short-term basis, regardless of the learning format. The overall cost of this solution might be prohibitive. Other solutions, such as an incentive plan, may have little up-front cost but a tremendous long-term expense—one that may exceed the actual payoff. Major change programs are usually long term and require careful consideration before implementing. The short-term versus long-term cost implication must always be considered.

Consider Forecasting ROI

A forecast can be developed showing the expected monetary benefits compared with the projected cost of the solution. The solutions with the highest forecasted ROI value become the best prospects for implementation.

Time Needed for Implementation

Some solutions are implemented quickly, while others take a long time. This may mean that long-term solutions should be implemented in conjunction with short-term fixes. In other words, the organization should recognize that both quick fixes and long-term changes are necessary. This approach shows employees that the organization is taking steps now and also building for the future, which results in enhanced commitment and loyalty.

Avoid Mismatches

The impact of a mismatched problem and solution can be significant. For example, having to discontinue an employee incentive plan can affect job satisfaction. Or if a costly virtual learning solution is implemented when a simple job aid would have sufficed. Mismatches can cause three major problems:

1. Funds are wasted, because money is spent on a solution that did not correct the problem and drained the organization's resources.

2. Inappropriate solutions have a negative impact. For example, if virtual learning is implemented as a solution when there isn't deficiency in knowledge and skills, the impact can be adverse. The participants being trained (such as supervisors and managers) may resent it, because they believe they were coerced into participating in a solution with no value for them or forced to work on skills they already possess.

3. When time, effort, and money are spent on a mismatched solution, it means there is a missed opportunity to implement the correct solution. An unmet need still exists, and the cause is still there, resulting in damage to the organization along with wasting resources on other solutions.

The message: Avoid mismatches at all costs!

Verifying the Match

After identifying possible solutions, a designer must verify that a match exists between the need and the solution. It is often helpful to return to the source of input (such as focus groups and employees) to affirm that the solution meets the need. This approach is not applicable for every solution, because employees may be biased. However, their input may provide insight into progress made or indicate whether a solution is on target or off base. If the initial input was obtained from interviews or focus groups, it may be easier to return to those groups to see if the solution is addressing the cause of the problem. The important point is to find a way to discover whether a mismatch exists. Upon initial implementation of the solution, obtain feedback to ensure that the solution is a fit and is working based on the early objectives. Early feedback can prompt adjustments that need to be made or, in worst-case scenarios, suggest abandonment of the solution altogether. Seeking feedback represents another opportunity to involve a group of experts.

In addition, communicate the early results quickly. Letting the target group know that a solution has been implemented and that the results are positive (or developing or need improvement) provides another opportunity to collect feedback. Employees need to see that action is being taken, progress is developing, and, most important, the organization is responsive.

Tackling Multiple Solutions

The answer to whether an organization should tackle a problem with more than one solution at a time is not clear-cut. To a certain extent, the answer depends on the relative priority of the causes. Clearly, too many solutions undertaken at the same time can reduce the potential effectiveness of each and result in confusion and waste.

It is essential to examine the top priorities to determine which solutions are feasible, the time needed for implementation, and the level of others' involvement. These factors may mean taking on three or four (five, at the most) solutions. Avoid the quick fix, especially if the issue calls for a longer-term solution. Most turnover problems are not solved through quick fixes and tend to be issues that have evolved over time (either internally or externally). As a result, they will take time to correct.

Consider the level of involvement and support needed for the solution. Most employees must be involved in the solution in some way, requiring time away from routine duties or time to keep track of what is being developed. The level of support from managers may also be an important factor. If managers need to be on board with solutions and their implementation, then how much they can (or are willing to) support is significant.

Finally, available resources play a key role in whether it's possible to implement multiple solutions. For most organizations, the costs of the solutions can be substantial, and taking on too many may drain available resources. The result may even have an impact on the organization's earnings, potentially creating another serious problem.

Should the Solution Be Virtual?

Once a designer is certain that the recommended learning solution matches the business need or opportunity, the next question to consider is the learning format. Should it be a formal in-person workshop? Or a facilitator-led virtual class? Or a self-directed e-learning program? Does it need a coaching component? Maybe it should be a combination of these items? The requester and other stakeholders will want a recommendation, and they may also possibly need to approve it.

Many factors contribute to this decision, including the information gained while researching the learning and preference needs. For example, if the participants are airplane mechanics who need to learn an updated repair process for an airplane part, and hands-on practice with the new process is critical to the learning success, then a hands-on experience must be replicated in the learning environment. This means application and impact are unlikely to occur through a self-led solution or a stand-alone virtual class. If the participants are new managers who need to learn how to effectively provide constructive feedback to underperforming employees, then the ability to role play realistic scenarios will be an important part of the learning program. Because role plays can easily be done in virtual classroom breakouts, virtual learning may be the way to go.

A simple place to start is to look at the learner demographics. For example, do the participants work together in the same building or are they geographically dispersed? If they work remotely, do they have sufficient internet bandwidth for virtual classes? Are they equipped with the necessary tools, such as headsets for crystal clear audio? Are they tech-savvy enough to easily connect to a virtual classroom and participate in learning activities? Do they all speak the same language, or would multiple virtual classes in different languages need to be supported?

Let's say an organization decides to improve efficiency and decrease administrative costs by switching to a new online customer relationship management system. Employees need to learn how to use this new system before the costs savings can be realized. After looking at travel costs, participant locations, and facilitator time, L&D determines that a virtual workshop is the best way to both demonstrate and answer questions about the new features. It also realizes that virtual training will reach the geographically dispersed audience and that the software skills training is suited to the virtual method.

Designers can use the following checklist to help determine if virtual learning is an appropriate solution:[5]

1. Are the participants centrally located or dispersed? If the organization is not going to save on travel expenses because everyone is in the same location, then consider sticking with in-person training. It may be just as fast for them to walk down the hallway to a training room as it would be for them to log in to a virtual classroom.

2. What technology barriers affect success? Participants and facilitators need to have the appropriate technology. The exact technology needed will vary depending upon the virtual software program used; however, a typical technology setup requires a high-speed internet connection, a sound card and speakers to hear streaming media, an external headset, a webcam, and administrative privileges to install the virtual classroom software.

3. Do you have qualified trainers and producers to facilitate the virtual training event? Classroom facilitators need a new skill set to effectively deliver virtual training. They need to be comfortable with technology, able to multitask well,

and know how to engage participants they can't see. These skills come with training and practice; however, this facilitator preparation time should be factored into the decision. In addition, a virtual training event will go much smoother with a producer, who assists the facilitator with technology, troubleshooting, and running the virtual event, and helps create a seamless experience for participants. Is your existing training staff large enough to support facilitators and producers for virtual events? If not, can a budget be secured to add staff or to outsource this capability?

4. Will every participant and facilitator have an appropriate learning environment? Participants and facilitators need to have their own computer connection with sufficient internet bandwidth to attend the virtual event. They should be in a quiet area conducive to learning.

5. Who will administer the logistical details for the virtual learning program? The online environment creates a long list of logistics that need to be executed for a successful program. This includes creating the virtual classroom events within the software's administrative tools, getting links and passwords to everyone who needs them, distributing electronic handouts and other class materials to participants, and helping participants troubleshoot technical problems prior to the class.

6. Do all participants speak the same language? Virtual training can be an excellent way to provide training to an international population, as long as language barriers do not get in the way.

Next Steps

This chapter focuses on step two in the eight-step results-based process: Make it feasible. The overall objective of making it feasible is to ensure that you have the right solution. This chapter builds on the previous chapter, where business alignment begins with answering the question "Why?" Making it feasible can help the learning and talent development team move from order takers to business makers. It can lead the team toward the right solution for the business need. With the project connected to the business and knowing that it is the right solution, the next step is to design for success. Ensuring that the success is now defined at the business level allows you to set specific objectives for reaction, learning, application, and impact. Share the objectives with each stakeholder in the process, including designers, developers, coordinators, implementer, participants, and participants' managers. Challenge them to design a program that can deliver impact with tools, templates, processes, enablements, support, encouragement, and other approaches.

PART 2

Designing for Results

Expect Success:
Design for Results

Designing for Results

After suffering through a series of safety incidents, a manufacturing organization implemented a thorough review of its policies and processes. The training team did a careful analysis and came up with a hybrid solution. Part of that solution was to provide supplemental lockout and tag-out training to everyone on the manufacturing floor in every company location. The team identified five learning objectives for the program:

1. Recognize the importance of lockout and tag-out procedures.
2. Identify when lockout and tag-out procedures should be used.
3. Identify the responsibilities of all authorized, affected, and other employees during lockout and tag-out procedures.
4. Recognize different types of lock and tag devices.
5. Follow seven key procedural steps for lockout and tag-out.

The first four objectives for this supplemental training were primarily knowledge-based, providing refresher content on information that participants would already know. Because the participants were also scattered among the company's 10 US-based locations, the designer recommended creating a series of short e-learning modules covering the content in the first four objectives. These asynchronous assignments were required prerequisites for a series of virtual learning classes covering the fifth objective, following the seven key procedural steps. This last part of the training program was composed of two 45-minute synchronous virtual classes, allowing the facilitator to engage participants in meaningful learning activities that led to application and impact (Figure 4-1).

Figure 4-1. Sample Lockout and Tag-Out Program

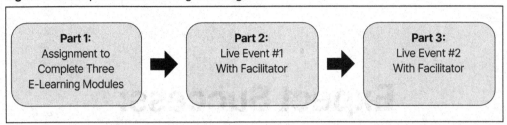

One of the most important considerations for designing live online classes is whether the virtual event will be perceived as worth the participants' time. Remember, you need to design training programs for application and impact, not just learning. This requires defining impact objectives (connecting the program to business measures) and application objectives (selecting the right solution) to deliver application results (they are using what they have learned) and impact results (the consequences of application). If a designer simply takes the knowledge objectives and creates a program where the facilitator just lectures and demonstrates, the program likely won't lead to learning, application, or impact. As we've already established, engaged participants are more likely to learn and apply the new knowledge.

There are many variations on the saying, "If you expect success, you will get it. If you don't expect success, you will not." However, we like Peter Drucker's version—"You have to create your own success." You must not only expect success from learning programs but create it by designing them for results.

The two previous steps in the ROI Process Model ensured that the program was aligned with the business, and that you were on the right path to get there. Now we'll turn our focus to designing for results. This chapter provides a blueprint for going beyond designing virtual learning that is simply engaging, focusing instead on how to ensure you're able to get the application and impact results you need.

The ROI Process Model breaks the design stage into two parts. In part one, your focus is on ensuring specific objectives are set at multiple levels, detailing how participants should react to the program, and identifying what they will learn, how they should use it, and the impact it will have on their work and the organization. Once the objectives are set, you move on to part two, where you'll design the virtual program in a way that fully engages participants in the learning experience. If they are not engaged, they are not learning, and if they are not learning then there will be no business impact.

Designing for Results at Each Level

To frame the importance of learning objectives in the success of virtual learning, let's return to the levels presented in Figure 2-1. As a reminder, levels of success define the chain of impact, which must occur as participants react, learn, apply, and have an impact. It all starts with Level 0 (input). Figure 4-2 summarizes the topics around which designing for results should occur.

Figure 4-2. Design Considerations by Level

Level		Design Considerations
0	Input	Who, what, where, when, how long, how much cost
1	Reaction	Important, necessary, relevant, intent to use
2	Learning	Action-oriented, knowledge gained, skills acquired, confidence
3	Application	Ease of use, timing, frequency, success, inhibitors, enablers
4	Impact	Alignment, line of sight, access, connectivity
5	ROI	Efficiency, effectiveness

Level 0: Input

Success begins with involving the right people in the program at the right time with the right amount of content at the lowest costs possible to achieve the desired results. Too often, virtual programs miss the mark with the target audience and the timing—sometimes with too much content and too much cost. So, designers need to consider the program's who, what, where, when, how long, and how much cost.

Level 1: Reaction

Determining the desired reaction is important. The principal targets for reaction are the participants. Will they see the content as important, relevant, easy, and something they intend to use? Do they think spending time in a virtual learning program is worthwhile? Clarifying these questions helps us design the structure, flow, content, examples, activities, communications, and all the other elements that motivate participants to actively contribute to the online class, use the content, and have an impact.

Level 2: Learning

At the heart of the process is the learning. The key to designing for learning is that it must matter to the individual and the organization. The content must be action-oriented so that skills and knowledge can be enhanced. And it must be contained in short, relevant bursts to keep the participants' attention and interest. Participants must leave the program with the confidence and determination to use what they learned. These factors drive many design decisions in virtual classes.

Level 3: Application

Simply learning the content doesn't ensure that participants will apply it. There are many design opportunities to help ease this application of content. Participants need to know when they should use what they learn, how often they should use it, and how to identify success; they should then go on to actually do these things. In addition, the program's design should limit inhibitors and enhance enablers that support application. These activities must be designed into the learning process to achieve business results.

Level 4: Impact

Ideally, the program's desired impact should be clearly understood from the beginning. That is why this is the focus of step one (chapter 2). The designer must then determine which solution will deliver that impact, as illustrated in chapter 3. Participants must be able to clearly understand business alignment and see a direct line of sight from what they are doing to those impact measures. They should have access to the impact data and understand their connection to it. There are many design issues that influence the impact requirement.

Level 5: ROI

Even if you aren't going to calculate ROI for a particular virtual learning program, it is helpful to think about it from a design perspective. ROI has two key components: impact outcome and efficiency. Impact outcome is converted to monetary benefits and focuses on the program's effectiveness. The efficiency is the cost of doing the program. In the design phase, the focus is on achieving greater impact while keeping costs low. Together, these concepts will keep the ROI on track.

Moving Beyond Learning Objectives

Objectives are powerful because they provide direction, focus, and guidance for all stakeholders. So, to deliver results you'll need to set objectives, especially at the application and impact levels. This step is noteworthy because higher-level objectives (particularly the business impact level) position the program to achieve business results. We must set objectives at the reaction, learning, application, and even ROI levels to generate business impact (Figure 4-3).

Figure 4-3. Multiple Levels of Objectives

Levels of Objectives	Focus of Objectives
Level 1: Reaction	Defines a specific level of reaction to the project as it is revealed and communicated to the stakeholders
Level 2: Learning	Defines specific levels of knowledge, information, and skills as the stakeholders learn how to make the project successful
Level 3: Application	Defines specific measures and levels of success with the application and implementation of the project
Level 4: Impact	Defines the specific levels that business measures will change or improve as a result of the project's implementation
Level 5: ROI	Defines the specific return on investment from the project, comparing the program's costs against the monetary benefits

Reaction Objectives

For any program to be successful, participants must react favorably to it. Ideally, all stakeholders, especially the participants, should be satisfied, because the best solutions offer win-win outcomes for all. Reaction objectives are necessary to maintain proper focus. Many programs do not have specific objectives at this level, because the designers and developers assume a particular reaction.

However, because it's very easy to collect this data in a virtual learning class using polls or survey links, it's best to drive the reaction with specific objectives (Figure 4-4).

Figure 4-4. Sample Reaction Objectives

At the end of the program, participants should rate each of the following statements at least a four out of five on a five-point scale:
- The program was organized.
- The virtual classroom platform was easy to use.
- The facilitators were effective.
- The program was valuable for my work.
- The program was important to my success.
- The program was motivational for me.
- The program had practical content.
- The program kept my interest and attention.
- The program represented an excellent use of my time.
- I will recommend the program to others.
- I will use the material from this program.

Learning Objectives

A common question for designers, especially when converting a classroom program to a virtual one, is "What content should I include in the virtual class?" Remember, an eight-hour classroom program will not equate to an eight-hour virtual program. While it may take a participant eight hours to learn the new content, not all of that learning needs to happen in the virtual classroom space with the facilitator. Instead of transferring an in-person classroom agenda directly to a virtual program, the designer should transform it. And this conversion should be driven by the learning objectives (Figure 4-5).

Figure 4-5. Sample Learning Objectives

After completing the program, participants will be able to:	
• Name the six pillars of the division's new strategy in three minutes.	• Determine whether a customer is eligible for the volume sales discount.
• Identify the six features of the new ethics policy.	• Demonstrate all five customer-interaction skills with a success rating of four out of five.
• Demonstrate the use of each financial calculation used in the weekly report.	• Explain the five categories for the value of diversity in a work group.
• Use problem-solving skills, given a specific problem statement.	• Identify five new technology trends explained by the subject matter expert.

Learning objectives are also important for designers creating virtual learning programs from scratch because they'll drive the decision around program structure. Cindy's three-step virtual learning design model, introduced in her 2014 book, *The Virtual Training Guidebook: How to Design, Deliver, and Implement Live Online Learning*, begins by determining the learning objectives:[1]

- Select the best format for each learning objective.
- Shape appropriate learning activities.
- Structure a logical flow.

The objectives determine which learning components should be self-led asynchronous assignments and which should be part of the synchronous facilitator-led classes.

Basic knowledge can almost always be learned by self-led asynchronous activities. For example, you won't find a formal training program on how to withdraw cash from a bank's ATM or how to operate a home coffee machine. You are probably like most people, who search the web when learning a simple new task or watch a YouTube video to figure something out. Other examples include:

- Following a job aid to complete simple tasks
- Reading an article to discover simple tips and hacks for doing something more efficiently
- Watching a video to learn a new process
- Clicking through an e-learning program to learn the fundamentals of a new procedure

Of course, there are always exceptions where asynchronous assignments aren't the best solution. Your analysis may reveal that participants aren't able to complete self-led assignments; for example, they might be new hires who don't yet have equipment or their work schedule may prevent them from completing self-led assignments while on the clock. Some training, such as for interpersonal or communication skills, is simply better when people come together because interaction plays a key part of the learning experience.

A Look Ahead to Steps 2 and 3 of the Three-Step Process

Once a designer looks at each learning objective to determine if the topic it represents should be synchronous or asynchronous, the next step is to shape the appropriate learning activities. In other words, you'll create a design document that maps out each exercise and activity, using the objectives to drive the details (we'll cover this in more detail in the next two chapters).

In step three, the designer uses this information to structure a logical flow for the learning solution. When this step is done well, it's an art form—like a child's building block set that can be pulled apart and put together in many different ways. When a designer builds a curriculum, they put the learning components together in a way that makes the most sense to the organization, stakeholders, and participants, and for the learning to happen at the impact level. This step encompasses sequencing as well as creating the overall flow of the blended learning journey.

Application Objectives

Program implementation should be guided by application objectives that clearly define what is expected and to what level of performance. They also involve milestones indicating when steps or phases of the process are complete. Application objectives are critical because they describe the expected outcomes of the intermediate area between learning what is necessary to make the program successful and the actual impact that those outcomes will achieve. The emphasis of application objectives is on tasks, action, or activity—they describe how participants should perform, the process steps that should be taken, or technology that should be used to implement the program.

The best application objectives identify behaviors or action steps in a process that can easily be observed or measured. They specify what the stakeholders will change or have changed as a result of the program. To be effective, they must clearly define the environment where the program is successfully implemented. As with learning objectives, application objectives may have three components: performance, condition, and criteria. Figure 4-6 shows typical application objectives and key questions asked at this level.

Figure 4-6. Typical Application Objectives

Typical questions for application objectives include:

- What new or improved knowledge will be applied to the job?
- What is the frequency of skill application?
- What specific new task will be performed?
- What new steps will be implemented?
- What new behaviors need to be adopted?

- What new procedures will be implemented or changed? What new guidelines will be implemented?
- Which meetings need to be held?
- Which tasks, steps, or procedures will be discontinued?

Impact Objectives

Most programs should have impact objectives. Business impact objectives are critical to measuring business performance because they:

- Are expressed in terms of the key business measures that should be improved as the application objectives are achieved.
- Define business-unit performance that should be connected to the program.
- Place emphasis on achieving bottom-line results that key stakeholders expect and demand.
- Ensure business alignment throughout the program.

The best impact objectives contain data that is easily collected and well known to stakeholders. They are results-based and clearly worded, and specify what the stakeholders accomplished in the business unit as a result of the program.

The four major categories of hard data impact objectives are output, quality, cost, and time. Major categories of soft data impact objectives are customer service, work climate, and image; this data is usually intangible. Figure 4-7 shows examples of impact objectives.

Figure 4-7. Sample Impact Objectives

After program completion, the following conditions should be met:

- The company-wide employee engagement index should rise by one point during the next calendar year.
- After nine months, grievances should be reduced from three per month to no more than two per month.
- Turnover of high potentials should be reduced to 10 percent in nine months.
- The average number of new accounts should increase from 300 to 350 per month in six months.
- Tardiness should decrease by 20 percent within the next calendar year.
- Employee complaints should be reduced from an average of three per month to an average of one per month at the organization's headquarters.
- By the end of the year, the average number of product defects should decrease from 214 per month to 153 per month at all plants in the Midwest region.
- Customer returns per month should decline by 15 percent in six months.

Return on Investment (ROI) Objectives

The fifth level for program objectives—the ROI—defines the minimum payoff from the project and compares its cost with the project's monetary benefits.

The traditional financial ROI is expressed as a percentage; in formula form, the ROI calculation is:

$$\text{ROI (\%)} = \frac{\text{Net Program Benefits}}{\text{Program Costs}} \times 100$$

Net benefits are program benefits minus costs, which is essentially the same formula as the ROI for capital investments. For example, when an organization builds a new building, the ROI is developed by dividing annual earnings by the investment. The annual earnings are comparable to net benefits (annual benefits minus the cost). The investment is comparable to fully loaded program costs, which represent the investment in the program. A program ROI of 50 percent means that for every dollar invested, that dollar is recovered, and an additional 50 cents is returned. An ROI of 150 percent indicates that after the invested dollar is recovered, $1.50 is returned.

Using the ROI formula essentially places program investments on a level playing field with other investments by using the same formula and similar concepts. The ROI calculation is easily understood by key management and financial executives, who regularly use it with other investments.

Defining Roles and Responsibilities

Before we dive deep into how to design, let's consider the who in the context of learning objectives. Remember from chapter 1, it takes a village for virtual learning to be successful. Many stakeholders are involved in the learning and talent development process, and they all have a role in delivering results. For the purpose of this section, we'll also assume that they have a role in creating expectations for success. Figure 4-8 shows how the different stakeholders are involved in a virtual learning program; the set of numbers under each role represents the objectives that role needs to drive their work and the success of the program.[2]

Figure 4-8. Objectives Needed for Important Stakeholders in Virtual Learning Programs

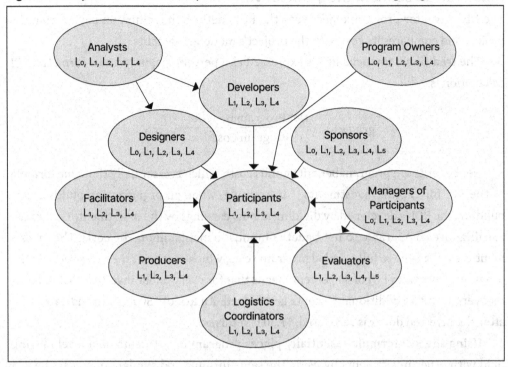

Analysts

The role of the analyst (or performance consultant) is to align the program to the business needs in the beginning by selecting the proper solution. As part of this process, they develop objectives—ranging from Level 0 (input) to outcomes at Level 1 (reaction) through Level 5 (ROI)—essentially creating the expectations for the program and clearly defining minimum expectations at each level. ROI objectives are usually developed when an ROI evaluation is planned. These objectives are approved by the requestor (or key sponsor), SMEs, and the program owners, and it is important to confirm whether it is possible to achieve the stated objectives for this program and audience within the timeframe. The objectives are created in a principal document using the SMART format (specific, measurable, achievable, relevant, and time-based).

Designers

The designer focuses on creating a solution that maximizes results. They select virtual activities that support learning, application, and impact. Having Level 3 and 4 objectives provides clear guidance so the designer can ensure they are reaching the right audience in a convenient time and place and realizing the proper reaction. Participants should find it easy to acquire the skills and knowledge and the application should be feasible, before the desired impact can be achieved.

Developers

In concert with the designer, the developer role acquires or writes the content based on the skills and knowledge needed in the program. They build virtual classroom templates and online interactions, bringing to life the designer's vision. The content is driven by multiple levels of objectives (Levels 1–4) and the need to develop materials that clearly help participants achieve those objectives at each level. The content's flow and sequencing are arranged to ensure proper learning. At Level 3, job aids, application tools, templates, and action plans are developed so participants can see how they're expected to use the information on the job. For example, cases and scenarios show participants why they are in the program, and share typical impact data from impact objectives.

Program Managers

The program manager is the person who owns the program and communicates information about it to all stakeholders. Armed with objectives at Levels 1–4, program managers prepare the communications, correspondence, and materials that are focused on the desired results, particularly at Levels 3 and 4. Program managers can be very influential, creating the expectation of results. They remind the participants that the program is not successful unless they actually use the content they learn on the job and show a corresponding impact in their work.

Facilitators

The facilitator's role is to explain, encourage, and validate expectations because they have Level 1–4 objectives. In the past, facilitators operated from Level 2 objectives to teach the skills and knowledge and measure improvements in the session, making sure participants learned the content. Most facilitators are comfortable in that role because it's familiar to them. But if the program has Level 3 and 4 objectives, the facilitator's comfort level may change (especially with remote participants) and they may resist these higher levels of the objectives.

Skilled facilitators can push the discussion beyond learning when they teach to Levels 3 and 4. For example, they can discuss application, explain how the content should be used, and provide tips and advice based on their experience with the use of the content. They can provide documents to help plan for application. And they can discuss the importance of impact and the typical impacts from these types of programs.

Producers

Producers are essential to the success of a virtual learning class. They support participants by helping them connect to the virtual classroom and then stay connected. They also support facilitators by running the behind-the-scenes technology. The producer may also serve as a co-facilitator and assist with program facilitation. Whether they stay in a support function or co-facilitate, skilled producers enable facilitators to focus on facilitating and allow participants to focus on learning. Because they support the learning program in such an important capacity, their objectives are the same as the facilitator's.

Participants

While the other stakeholder groups expect and support success, participants must deliver the results. If they don't, the program is a waste of time from the organization's perspective. Participants need clearly defined expectations, with objectives at Levels 1–4:

- Level 1 objectives show the expected reaction as participants shape their perception of the program.
- Level 2 objectives clearly show what they must learn, how they demonstrate the learning, how long it should take, and to what level they must achieve.
- Level 3 objectives clearly define what participants should be doing with what they have learned, how they should use it, how often they should use it, and the success they should have with it. Those important issues can otherwise be a mystery.
- Level 4 objectives address the impact. Participants should not complete a program and be left wondering "Why are we here?" Level 4 objectives describe the impact the program will have and whether that impact represents an improvement in a measure or maintaining their good record.

Logistics Coordinators

The attention to detail required for successful virtual learning requires logistical support. From sharing links to posting materials to communicating with participants, the coordination must be seamless. Participants and other stakeholders don't notice these details when they happen as planned, but it's obvious when something is missed. Therefore, coordinators need to be in tune with all program specifics, including the objectives and desired outcomes, so they can provide ample support and appropriate communication.

Sponsors

The sponsor is the individual or group that wants the program. They have supported, requested, or funded it; are very interested; and are powerful and influential. Sponsors have objectives at all levels, including Level 5 if the project's ROI will be evaluated. Sponsors often drive these expectations and analysis. Impact and ROI objectives are developed in discussions with the sponsor during the initial analysis phase. They have expectations and communicate them in correspondence, discussions, and kickoff sessions.

Managers of Participants

The participants' managers are an influential group when it comes to ensuring that participants are using what they have learned and that there is a corresponding impact once they're back on the job. Managers must be involved in the process of creating expectations before the program and in following up afterward to make sure the expectations are met. Manager activities can help ensure the transfer of learning takes place and the material is used on the job.

Organizational Leaders

The organization's leaders set the tone for expectations of results, defining the success of learning at the impact and ROI levels. They often review results, creating goals and challenges along the way to manage for value. If an organization adopts a leaders-as-teachers mentality, executives are typically involved in learning programs and create expectations with their comments, emails, and town hall communications. They'll also create expectations through facilitating the programs, pushing success to Levels 3 and 4.

Evaluators

Whether it's a distinct role or just part of someone's responsibilities, the evaluators collect data along each of the four levels. To be successful, they need the four levels of objectives and, if the program is set for an ROI evaluation, data for the ROI calculation. The evaluators position evaluation as process improvement for the program and provide participants and their managers with data to see the program's value.

Other Stakeholders

If your system has other appropriate stakeholders, they need to be defined and you need to communicate Level 1–4 objectives as they are developed. This will allow the stakeholders to clearly see where the program is going and their role in its success. Then they can help create the expectations from their perspective.

Keep It Sensible

We realize that there are many defined roles and stakeholders. While these roles may be clearly defined by job titles and full-time responsibilities, it is also possible that many roles will be accomplished by one individual (especially in smaller organizations). Even if one person has four different roles in the process, they have to think about the issues that are described in this section for each individual role. So, let's keep a sensible approach here. We are not suggesting added staff, only clarification of the roles established. The power of these objectives to make a difference in those roles will drive the needed business success.

Designing for Application and Impact: The Journey

This chapter sets the stage for designing for results and gets you started on the right path. However, the heart of this book is the next four chapters, which focus on designing for application and impact. When considering the transfer of virtual learning to the workplace, we can think about three different timeframes:

- Things we do before the journey.
- Things we do during the journey.
- Things we do after the journey is complete.

The terminology may be a little messy. With modular, virtual learning, and the concept of virtual learning assets, it may be harder to categorize clear timeframes for before, during, and after. As mentioned in the first chapter, we've broken down this modality as follows:

- Before is represented by the preparation phase. This is when you are preparing the learning module or asset.
- During is the learning phase. This is when the learning actually takes place in some formal or informal way.
- After is represented by application. This is when the learning is applied on the job and you want to evaluate the success of the program. You can evaluate a module, program, series of programs, learning asset, or learning component individually, or they all could be evaluated together.

The next three chapters of this book are devoted to these concepts. Chapter 8 then presents a growth area for the transfer of learning by introducing technology-enabled actions and techniques. These four chapters comprise the heart of the material to design for the results stakeholders want to see. We recognize that this is not an exclusive list, and encourage you to explore other techniques and report and share the outcomes.

Next Steps

This chapter set the stage for designing virtual learning for application and impact. First, the learning and talent development team must push success—beyond having a great reaction and acquiring the knowledge and skills—all the way to applying the new knowledge on the job and having an impact on business measures. Additionally, expectations must be created with SMART objectives at each level that define success. Ideally, they are needed for reaction, learning, application, and impact. If the ROI is pursued in a program, then an ROI objective is also needed. Level 3 and 4 objectives are powerful because they connect learning to the bottom line for all the stakeholders.

Once program objectives are determined, they drive the initial design decisions for virtual learning programs. This is the last step before program implementation. At this point, it is helpful to pause and look at how to more specifically design for application and impact. The next four chapters detail how this is accomplished. First, we'll focus on actions we can take before the program, module, or session is conducted, getting participants ready for the impact even before they attend.

Actions to Take Before the Program

Olympic athletes come together every four years to compete on the world stage. Each athlete's goal is to perform their best, and ultimately stand on the podium to receive a medal for their country. It's the realization of all the time, energy, and effort they've poured into their performance. The Olympics represents the pinnacle of their journey in their sport, considered by many to be the greatest accomplishment of them all.

No athlete would dream of "just showing up" to the Olympics. They come prepared—even overprepared: A swimmer brings extra goggles; a runner practices in all types of weather; a skater watches hours of video playback to improve one small technique. It's an opportunity of a lifetime, so they do everything they can to increase the chance they'll win.

While this analogy stops short of being perfect, it illustrates the type of advance preparation needed to design a virtual learning program for application and impact. The medal represents the program's end goal of business results. And the practice and preparation steps symbolize the work that must take place before a learning program occurs. Facilitators can't just switch from in-person classes to virtual ones and assume they can create engagement. Designers will not create a successful program without paying attention to the preparation phase. And participants cannot "just show up" for an online class and expect results to happen. Effective virtual learning that leads to application and impact requires setting the stage for success.

Design Techniques Prior to the Journey

Now that you have the foundation set (business alignment, appropriate learning objectives, and the right solution selected), it's time to start building the learning experience. In this chapter, we will explore 15 techniques that can be done prior to a virtual learning program to help lead to application and impact. The techniques include tasks for designers, facilitators, and participants. By applying these simple yet powerful methods, you can make sure the participants can engage in the program, learn new knowledge and skills, and apply their new knowledge back on the job.

Technique 1: Define Virtual Learning

As we said in an earlier chapter, if you ask 20 people to define *virtual learning*, you're likely to get 20 different answers. Some may think it's any type of online training, including asynchronous e-learning or watching a video on the company intranet. Some might reference using mobile devices in a classroom, while others assume a series of synchronous online events. And with the evolution of technology, some might think we've jumped to virtual reality simulations. While this subtle difference of definitions might not seem significant, if different stakeholders use different terminology and have varying expectations, there is bound to be trouble in achieving desired results.

In chapter 1 we defined *virtual learning* as:

> A synchronous, live online, facilitator-led training program. It has defined learning objectives, and a geographically dispersed audience. Each participant is individually connected to an online classroom where they can connect, communicate, and collaborate.

The emphasis is on using the virtual class for group discussion and dialogue. There's a distinction between a presentation-style webinar and an interactive virtual learning event.

This technique—defining virtual learning—is the foundation of all other techniques to use before a program. It may seem obvious, but it's not. Your organization's definition of virtual learning will guide the decisions made about its design, which will in turn affect the expectations around learning, application, and ultimately impact. Your definition will help determine things like how many participants join and how long each live event will be. For example, if some stakeholders think that a presentation-style webinar with 100 people is the same as an interactive virtual training class for 20 people, then getting on the same page with a standard definition will help smooth out the discussion around solutions.

This technique may be as simple as creating a statement like "Virtual learning is learning together, online," or using a statement as detailed as our definition. The point is to come to an agreement among all designers, facilitators, and other stakeholders, so that when a learning and talent development department proposes "virtual learning" as a solution to a business problem, everyone knows exactly what that means.

Technique 2: Design for Interaction, Engagement, and Application

Simply watching a documentary on television does not make one an expert on its topic. A doctor doesn't watch a video on surgical procedures and expect to perform them on a patient. The same holds true with virtual learning. A participant won't learn if they only passively watch a demonstration or listen to a speaker share a presentation.

As established in chapter 1, one of the challenges of virtual learning is a participant's tendency to multitask. People are not learning when they only half pay attention to a lecturing facilitator, and if they are not learning then business impact has no chance. While some of this challenge rests on their participants' shoulders—they need the discipline to put away distractions and choose to be present for the learning experience—the root cause of the issue often goes back to the program design.

Unfortunately, organizations that see virtual learning as an opportunity to pack as many people as possible into an online classroom just to lecture at them are missing the point. Presenting information online is not the same as creating a virtual learning experience that leads to application and impact. It's important to break out of this check-the-box mentality.

Therefore, the point of this technique is to be intentional about designing the virtual learning program for interaction, engagement, and application. And to ensure that everyone is on the same page about it. This is the next logical step after defining virtual learning, and it requires an intentional, coordinated effort.

One way to ensure a program is designed for interaction and engagement is to create a set of virtual learning standards to serve as consistent guidelines that spell out the expectations. By resolving to create an interactive virtual learning program, and then ensuring that all are in agreement about it, the talent development department has a pathway to engagement and application. Figure 5-1 presents a sample set of interactive design standards.

Figure 5-1. Sample Definition and Design Standards for Virtual Learning

Our Organization's Definition and Virtual Learning Standards
Virtual learning—also known as *virtual instructor-led training (vILT), virtual training, live online learning, synchronous online learning*, and other terms—is a method for our employees to learn in a social setting with a facilitator in an online environment. It's learning together, online.

Virtual learning at our organization consists of a highly interactive, live, facilitated, synchronous, online training event that uses a virtual classroom platform, where learners and facilitators engage with one another. It may be a stand-alone event or a series of online events. It has learning objectives and measurable learning outcomes.

What It Is Not
Virtual learning at our organization is not a one-way online presentation, nor is it solely an asynchronous self-directed experience. While those learning methods can have value in certain contexts and may be included as components in a virtual learning journey, they are not our definition of virtual learning.

Figure 5-1. *(cont.)*

Virtual learning at our organization fits the following characteristics:

- Small groups of attendees, typically 15–20
- Short (45-to-90-minute) interactive live online events (and no more than two hours), which are often part of a series
- Focused on dialogue and conversation instead of lecture
- Led by two facilitators (whenever available, for example, a facilitator and a technical producer, or two facilitators with shared responsibilities)
- Rarely recorded, instead requiring live attendance and participation (learners who are unable to attend a live event will either be rescheduled for a future session or directed to other learning resources)
- Conversation and dialogue are the core of each live event
- An opening activity (such as an icebreaker question) is displayed onscreen as learners join in to immediately capture attendee attention
- To establish an engaging environment, learners are invited to engage with the facilitator, the tools, and one another within the first few minutes of the session start time
- To help minimize distractions and multitasking, live events are designed to engage participants via interaction approximately every three to five minutes or through small group breakout activities
- Learning activities are both meaningful and relevant (i.e., learners don't have to answer a poll question just to take a poll)
- Learning activities take advantage of the full set of tools available in the virtual classroom platform (e.g., chat, polls, whiteboards, and breakouts) to create an interactive learning experience

Technique 3: Select the Right Platform

Because application and impact stem from engagement and learning, the virtual class must be interactive. Many platforms are available for online events, but only some were created with interactive training in mind. One of the most common mistakes made when designing virtual training programs is using a meeting or event platform. That's because many platform features essential for engagement, such as polls, chat, reactions, breakouts, and drawing tools, are not available in all meeting and event platforms. Learning professionals may attempt to use this type of platform because they're told the organization is already using it or that there isn't room in the budget to support a separate training platform. Unfortunately, this is like trying to hold an interactive in-person class in a corporate boardroom—it's possible but not ideal because that type of room isn't outfitted properly for small group collaboration.

For context, in the past, online platform vendors would offer a suite of products for online events. For example, one vendor would have a product for meetings, another product for large events (webinars), and a third product for training. (A familiar example may be GoToMeeting, GoToWebinar, and GoToTraining.) This made it easy to pick the appropriate solution. However, some vendors have now morphed features together, making it harder to tell which platforms are best for each type of online event. Now talent development teams have to go through a dedicated selection process to ensure the platform will allow the virtual learning program to achieve its goals (namely application and impact).

There is no one best vendor or best platform for every organization. Each one has its benefits and drawbacks. One platform may excel in its ability to share training templates among a team, while another platform may have superior whiteboarding capabilities. When seeking the best platform for your organization, start by comparing its features with the needs of the learning program (Figure 5-2).

As a general set of guidelines, consider asking these questions when selecting a virtual training platform:

❑ What activities do participants need to do to achieve the learning outcomes? What tools does the platform have to support these activities?

❑ How much internet bandwidth is required for the platform to operate smoothly (and how does that compare with typical participant bandwidth capabilities)?

❑ What is the platform's compatibility with other existing programs (such as the organization's LMS)?

Figure 5-2. Sample Platform Selection Tool

Features	Vendor 1	Vendor 2	Vendor 3	Vendor 4
Screen-sharing capabilities	❑	❑	❑	❑
Shared document file type requirements	❑	❑	❑	❑
Media file playback (audio and/or video)	❑	❑	❑	❑
Chat	❑	❑	❑	❑
Annotation and drawing privileges	❑	❑	❑	❑
Whiteboard collaboration	❑	❑	❑	❑

Adapted from Huggett (2017).

Technique 4: Prepare Facilitators to Support Learning Transfer

Skilled facilitators are known for their ability to present any type of content. They can lead engaging discussions, share captivating stories, and capture interest with interactive exercises. But if the ultimate goal goes beyond engagement to application and impact, then the facilitator has to do more. In addition to being engaging, they must also be relevant and informed. They must be deeply knowledgeable about the anticipated learning outcomes, and familiar with how the participants will be expected to apply their new knowledge. The facilitator must also recognize the significance of the business impact needed for the learning program to be successful. Once they truly understand how the learning will be applied in the workplace, the facilitator can support participants in reflecting and finding ways to apply the information relevant to their role and context. It is the role of the facilitator to help participants see how they can apply what they've learned and make commitments to what they will do after they leave the virtual classroom. Preparing to be able to support participants in this way is key.

Experienced facilitators with a background in the business may find this recommended technique easier to undertake. For example, a former bank teller who moved into a training role will quickly identify with the business realities of new tellers going through a customer service program. However, most facilitators will not have this prior background knowledge and thus will need to take time before the program to properly prepare.

In chapter 1, we introduced design thinking as a process for achieving learning success. One of the design thinking principles is empathy for the learner. Facilitators who put themselves in participants' shoes to uncover their challenges and get to know their situations are using this design thinking principle to create a better participant learning experience. This better equips them to relate the content to the participants, and help them apply the learning. These steps help lead to business impact.

Specific actions for facilitators to take include:

- Job shadow or observe to become immersed in the participants' world.
- Interview participants to learn about the types of situations they encounter.
- Review participants' job descriptions and other documentation to gain insight into performance tasks.
- Talk with participants' managers to gain clarity on performance expectations.
- Scan the organization's current business environment to learn more about the realities and challenges it faces.

Technique 5: Send More Than a Calendar Invite

A typical employee spends up to a third of their workweek in meetings.[1] And, because most calendar invitations look exactly the same, there's nothing to distinguish a virtual learning event from any other online meeting. Because interactive virtual classes have vastly different participant expectations than a typical meeting, sending a standard calendar invitation won't communicate enough information. This leads to this simple but effective technique: Send more than a meeting invite.

It's not that we should avoid sending a meeting invitation. In fact, they are important because they block the participants' time on their calendar. It's just that simply sending an invite isn't enough to support a learning program that's designed to achieve application and impact.

We recommend sending personalized messages to each participant in advance of a virtual learning program. Launching at least one email message upon registration, along with reminder messages, is ideal. The exact number of messages to send depends upon the scope of the virtual learning program. For example, in one of Cindy's six-part virtual learning journeys, participants receive a personalized message upon registration, another about a week before the program's start date, and two messages at designated time intervals during the program. These messages, which are above and beyond the calendar invitations, are tailored to the participants and sent directly from the facilitator.

These messages should be intentionally scripted by the instructional designer and included in the program materials. For small-scale virtual learning programs, the facilitator or another member of the talent development team can send out the email. Emails can also be automated—if needed—using a learning management system (LMS); this can be especially helpful in large-scale learning programs, which have more volume. However, research shows that email messages are more likely to be opened if the sender is a person instead of a system.[2] So, make sure to use someone's name in the "sender" field so that the messages look like they come from "Maria, Your Facilitator" instead of "No-Reply at LMS Name.com."

At the time of this writing, email remains the communication tool of choice for most organizations. However, as video communications, text messaging, and other platforms become more common, this technique could easily be accomplished using those tools as well. We advocate using the best communication method available for your audience.

As you'll see in the recommended techniques that follow this one, these advance messages can be used for multiple purposes. This technique's focus is on capturing participant attention and interest. It sets the stage for the engagement that will eventually result in our end goal—achieving business impact.

Technique 6: Set Participant Expectations in Advance

Many participants are used to attending passive webinars where they can easily multi-task throughout. So they may be taken by surprise if they join a virtual class and find that they're expected to get involved. In addition, participants in a traditional training program would leave their workspace to go to a classroom. But for virtual learning, they stay at their desk or office location. They are asked to stop what they're doing, often in the middle of their workday, and make a mental shift to focus on learning. We ask them to concentrate on practicing new skills even while their daily to-do list keeps catching their eye from the corner of their desk. Distractions abound and entice their attention away from the online program. Even the most disciplined of learners are likely to struggle with this challenging task.

Setting expectations in advance helps participants know exactly what to expect when attending a virtual class. It also helps drive the behaviors that you strive for in a virtual learning program that's designed for application and impact. If participants aren't engaging, then they aren't learning. And if they aren't learning, then there's no chance of achieving application and impact.

The exact expectations to set in advance will depend on the learning program. For example, some programs might require participants to log in to a software program so they can follow along with a brief demonstration and complete case study practice exercises. Other programs might need participants to be near a certain location, such as the factory floor, so they can quickly access equipment during an activity. Or perhaps it's simply the expectation of participation with webcams on. Each program is different.

The most obvious way to set expectations in advance is to send an email, as described in technique 5. Other methods include updating the program description to be clear about engagement expectations or sharing a checklist of preparation tasks to complete in advance of the program.

Tip

Avoid using the word *prework* to describe tasks that participants should complete in advance of the program. Instead, call it *preparation*, *action assignment*, or *part 1*. Because the phrase *prework* doesn't sound important, participants are more unlikely to complete it. Changing the description helps with perception, which then helps with motivation to do it.

Technique 7: Clearly Communicate Objectives

The learning objectives are the heart of the program and guide design decisions. Everyone involved in the program—from the stakeholders to the facilitators to the participants—should understand the objectives and how they lead to application and impact.

For participants to know why they are in attendance, the objectives need to be clearly communicated multiple times. Because most virtual learning events occur in the middle of the workday, people need a reason to stop what they're doing and focus on the facilitator and their fellow participants. If they know the program's "why?" (the business impact), they will be more likely to engage, and if they are aware of the objectives, they are more likely to achieve them.

"What sets us up for success are the strong learning objectives that come from a robust needs assessment," explains a senior learning consultant at a large US healthcare facility.[3] "These learning objectives have a prominent role in every training program. Facilitators make frequent references to them, not just at the beginning, but throughout. Because learners are exposed to the objectives multiple times, they are able to see the progress they're making toward the outcomes. Therefore, when we go to measure post-program results, we are able to use those objectives and refer back to them. Learners are so familiar with them that they know what we're measuring. It helps us determine results."

Getting everyone familiar with the objectives leads to a more successful virtual learning program. Figure 5-3 presents an example message.

Figure 5-3. Sample Participant Preparation Message With Expectations and Objectives

Hello everyone! My name is Cindy Huggett, and I'm looking forward to spending time with you in our How to Facilitate Hybrid Meetings online workshop, on Thursday, May 19, from 9:30 to 11 a.m. CT. As we prepare for our organization's new hybrid working model, this workshop will provide the practical information you need to effectively lead hybrid meetings. More specifically, it will equip you with the skills needed to create clear communication between your co-located and remote team members so your team can continue to reach its quarterly targets in this new environment. This message has all the information you'll need to have a successful learning experience.

First, please plan ahead to set this time aside, so that you are ready to learn and engage with your peers in this highly interactive, hands-on program. It may be a different online experience than you are used to—you will be working in small groups, participating in activities, and typing, clicking, and talking. We will use the webcams to see one another throughout the session, so please plan to join with your webcam on.

Also, to be ready to engage with your peers, please do three quick things before the program starts:
1. Send me a message with a brief "hello" and let me know what you are most looking forward to about our workshop. If we haven't already met, please include a brief introduction. What would you tell me about yourself, your role, and your experience if we were meeting in person over a quick cup of coffee or tea? Do you have any burning questions about facilitating hybrid meetings? If so, please share them.
2. Test your virtual classroom connection here: (insert link).
3. Read the attached article as it will set the stage for our time together. Come prepared to discuss what resonated with you most.

On the day of the workshop, about five minutes before our start time, get ready to learn, set aside your distractions, click on the virtual classroom link, connect your audio, and turn on your webcam.

See you online soon!

Technique 8: Create an Evaluation Plan

We cannot overemphasize the critical task of creating an evaluation plan as part of the design process. To achieve success, a designer must begin with the end in mind. They need to keep their eye on the program's primary purpose, which is for participants to apply new learning that leads to positive business impact. By creating an evaluation plan as part of the design process, the designer, and all interested stakeholders, will know how to measure and evaluate success.

The evaluation plan should encompass the entire scope of the virtual learning program, including virtual classes combined with other components that support learning transfer. We want to capture behavior change and impact.

There are many formats of evaluation plans, from a simple one-page list of tasks to complete, to a full-blown project plan with multiple lists of stakeholder actions. For a sample evaluation plan, see the additional resources available on the ATD website (td.org/DVL).

Technique 9: Create Job Aids and Application Guides

In a traditional classroom setting, participant workbooks are a standard part of the design and development process. These workbooks provide content and reference material, along with worksheets and other information about the in-person class. A common question is whether to create workbooks for participants in virtual learning programs as well.

The answer is "yes, and." Most virtual classes don't provide printed workbooks, although there are some exceptions (for example, programs that benefit from product documentation or other printed reference material). In lieu of printed guides, it's become common to distribute electronic materials.

But here's where the "and" comes in. It's not enough to simply provide a participant workbook for virtual learning. Printed training materials often ended up on a bookshelf never to be looked at again. Likewise, electronic training materials may get lost in the jumble of files and folders on a computer's hard drive or in the cloud. While participants may find a workbook useful during the program, they often forget about them after the program ends and so the workbooks are discarded.

Therefore, we suggest that designers should move beyond the traditional participant workbook and instead create a collection of job aids and application guides. Application guides are reference documents that provide support and learning reminders. More complex than job aids, these guides may be manual, detailed documentation or a dedicated online website.

A job aid provides a step-by-step guide to help participants go through a task once they're back on the job. Job aids can be printed or electronic and serve to reinforce what participants have learned. There is no one right format for job aids in virtual learning programs. They could be a checklist, a diagram, an e-book, or any other takeaway resource that assists participants with the application of content.

By focusing on application-based participant materials, a designer creates the pathway toward behavior change, which ultimately will contribute to the business impact we are seeking.

Technique 10: Create Custom Self-Objectives

Adult learners appreciate relevancy, so they are more likely to engage in learning if they know the direct impact it will have on their daily activities. If participants can see the specific, personalized benefits of a learning program, they will be more engaged and more likely to want to use their new skills back on the job. Thus, this technique is designed to get the self-motivation process started before the program even begins. (In chapter 7, we will discuss more about self-regulated learning and how autonomy can drive motivation to apply the new information.)

In this technique, designers create a preparation assignment where participants (and their manager, if appropriate) outline custom self-objectives after reflecting on the planned learning content and its relevancy to job tasks. These customized impact objectives involve two possible actions:

- If a program's impact objective is already set for the participants (such as to obtain new clients), participants may be able to customize the objective to their specific situation. For example, they could include how many clients to obtain and in what time.
- If participants are in a soft skills program, there may be many different impact objectives depending on their exact role. For example, a leadership program designed for all first-level managers in an organization will have a variety of measures depending on which department each manager works for. This provides a great opportunity for customization—participants can select the one or two measures to improve using their newly learned soft skills with their team.

This technique creates a customized objective just for a participant and motivates them to improve it. Figure 5-4 shows a customized self-objective preparation assignment we've adapted from ATD's Master Trainer Program.

Figure 5-4. Sample Learning Prioritization and Self-Objective Worksheet

Use this worksheet to prioritize your learning goals for the upcoming program. If possible, use it as a discussion guide with your immediate supervisor.					
Core Skills	**Learning Objective 1**	**Learning Objective 2**	**Learning Objective 3**	**Learning Objective 4**	**Learning Objective 5**
Preprogram review (enter one self-objective for each topic)					
Post-program reflection (items for application and an action plan)					

Adapted from ATD's Master Trainer Program.

Technique 11: Create a Kickoff Event and Include Managers

Also known as a *program orientation* or *part 1 of the curriculum*, the kickoff event is a separate session that designers often include in virtual learning series to set the stage for participant engagement and ensure the technology is working seamlessly. (See Figure 5-5 for a sample agenda.) Program kickoff events also increase participant motivation because they can give the learners a clearer view of the big picture and desired results. In our experience, participants are more likely to complete the self-led assignments series if they have met others in their cohort, recognize the learning expectations, and understand the important role they play in the learning process. These things are accomplished in a kickoff event.

In this technique, we also encourage the additional step of inviting each participant's manager or direct supervisor to attend. We know that managers can be a critical factor in learning transfer, so including managers in this initial kickoff event will help you gain their buy-in and accountability. While it's unrealistic to expect them to participate in the program alongside their employees, it's a helpful addition to invite them to the program's initial start.

Another, similar option is to hold a separate virtual event specifically for the participants' managers. While this requires extra time and effort for the facilitators, it may pay off in dividends with manager involvement. Having a quick check-in meeting to inform managers of the expected program requirements and the desired outcomes could be the difference maker that allows for application and impact.

Figure 5-5. Sample Virtual Learning Kickoff Agenda

This 30-minute virtual orientation will introduce you to the ABC Learning Program. You'll meet your facilitator and colleagues, learn about program requirements, and receive your first assignment. In addition, your managers will hear firsthand about the program's time commitments and expected learning outcomes.

Orientation agenda:
- Welcome from the facilitator team
- Virtual platform tour of tools
- Program outcomes, expectations, and required time commitments
- Meet your colleagues (This small group breakout activity includes a manager roundtable with the facilitator team.)
- First assignment overview

Technique 12: Design a Manager Guide to Accompany the Learning Experience

If managers will play a role in the participants' learning application, then they should be informed and involved with the learning program. One way to accomplish this is to design a companion guide for managers. It's like a participant workbook, but in a much shorter and more streamlined format.

The manager guide is designed to inform managers of the application learning objectives as well as provide an overview of the learning program. This can be especially useful during an extended learning journey because it helps the manager keep track of what the participant is learning and when they are learning it. It can also be used as a discussion guide with question prompts and sentence starters for managers to use with participants.

For example, a three-month management development program for high-potentials included multiple components, including in-person classes, self-directed assignments, virtual classes, coaching sessions, and many practice opportunities for participants. In addition to participant and facilitator materials, the designer also created a manager guide for the participants' direct supervisors. This guide included everything a manager needed to know about the learning program logistics, and the expected application outcomes. The guide also included a weekly discussion guide with questions written to create thoughtful discussions to spur participants to apply their new knowledge.

For this recommended technique, the designer should add the manager guide to the list of program materials that need to be developed in advance.

Technique 13: Ensure Easy Access to Application and Impact Data

It's said that what gets measured, gets done. As designers work through the entire process of creating virtual learning for application and impact, they have to examine a lot of data as they align the program to business needs. By making this data easily accessible to participants, the talent development team can increase the likelihood of buy-in to the program. In some situations, organizational processes are already in place for participants to easily apply what they've learned. For example, a posted procedure checklist can be used for participants to mark their completed steps. In other situations, there may be an online performance dashboard that allows participants to track application and performance. The key is to make it as easy as possible for the participant to follow through with what is needed as they apply the learning.

Technique 14: Use a Commitment Contract With Participants

There are several reasons a commitment contract can set up a virtual learning program for application and impact. For one, it encourages motivation throughout the learning journey. Remember, most virtual learning programs are part of a larger training curriculum with self-directed assignments that extend over time, so it's easy for participant motivation to wane. Assuming that each learning component adds value to the overall intended outcomes, then participants must complete each learning task.

For example, let's envision a blended training program for new first responders that includes sessions on basic life support, first aid, and emergency response. New first responders must learn all aspects of these items before they can be effective on the job. If they skip out on the lesson about wound care and don't learn how to properly suture a cut, then an injured patient may end up with an unnecessary scar. A commitment contract could prevent this from happening.

Commitment contracts ask participants to intentionally agree to complete every component of the learning program, with the ultimate goal of application and impact on the job. While it may seem pedantic to include this type of contract in a program, it may make the difference for some participants. This contract could represent a personal commitment that the participant acknowledges on their own behalf, or it could be shared with the facilitator, a trusted colleague, or the participants' direct supervisor.

A commitment contract could also go a step further by asking participants to take specific actions (application) and achieve a consequence (impact). In this case, the focus is usually on impact, and the participant commits to improve the impact by a certain amount by a particular time. This type of contract assumes that both the facilitator and the participant's immediate supervisor will agree and sign off on it. This essentially creates a three-way contract for performance improvement that is agreed to by participants, supported by their manager, and reinforced by additional efforts from the facilitator, administrator, and program owner. (See Figure 5-6 for a sample commitment contract.)

Figure 5-6. Sample Commitment Contract

Safe Workplace Action Plan

Name: Ellie Hightower

Facilitator Signature: _____

Immediate Manager Signature: _____

Follow-Up Date: June 1

Objective: Improve workplace safety

Evaluation Period: December to May

Improvement Measure: Monthly slips and falls

Current Performance: 11 per six months

Target Performance: Two per six months

Action Steps		Analysis
1. Meet with team to discuss reasons for slips and falls.	December 2	A. What is the unit of measure? 1 slip and fall
2. Review slip and fall records for each incident with safety—look for trends and patterns.	December 18	B. What is the value (cost) of one unit? $1,750
3. Make adjustments based on reasons for slips and falls.	December 22	C. How did you arrive at this value? Safety and health
4. Counsel with housekeeping and explore opportunities for improvement.	January 5	D. How much did the measure change during the evaluation period? (Monthly value) 8 (11 - 3)
5. Have safety conduct a brief meeting with team members.	January 11	E. What other factors have influenced this change: A new campaign from safety and health.
6. Provide recognition to team members who have made extra efforts for reducing slips and falls.	As needed	F. What percent of this change was actually caused by this program? 70%
7. Follow up on each incident and discuss improvement or lack of improvement and plan other action.	As needed	G. What level of confidence do you place on the above information? (100% = Certainty and 0% = No confidence) 80%
8. Monitor improvement and adjust when appropriate.	As needed	
Intangible Benefits: Image, risk reduction		

Technique 15: Use the Platform's Welcome Message to Reinforce the Program's Purpose

What do participants see onscreen when they join a virtual learning event? If you're using a platform designed for training (see technique 3), then you'll likely have a lobby or waiting room that can be used to set the tone for the program, as well as to communicate and reinforce previous messaging. This onscreen reminder of expectations and objectives will put the information at the forefront of each participant's mind. Going into a virtual learning program with the right mindset—to engage and to learn—will help participants apply the new knowledge. Figure 5-7 provides a sample welcome message.

Figure 5-7. Sample Welcome Message

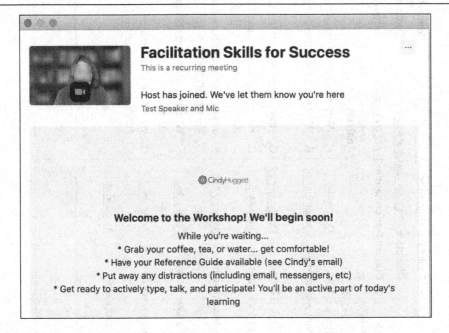

Next Steps

In this chapter, we provided 15 critical techniques to set the stage for program success. If you think in terms of the common ADDIE instructional design model, we are in the design and develop phase. We are building actions and activities that will continue the path to application and impact. These basic but powerful techniques help lead the way.

6

Actions to Take During the Program

Malaysia's minister of innovation is very interested in making his country one of the most innovative in the world. To do that, he is asking many organizations, particularly universities, to focus on innovation activities. In response, one university created a six-month program—Innovation Champions—for faculty and staff interested in identifying a product or service that could then be shared with another organization for development, use, or sale to the public. The selected participants wanted to explore new possibilities and define new ideas for products or services to implement in the country.

Four *R*s describe the purpose of the program:

- Make the university *relevant* in the innovation process.
- Increase *revenue* back to the university (because some organizations would develop the products and services in the marketplace, sell them, and pay a royalty or a lump sum to the university to use the idea).
- Build *relationships* with various organizations as the university faculty and staff develop the ideas.
- Gain *respect* for the quality of the faculty and staff and their ability to be creative and innovative in today's climate.

During the six-month program, participants engaged in various creativity and brainstorming sessions before deciding on the idea they wanted to develop. They were also given the resources and support they needed to create a usable product or service.

Midway through the program, participants were asked to write a press release detailing their vision of the finished product or service. It would describe the idea that led to the product or service offered, and explain why it was needed, who needs it, and the type of organizations that may be interested in it. This activity enabled the participants to visualize the final result of their effort. It was a great motivational and learning tool that allowed participants to extend what they learned beyond the virtual sessions into what would happen after the virtual program.

In the previous chapter, we recommended techniques to take prior to a virtual learning program. Many of those tasks focused on setting the stage for interaction. If you can overcome the challenge of multitasking participants to create an engaging environment, then the learning can happen. When participants are involved in the learning, they are more likely to apply it. And with application comes business impact.

Specific Techniques

In this chapter, we continue the design process by recommending effective techniques to use during a virtual learning program. A successful program—one that's interactive, engaging, and focused on learning outcomes, application, and impact—needs to have both an interactive design and engaging facilitator. Therefore, these techniques include methods that span both design and delivery. Most of the 17 techniques in this chapter are quite simple, yet they create a path to success. By using these techniques, you will make sure the participants can engage in the program, learn new knowledge and skills, and apply the learning on the job.

What's in a Program?

The most common length of a virtual class is 60 minutes; however, that doesn't mean that you need to fit all the learning required for application and impact into a one-hour timeframe.[1] Learning takes place over time, and most modern training curriculums consist of multiple learning events. A blended learning journey includes both facilitator-led synchronous components and self-directed asynchronous activities. Learning and application naturally extend beyond the boundaries of the official training program. For the purposes of this chapter, and this book, we use the terms *program* and *journey* to refer to a defined set of learning components that are intentionally woven together as a learning solution designed to meet a business challenge or opportunity.

Technique 16: Create a Warm Welcome

In any advanced messaging you send, invite participants to join a virtual class five to 10 minutes early. This is especially important if it's the first event in a series because it allows you to sort out any tech issues in advance. It's also important because it ensures that everyone is ready to start at the actual start time. Think of it this way: In an in-person class, it would be strange if participants walked in the door at 9:59 or 10:01 a.m. for a 10 a.m. class. Participants typically arrive early for in-person sessions so they can select a seat and get settled. Virtual classes should be the same.

If your organization struggles to get participants to join virtual classes on time and/ or early, consider the root causes. Are all virtual events—meetings, webcasts, and training events—seen as the same type of experience and thus have the same norms? The techniques presented in the previous chapter will help with this issue because they'll distinguish virtual learning activities from other online events. Or, perhaps the organization has a meeting-heavy culture, which leads to meetings running back-to-back throughout the day. Not only does this encourage tardiness, but it is also detrimental to the participants' ability to actively focus on learning.[2] To overcome this issue, ask organizational leaders and other stakeholders to model the importance of spending less time in meetings and prioritizing learning. In addition, if participant timeliness is a known challenge, then the L&D team should be intentional about when virtual classes are scheduled. For example, they can schedule classes for first thing in the morning or start learning events at half-past, rather than on the hour.

Now that we've established that joining a virtual class early is possible and preferred, the next step is to make it matter. Participants entering the room should be promptly acknowledged and warmly greeted. The online atmosphere should feel welcoming and inviting, to encourage participants to get involved. Instead of stark silence, spark conversation. Have a soft opening that invites participants into the experience. Be intentional about what's displayed onscreen when they join the room. Use the time to set the tone, teach participants how to use the interactive platform tools, and preview the training topic. Generate excitement and capture their attention.

Using Producers

The most effective virtual classes have a facilitator and a producer. The facilitator leads the learning portion of the program, while the producer manages the technology. Producers may stay completely behind the scenes, or they may have an active co-facilitation role. Either way, they are responsible for supporting both the facilitator and the participants. While it's possible for a single facilitator to lead the entire virtual class, we don't recommend it. Without a producer, if even one participant struggles with the technology, the facilitator has to stop facilitating so they can help the participant, which affects the learning experience. Producers are a small investment of resources that pay big dividends in quality.

If you're having trouble picturing this technique, consider how stage shows use warm-up acts or preview moments to generate excitement. Or think about the trivia questions that play on theater screens prior to a movie. The idea is to capture the audience's attention and prepare them for the main act. The exact implementation of this warm welcome will vary depending on the platform used, the training topic, the intended design, and the facilitator's style. However, regardless of the implementation, this technique will help participants realize that they will be expected to get involved. See Figure 6-1 for a sample slide.

Figure 6-1. Sample Warm Welcome

Welcome to the Program!

While we're waiting to begin . . .

1. Connect your audio and video

2. Get ready to learn by putting away distractions and closing your email

3. Introduce yourself in chat (name, role, location)

4. Submit your best guesses to the following questions?

What percent of all transactions have been with new clients so far this year?

What's the most common request that new clients make?

Technique 17: Create Immediate Interaction

The Warm Welcome technique primes the pump for interaction by setting the tone for conversation and collaboration. This technique, Create Immediate Interaction, is designed to come immediately after, picking up at the official start time of a virtual training class.

A traditional class usually begins with a facilitator spiel. They welcome everyone to the program, review the platform tools, talk about the program timing, and share the agenda. While this information may be useful, it keeps participants in passive mode. When the information is presented this way in a virtual classroom, however, it leads to a common virtual learning design mistake: waiting too long to get participants involved.

We recommend immediate interaction, within the first two minutes of the virtual class start time, to get participants clicking, typing, or talking right away. It doesn't need to be a complicated activity—a simple interaction, such as a poll question or a chat prompt, is sufficient. What's important is taking advantage of this prime opportunity to set the stage for an interactive learning experience, which won't happen unless participants interact with the tools and one another within the first few minutes of the program. The housekeeping content can either wait a few minutes or be converted to an engaging exercise.

For example, you could immediately ask everyone to introduce themselves in chat. Or post a short-answer poll question that requires typing. Or have everyone complete an exercise using the onscreen drawing tools. Or put everyone into small breakout groups with an assignment to complete. The main point of these ideas is that every single person should be clicking or typing in this first activity to reinforce the notion that they will be expected to participate throughout.

A virtual class designed for interaction will keep participants involved in the program. But it's not about interactivity for the sake of interactivity. Most participants want more than entertainment—they want results. Organizational stakeholders want this too. Instead, the interactivity is there to help participants stay engaged in the program. Remember, if they aren't engaged, they aren't learning. And if they aren't learning, then the ultimate goal of application and impact won't be achieved.

See Figure 6-2 for a sample interactive opening.

Figure 6-2. Sample Opening Script With Immediate Interaction

"Hello, my name is Maria; welcome to the program. It's great to see everyone on webcam! Please introduce yourself in chat: Share your name, role, and location, as well as your response to the onscreen question. Let's get to know one another."

[Maria gives everyone time to type and then invites several participants to speak and elaborate on their comments to create conversation and dialogue.]

"As you know, we'll be focused on topic ABC today. Here's a poll question to find out your experience with it."

[Maria opens the poll, gives everyone time to respond, and then invites several participants to comment on their experience.]

"Thanks everyone! Now that you've told me about yourself, I'd like to introduce myself. I'm joining today from the Harrisonburg site and have been with the company for 12 years. Before joining the training team, I spent almost 10 years on the factory floor. I'll share more as we go through this learning journey.

"We have posted three guidelines for virtual learning success onscreen. Take a moment to read them. *[Pause for a few moments while everyone reads.]* Can we all agree to these guidelines? Click on the raise hand button at the bottom of your screen to agree. *[Acknowledge responses.]*

Technique 18: Include WIIFM at the Start

Help participants prioritize the virtual class over any other distractions surrounding them by sharing the WIIFM at the start of each virtual session. *WIIFM—or What's in it for me?*—refers to someone's willingness to pay attention to something. If someone understands the benefits of the program and how it will benefit them, they'll be more likely to pay attention and take in the information.

Even if it's the third virtual class in a series, circling back to the WIIFM each time reminds participants of the program's importance. You can share the WIIFM in multiple ways, such as through a static visual aid or a small group (breakout) discussion. However, remember that it's preferable to use activities that get participants involved and thinking, rather than simply passively listening.

Technique 19: Make It Social

A design that emphasizes social connections makes for a better overall learning experience because fostering a sense of community is critical for engagement in the virtual environment. When there is robust conversation and collaboration, remote participants are able to learn from one another and feel less isolated because they realize they're part of a group. By designing conversation and teamwork into virtual learning, you create a community. When participants feel connected to one another, they are more likely to get involved. On the other hand, when participants stay anonymous, they are more likely to tune out and multitask.

Here are a few simple ways to make a virtual class social:

- Encourage small talk between and among participants. This chatter can be verbal, via chat, or in small group settings.
- Use poll questions to gather input, share the results for all to see, and allow the group to comment on the collective responses.
- Use small breakout groups for deeper discussion and dialogue.
- Allow time for conversation in the program agenda.
- Assign participants to teams at the start of a session and encourage them to work together throughout the class.
- Ask participants to choose a learning partner with whom they can privately chat throughout the session to share insights.

Technique 20: Select Activities for Maximum Involvement

Once you have set the stage for an engaging virtual class that's focused on application and impact, it's important to keep the momentum going. You've established that participants are expected to take an active role in their learning, gotten them involved from the start, and asked for their commitment. Now it's time for them to deliver on that promise.

In a cohort of 20 participants, for example, it's essential that everyone can apply the learning—it's not enough for just five or 10 participants to be active and "get it." All 20 participants need to be on board. Stakeholders expect it, their managers expect it, and the facilitator should expect it as well.

Thus, when planning class activities, the designer should create interactions that purposefully include everyone. For example, poll questions that allow everyone to provide input and reactions are a fast way for everyone to respond. Breakout activities should be designed for small groups (three to four people) so that everyone can be involved. Minimize times when only one person gets to talk and make the most of whiteboards and other collaboration exercises. While this may all seem obvious, it's easy to forget when designing the program.

Skilled facilitators should also make a point to include everyone in the activities. For example, they could deliberately phrase questions in ways that invite all to participate: "There are 18 of you, so let's get 18 responses in chat before we continue." (We'll cover this more in technique 21.) It's the facilitator's responsibility to keep track of participation, openly ask for input, and seek everyone's involvement in the learning.

Number of Participants?

Most virtual classes (77 percent) have 25 or fewer participants.[3] The larger the group, the easier it is for a facilitator to present content rather than enable learning. Therefore, be intentional about the number of participants in a virtual class.

As facilitators carefully monitor participant involvement in the learning activities, they need to pay attention to engagement clues. For example, if a participant doesn't respond to discussion questions for a lengthy period of time, then the facilitator should check in to see what's going on. A passive participant may simply be reflecting on the content or more comfortable remaining silent, but facilitators need to be aware if lack of engagement is hindering their ability to learn. There's a difference between participants who connect but don't engage because they're multitasking and not paying attention, and participants who don't engage because they prefer to stay silent. When facilitators notice that a participant is remaining passive, they should find out if that choice is affecting their ability to learn. The facilitator could send the participant a private chat, keep them in the main room for a moment at the start of a breakout activity, or connect with them between sessions.

It's also possible for technical problems to get in the way of learning, such as a participant who can't stay connected to the class due to bandwidth issues. When this happens, the facilitator could reschedule them to the next class offering, have a producer work with them for quick solutions, or provide back-up application activities for them to complete.

Technique 21: Ask Questions With Intent and Inclusion

In the traditional classroom, discussion questions are usually open ended. However, most open-ended questions are met with silence in the virtual classroom environment because they aren't specific enough to jump-start a conversation. In addition, virtual participants can get confused about whether they are supposed to speak up, type in chat, or wait for further instruction. Or they may not want to be the first person to speak. Or they assume someone else will respond.

Virtual facilitators can generate dialogue by asking an initial discussion question that's both *precise* and *prescriptive*. The question should include directions on how to respond; for example, instead of asking, "How will you apply this information to your job?" it's better to ask, "What is one specific way you can apply this information to your job? Please type it in chat." Or you could say, "Click on the raise hand button if you can think of at least one specific way this information applies to your job." The facilitator can then use the typed comments or raised hands to ask follow-on questions and continue the conversation.

This technique not only jump-starts conversation; it also intentionally includes all participants. For example, only a few people may respond to a facilitator's question of, "Who else has a comment about this topic?" But if the facilitator says, "Raise your hand if you have a comment, otherwise click on the 'no' button," this phrasing implies that everyone is expected to give input. Skilled facilitators who adopt this technique can keep all participants immersed in the learning, which will then enable application and impact.

Technique 22: Use the Tools Creatively

Virtual classroom platforms provide an abundance of tools to keep participants engaged and involved. For example, facilitators can use:

- Polls for conversation starters
- Chat for group conversations
- Webcams for deeper dialogue
- Whiteboards for team collaboration
- Breakouts for practice and feedback

But remember—it's not about using the platform tools just to use them. It's about using them to further the learning results. For example, if participants have to learn a new technique for responding to customer requests, they could respond to a poll question about their experience with the technique, watch a three-minute video demonstration, brainstorm application ideas with their peers on a whiteboard, and then go into breakouts to practice the new technique.

It's also important to maintain interest by using different activities, rather than using the same one over and over again. Participants will get bored quickly if the only activity is "type your response in chat." Designers should get creative with the available tool set to keep the content fresh and exciting. Table 6-1 presents some sample activity ideas to use with different tools.

Table 6-1. Sample Activity Ideas by Platform Tool[4]

Tool	Sample Activity Idea
Chat	Pair up participants to have a private, typed discussion about their action plans. Then ask each pair to report out one or two highlights from the discussion.
Annotate and draw	Draw a line that divides a slide (or whiteboard) in half. Ask half of the audience to type action plan obstacles on one side of the slide, and the other half to type action plan enablers on the other side.
Whiteboard	Ask participants to collectively design and draw an image that represents their topic takeaways, which will help them remember to apply them back on the job.
Reactions	Pose a challenging question and ask participants to respond using a status indicator. For example, use a smiley face for "strongly agree" or an away symbol for "strongly disagree."
Raise hand	Ask anyone who's experienced XYZ to please raise their hand. Then invite each person to share a brief synopsis of their experience either verbally or in chat.
Poll	Create a competition by assigning point values to the correct responses of each poll question. Run the competition throughout the virtual event, using polls to ask application questions that check for knowledge transfer. Have a simple prize for the participant who accumulates the most points.
Breakouts	Divide participants into small groups and place them into breakout rooms. Have each group brainstorm solutions to a common challenge and report out on their recommendations.
File or material distribution	Post a scavenger hunt list and ask participants to search for information on a support website they'll use after the program. The first person to raise their hand, indicating they've found everything, wins a fun prize (such as bragging rights).

Technique 23: Use Visuals to Keep Attention

Most virtual classroom platforms emphasize screen sharing and document sharing, which means slides take center stage. However, the longer a slide stays on the screen, the more likely a participant is to grow visually tired, look away, and check out. Unfortunately, passive participants are usually not learning, which negatively affects their ability to apply new skills. Instructional designers need to combat this by intentionally creating slides that align with an interactive virtual class.

Slides should enhance the content and provide activity instructions. When used during short teaching sections, they should be visually appealing and follow generally accepted best practices for slide design:

- One thought per slide (not text-heavy or laden with bullet points)
- San serif fonts (easier to read onscreen)
- Use of photos or vector graphics (not clip art)

Also, remember the difference between visual aids and reference material—the best slides make the worst handouts. As we recommended in the previous chapter, provide job aids or application guides for the how-to content, and use the slides as visual aids.

Finally, because participants may be joining from many different device types, each with a different screen size, pay attention to the selected font sizes. The smaller the screen, the larger the font needs to be for readability. As a general guideline, fonts should be at least 34 point to be read on most screens.

Technique 24: Use Realistic Scenarios

Our design process emphasizes application and impact. It's not enough for learning to take place during a virtual class; that learning needs to be applied so that it has business impact. One aspect of this learning transfer incorporates using realistic scenarios that participants can easily recognize themselves in without having to reach too far to make a connection. Stories should make sense in the context of the participants' workplace and the organization's realities.

This technique extends beyond storytelling to designed program activities. Role-play activities, video scenes, and other scenarios should be as close to real-world as possible. Designers can partner with subject matter experts to create believable application activities, and use pilot programs to verify their validity.

With the rising use of augmented reality and immersive simulations in workplace learning, it's also time to consider whether to use them in virtual learning solutions (if they are not in use already). These technology-enhanced activities create extremely accurate replicas of the real world that allow for very realistic practice scenarios.

For example, a virtual class could include a facilitator-led virtual reality (VR) simulation. Participants meet in the virtual classroom platform before starting the VR activity (typically by following a link the facilitator has placed in chat). Participants may put on a VR headset for a fully immersive experience, or they may be able to view the simulation via a web browser. At the end of the VR activity, participants return to the virtual class to debrief the learning and continue with the program. Research on realistic immersive learning simulations has found that participants are 275 percent more confident to apply skills learned after training.[5]

Technique 25: Incorporate Formative Feedback

Facilitators should gather formative feedback during a program. Fortunately, this is relatively easy if they leverage the tools in the virtual platform:

- Polls allow for multiple-choice and even short-answer responses.
- Chat opens up the ability to type and provide open-ended input.
- Whiteboards let participants freely write and draw.
- Reactions can be used to quickly gauge participant sentiment.

Designers should build in knowledge checks throughout the event to assess understanding and comprehension. These should go beyond simple recall-type poll questions and instead use relevant application questions. In addition, it's possible to have knowledge checks in the form of hands-on activities and other exercises. For example, in a selling skills program, participants could review common objections and role play their responses to each. This activity mirrors what they'll do when talking with customers and allows the facilitator to gauge their comprehension and application abilities. The facilitator can then use this information to determine whether more application practice is required or it's time to move to the next topic.

Technique 26: Include Self-Reflection Time

Short virtual classes often mean a fast-paced experience with frequent activity to keep participants involved. Some training topics lend themselves to this quick pace, while others benefit from a slower deep dive. As long as participants are engaged, learning, and moving toward the endpoint of application and impact, either speed is fine. However, it's not OK to skip over self-reflection time. Kolb's Learning Cycle insists that reflection must be included if application is the goal.[6]

The challenge with self-reflection in a virtual class is how to design the activity so participants don't multitask. Help them prevail over the temptation to disengage by providing built-in scaffolds. Here are a few ideas for self-reflection activities with boundaries:

- Provide a short break in the agenda before self-reflection time to give participants time to take care of any pressing needs.
- Place a countdown timer onscreen, so participants can see how much time they have for each self-reflection question.
- Put participants into individual breakout rooms (just one person per room) with individual activity whiteboards. Watch as participants complete the questions on the whiteboard in their assigned rooms.

- Inform participants that they will be reporting out the results of their self-reflection to a partner, a small group, or the large group.
- Include self-reflection in an action assignment activity between virtual classes.

When planning a self-reflection exercise, encourage participants to use the time to go beyond just recalling new information they have learned. Invite them to consider application of the content. How will they use the new knowledge and skills? How will the information assist them with productivity, efficiency, or other tangible measures? What could get in the way of application, and how can they overcome those challenges?

Technique 27: Teach to Application and Impact

When application objectives and impact objectives are developed and given to all stakeholders, it clearly shows what they should do after the program (Level 3) and why the program exists in the first place (Level 4). This helps the facilitator and producer teach toward the objectives. An instructional designer will ensure the content, exercises, activities, and materials speak to actual use and the impact. This places the focus on program success that's defined not by what participants learn but what they do with what they learn, and stakeholders can focus on that as the definition of success—impact and not learning.

This technique also represents the application of an important mind shift we have mentioned throughout this book. Many instructional designers think their work is finished once participants learn the material. Unfortunately, if participants don't use what they've learned, and there is no corresponding impact within the organization, then the program is a waste. The top executives who allocate budgets for virtual learning clearly want to see the program's impact. In their minds, the success of the learning program is not reached until the impact has been achieved. This mind shift puts a proper focus on all the activities to teach to those Level 3 and 4 objectives.

Technique 28: Integrate Application Activities

When sequencing a virtual learning program, application activities should be in the forefront of everyone's mind. By using the techniques we have described to this point, participants should be well aware of the expected level of success: The final goal is a positive business impact. Learning isn't enough. Application activities must be integrated into the learning experience.

In chapter 4, we outlined a process to distinguish between what content belongs in a virtual class and what can be asynchronous. Knowledge acquisition usually belongs in self-directed assignments. In most circumstances, participants can watch a video or read a document to learn fundamentals and background information, so that the virtual class time can be spent in discussion, collaboration, and practice.

A common design mistake in many learning programs, not just virtual classes, is to focus on rote understanding instead of applied knowledge. One way to tell if this is happening is to look at what kind of questions are asked on an end-of-program test: simple multiple-choice questions or scenario-based application questions. Multiple-choice questions test only knowledge, while scenario-based application questions test how the learner will apply that new knowledge back on the job. Think of it this way—would you want to share the road with a new driver who'd only passed a multiple-choice test before receiving their license? Of course not! We expect new drivers to gain ample practice time and pass a road test before they get behind the wheel on their own. It's not that knowledge is bad; it's just not enough. The focus of virtual class activities needs to be on application.

Role playing and case studies are two types of application activities. Role plays, especially in breakout groups, allow participants to practice and explore their new skills. Case studies can be tackled individually, in pairs, in small groups, or as a large group interaction. Their flexibility provides many methods for implementation.

Technique 29: Connect Content Between Sessions

A key benefit of virtual learning is the ability to provide practice and application exercises throughout a participant's blended journey. Because participants stay in their workplace for the experience, they likely have ample opportunities to quickly apply their new skills in real-world situations. This immediacy of rehearsal and application helps integrate the new skills into memory and use. If practice activities are placed between virtual sessions, the facilitator can link the content from one session to another while allowing learners to practice their new skills.

The instructional designer should create asynchronous application exercises for participants to do between sessions. They could be either self-led or group projects, and they may involve the participants' managers. For example, participants may spend time together in a virtual class from 8:30 to 10 a.m. and then receive an application assignment to complete before they reconvene the following day. Upon returning to the virtual classroom, participants discuss and review the project. This process could repeat over and over throughout the program. Participants get the benefit of immediate application, discussions with their peers, and expert guidance from the facilitator as needed.

Scheduling Virtual Classes?

When virtual classes are part of a learning journey, it's common to question how much time should pass between each facilitator-led event. There isn't one right answer because it depends upon many factors including the scope of the training curriculum, the activities required for learning and application, and the scheduling needs of the organization.

Here's one way to schedule a full-day program with three facilitator-led virtual classes and three self-directed application activities:

8–9:30 a.m.	Virtual Class #1
9:30–10:30 a.m.	Application Activity and Break
10:30 a.m.–12 p.m.	Virtual Class #2
12–2 p.m.	Application Activity and Lunch
2–3:30 p.m.	Virtual Class #3
3:30–4 p.m.	Application Activity

This same program could also be spread out over several days or even several weeks.

In general, there should be enough time between classes for participants to reflect on and apply the content. But don't leave too much time or learning momentum will stall and suffer.

Technique 30: Have Action Plan Presentations

The use of action plans traces back to the federal government in the 1950s as the Participant Action Plan Approach (PAPA).[7] To create an action plan, participants simply list the steps they plan to take to use the content they are learning in the program. In the last two decades, action plans have been used for application and impact. The action plan starts by stating the impact measure the participant wants to improve and then listing the actions they will take to do so. This not only serves as a way to organize and plan the action steps, but it increases the participant's motivation by creating ownership. It also acts as a data collection tool because completed plans are sent to the evaluation team to show the successes for application and impact.

To help shape action plans, we suggest using these types of goals:

• **Progress.** This type of goal focuses on making significant progress in eight to 10 weeks, which is a tangible period of time for focusing on a goal. If the task is too big, resulting in a longer goal, break it down into smaller chunks.

• **Stretch.** Stretch goals keep it interesting! Just make sure they're not too easy or too hard.

- **Continuous.** This goal is about a journey or continuous improvement—not yes or no. This makes for a richer reflection process and conversation.
- **Meaningful.** Make sure goals are meaningful to the participant, not someone else. A goal that someone chooses for themselves will be far more sustainable than a goal chosen for them.
- **Actionable.** This is a doing goal, not a knowing goal. Don't commit to knowing more or learning more content; instead, commit to doing something with what the participants have learned.

Action planning is the preparation step for great learning transfer. It's essential that this is captured during the learning experience, rather than waiting until after the program is complete. When participants create their action plans three-quarters of the way through the content and learning phase of the program, superior results and outcomes typically follow. While this may seem counterintuitive—shouldn't we cover all of the content before participants create their action plans?—it's a trade-off between the quality of the action plans and information that is covered. If we want application and impact, the plan's quality and completeness are paramount. And it's also fine to amend action plans after the session closes. Visit TurningLearningIntoAction.com to see a sample action plan, as well as create and share plans among the learner, facilitator, and manager.

In addition, commitment to an action plan increases if it's been presented to the group during the learning program. For example, each participant could share their plan with the large group, fish-bowl style, or they could break into teams, so each participant presents to a small group in a breakout room. The key is for each participant to share their plan with others to increase their commitment and enhance the likelihood they will follow through and do it. The only downside is that it does take time for participants to present their plans, which means you'll have to reserve time in the agenda.

Concerned About Accountability for Action Plans in Small Groups?

Virtual platforms designed for training programs (as opposed to videoconferencing or meetings) allow the facilitator to observe activity in a breakout room. They can see shared content, open whiteboards, and microphone movement that indicates active conversation. While it's important to give adult learners the benefit of the doubt, this virtual training room feature provides peace of mind that people are actively participating and an extra layer of accountability.

Technique 31: Finish With a Call to Action

Participants should leave each virtual session knowing exactly what to do next. For example, they should know if there's an application assignment to complete before the next gathering, or if it's time to finish the formal program and move into the next phase. Beyond recognizing what to do, participants should also understand why they need to do it. Therefore, finish each virtual class with a specific call to action that either builds on the action plans or provides a way to review and amend them. This helps participants feel energized, excited, and eager to apply their new knowledge and skills.

Just like the opening, how you close a virtual class is key. The closing call to action activity leaves a parting impression for the participants and is the springboard to the next step.

Here are three ideas for how to close a virtual class with a call to action:

- **Accountability pairs.** Have participants select a partner (or assign them) and use private chat to exchange contact information and arrange a follow-up conversation to discuss how they are each applying the lessons learned.
- **Note to self.** Ask participants to send a private chat to the facilitator that shares their email address and a short note to themselves about how they will apply the learning. The facilitator then saves those notes and sends them at a designated point after the program finishes.
- **Red light, yellow light, green light.** Use a slide or whiteboard divided into three sections labeled Red Light, Yellow Light, and Green Light. In the red section, ask participants to list anything that will stop them from implementing lessons learned. In the yellow section, ask them to list any potential roadblocks that could get in the way. In the green section, ask them to list any action items or ideas they have for applying the content.

Next Steps

Review the techniques outlined in this chapter. Which ones can you use now in the programs you are running or creating? Which techniques will help you create engaged learners who get involved in the learning and use the session to grow and develop?

The interactive program launches participants from learning to application and impact. Now, as the formal facilitated portion of the learning program ends, it's time to move to the next phase. In the next chapter we will delve into techniques that support learners as they apply the learning and deliver impact.

Actions to Take After the Program

Getting to Action

A global architecture membership body set out to deliver a new diversity and inclusion program. It identified several ambitious goals, including:

- Create an inclusive culture at the organization where all staff and members believe they belong.
- Hold staff and members accountable for inclusive action.
- Model how to drive an inclusive culture in the architecture profession.
- Deliver actual behavioral change in regard to cultural awareness and sensitivity.
- Drive a perception change of the organization among staff, members, and the public.

The organization decided to use the globally recognized cultural intelligence (CQ) framework. CQ refers to the ability to recognize and adapt to cultural differences and work effectively in culturally diverse situations. The organization developed three targeted virtual CQ learning programs involving a combination of assessments, virtual workshops, and e-learning sessions, which would be rolled out to executives, managers, and more than 300 staff.

The organization was acutely aware that without a robust approach to virtual learning, its diversity and inclusion initiatives would fail. Creating behavioral change in this context is particularly challenging because it requires the learner to acknowledge inherent biases and participate in some uncomfortable introspection to identify what about them needs to change. Achieving truly lasting change requires the most robust of training reinforcement approaches—one that creates measured learning transfer.

To incorporate a learning transfer approach, the organization integrated one-on-one coaching conversations that would take place either with a chatbot or on the phone with a coach at various intervals following the training course. This ensured that learners were able to slow down and participate in specific, structured, and accountable reflection to increase training ROI.

Each participant created up to three specific goals for how they would apply what they learned. Then, during their conversations with their coach or the chatbot, the learner was asked to score and rescore their progress against their goals and outline any actions they'd taken to illustrate that score. Participants were also asked what changes they had made and what benefits or results they perceived coming from the program.

Participants reported how they were applying the content in their day-to-day jobs, which allowed the organization to track behavioral change. In addition, the goals uplift was 64 percent, 106 percent, and 54 percent for the executives, managers, and staff, respectively, meaning that the participants had progressed with their individual goals and had a significant impact on the organization's equity, diversity, and inclusion (EDI) goals.

This is an excellent example of the importance of learning transfer in delivering genuine behavioral change, especially when the behaviors or context are complex. Supporting virtual learning programs through reflective conversations, action plans, reminders, and follow-up, whether human or technology-driven, are all important components for holding learners accountable and turning learning into action.

This chapter focuses on the application phase of learning, which can be called *transferring the learning, sustaining the learning*, or *embedding the learning*. Applying the learning drives impact. In other words, how can learning professionals ensure that what participants learn is transferred into behavioral change and creates an impact for an organization? Knowing what to do or being able to demonstrate what they've learned isn't enough. Instead, to create successful individual and organizational outcomes, applying the information day-to-day or when required is the key. In addition, with virtual learning, where the participant is physically distanced from the facilitator, extra support and a robust strategy for transfer is essential.

The Shift From Inputs to Outcomes

The definition of learning success has shifted from simply being when learning has occurred to when learning is used and has an impact—in other words, from knowing to doing. This new definition represents a mind shift for many learning and talent development stakeholders. Taking ownership of this shift and creating strategies to deliver it needs to be embedded across all learning stakeholders, including participants, facilitators, designers, content creators, learning and talent development managers, and the managers of the participants attending the program. Awareness that a different approach is needed to create these outcomes, as well as buy-in for that different approach, is critical to driving the program's success. Shifting the mindset from learning inputs to learning outcomes will help bring stakeholders along on this stage of the journey (Figure 7-1).

Figure 7-1. The Shift From a Focus on Learning Inputs to Learning Outcomes

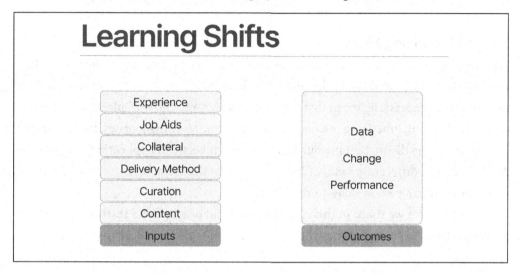

When it comes to delivering results from virtual learning, hope is not a strategy, luck is not a factor, and doing nothing is not an option. The accountability for virtual learning has shifted. It's up to each of us to make sure virtual learning delivers the desired results.

This chapter explores techniques to use after the virtual learning program is complete to enhance the application and impact of virtual learning programs. Committing to supporting and creating behavioral change and impact from your virtual learning programs will help realize the required results you identified in the alignment phase (chapter 2).

The Learning Professional's Role in Application

The job of a learning professional isn't done once the virtual facilitation is over. Learning is a continuous journey, but there isn't always a clear beginning, middle, and end. While learning journeys are a great way to think about your solution, don't forget that they have different phases. A learning journey will start with the design process before the learners are even engaged. Then, during the program, learners will move through additional phases as part of their learning journey.

As discussed in chapter 4, gaining clarity on the learning objectives can help break the journey into stages of knowledge, skills, practice, and application. The application phase, where the learning is transferred into sustained behavioral change and incorporated into the person's day-to-day role, is where the benefits of the program will be realized. This may take place after the learning program, or it may be broken into application phases within a longer pathway. Either way, the practice and application phases are two discrete stages in the journey. (Although it's worth noting that in a virtual learning context they often both happen in the workplace, not the virtual classroom.) This chapter supports the understanding of the learning transfer and application phase.

Beyond Practicing Skills

The learning transfer phase can often be confused with practicing the learning. However, practicing new skills—whether in the workplace or a controlled classroom environment—doesn't necessarily mean that they will transfer into the workplace on an ongoing basis (application). Practicing is a necessary part of the learning journey, but it is important to create the distinction in your learning design between application and practice. Application is a different phase, which occurs when the learning is fully implemented and adopted into a person's day-to-day role.

The strategies we share in this chapter go beyond practice and start with a decision by the participant to apply what they've learned or at the very least experiment with applying it.

Learning Transfer as Part of a Learning Journey

While this chapter is entitled "Actions to Take After the Program," it's imperative to embed the application phase into the overall program, rather than consider it a separate piece. To the learner, the virtual experience needs to be end-to-end, culminating in applying the learning and seeing the resulting business impact. In addition, adult learning principles have also shown us that the more people explore and discover for themselves, through facilitated conversations, the higher the integration with the learning and the impact of the learning. So, at the application stage, we have to switch our focus from thinking about the learning content to its application in the learner's day-to-day role.

Shifting From Content to Context, Reminding to Reflection

It's critical that the emphasis in the learning transfer phase shifts from information and content to reflection and context.

In the past, learning and talent development programs have used prompts with additional content and reminders about what participants have learned as a way to create behavioral change. This is based on the premise that people don't apply learning because they don't know what to do or they've simply forgotten. For more technical, knowledge-based training (such as a new product launch training), where remembering the information is the biggest barrier to success, this type of reminder could be relevant and is easy to provide by sharing reference guides or prompts.

Frequently though, training initiatives within organizations call for more complex soft skills changes as in the chapter opening story about the global membership organization that wanted to build cultural intelligence. In these circumstances, the issue isn't usually that the learner has forgotten the information, but that it is naturally challenging to change such ingrained behaviors. Thus, reminding people of the content and what they should be doing can feel like nagging.

For example, if your partner says they will paint the living room, but six weeks later there's still no action, how likely will you be to create a behavior change by continually reminding them of their promise? It won't help them take ownership. In fact, this approach can actually work against the application of the learning, because people may resist doing what they're asked or told to do if they don't have the ownership and it's not their idea.

Making Reminders Work

Reminders don't feel like nagging if the individual has selected the time or frequency they want to be reminded about an action they want to take. So, allow learners to choose how often to be reminded—every two weeks, every week, or every day. Because they have proactively selected that cadence, learners find the reminders helpful rather than annoying. We want to find ways throughout the behavioral change journey to allow the learner to choose, plan, and take ownership of how they will change and be supported in the application phase of the learning journey.

Why Reflection? What the Research Tells Us

Given that in the application phase we aren't focusing on reminding people or looking at additional content, you may be wondering how we plan to drive behavioral change and learning application. Each of the techniques discussed in this chapter focuses on the principles of reflection and accountability. We can draw on the research from a number of fields for the "why?" behind focusing on reflection and accountability, including motivation theory, self-determination theory, self-regulated learning, behavioral psychology, behavioral economics, and neuroscience.

Self-Determination Theory and Learning Transfer

Many training programs used to rely on carrot and stick approaches to motivate people to change their behaviors. However, Edward Deci and Richard Ryan's groundbreaking work in self-determination theory (SDT)—which highlights the importance of intrinsic motivation through the lenses of autonomy, competence, and relatedness—has changed the way we think about behavior change. Throughout the approach outlined in this chapter, the use of reflection drives autonomy by allowing the learner to internally process their decisions and commitments to change based on their own mental models of the world.[1]

Self-Regulated Learning and Learning Transfer

The theory and practice of self-regulated learning (SRL) includes the cognitive, metacognitive, behavioral, motivational, emotional, and affective aspects of learning. Looking at this research allows us to consider many variables that influence learning and learning application (for example, self-efficacy, volition, and cognitive strategies). While environmental factors are important in SRL, the metacognition phase takes center stage.[2] Zimmerman's SRL model is useful to consider here. It is organized into three phases—forethought, performance, and self-reflection—that align with the stages we will be looking at in this chapter. Zimmerman refers to the effectiveness of learning diaries, which could be compared to reflective conversations and journaling with technology.[3]

Behavioral Economics and Learning Transfer

The importance of Nobel Prize–winning author Daniel Kahneman's work shouldn't be overlooked. In his book *Thinking Fast and Slow*, Kahneman outlines the difference between System 1 thinking (the fast brain, which is instinctive, operating quickly with a low level of effort) and System 2 thinking (the slow brain, which is ponderous, allocating attention to mental activities, thinking, choice, and concentration).[4] Because people typically operate in System 1 mode, we need to find and create methods to help them slow down, reflect on their learning, and shift into System 2 thinking. This will help them change their behaviors and deliver learning transfer to drive a more considered way of thinking and behaving.

Neuroscience and Learning Transfer

Finally, neuroscience and the way the brain functions and changes can't be ignored when considering the factors that influence behavioral change. The old adage "You can't teach an old dog new tricks" has been proven wrong by Norman Doidge and others. According to Doidge, the brain changes and is more pliable, thanks to a level of neuroplasticity. Using levers that influence the brain to change—such as linking the achievement learning application to an individual's *why* or personal passion—creates a boost in dopamine and serotonin levels, which tells our brain that we are happy or pleased. We then seek to replicate this feeling, which drives our desire to change.[5]

The Manager's Role in Application

Another factor to consider at the application phase is the role of the learner's manager. As mentioned in chapter 1, it is important for the manager to be involved in the impact and application of the learning. In chapter 2, we outlined how critical it was to involve the manager in the alignment of business objectives with the overall learning program, because they are ultimately the ones held accountable for their team's performance. If managers understand the program's goals and are involved in selecting or creating the metrics for success, they will feel accountable for how their direct reports apply what they've learned. The manager may also have a role in setting expectations with participants and giving specific insights to help participants understand how the program is relevant to their role, and how and why it's specifically important to them.

Helping people identify skills gaps and where they can grow, particularly for high performers, is an area where managers can contribute and guide. High performers often struggle to identify their own areas for growth because it's not as obvious as it is for those who are underperforming. Regardless of performance level, however, growth can inspire and motivate people. It's an intrinsic human need to believe we are making progress.

Factors to Consider

The level of support and input from the manager at the transfer phase will depend on many factors including the specific program, the manager's time and availability, and the manager's skill level.

If your program is targeting behaviors that are relatively easy to change and have a straightforward application, a low level of manager support would be required. This could be as simple as a two- or three-minute conversation with the manager once the learner has completed a virtual module, focusing on what they learned and how it is relevant to their role. Regardless of where the learner is in the program, it is always welcome for the manager to offer encouragement and enthusiasm for the content.

We will explore how technology can be used to prompt this type of interaction in chapter 8.

Avoid a Negative Impact

Regardless of the specifics of the program, it is essential that managers are not actively disengaging or sabotaging a virtual learning program. For example, statements made by managers in an organization that will jeopardize program outcomes and indicate low levels of manager engagement include:

- "Oh, don't worry about the training. That's not what we do around here."
- "Don't worry about virtual learning."
- "Um, it's not really relevant to us. Our team/division/department skills are different."

In addition, if a manager is actively contradicting the content, mindset, or actions an individual has gained during the program, this needs to be tackled immediately. Note that this scenario is unlikely if the manager is involved from the outset, but it's worth taking caution.

It's equally important for the manager to avoid staying silent. If a manager doesn't say anything—especially if they've been briefed on the overall virtual learning initiative and asked to play a specific role—it will negatively affect the participant's ability to succeed. In fact, a manager is essentially sabotaging the program if they have specifically been asked to support it in some way and they don't.

Other Support Roles

Make sure to carefully consider the management bandwidth in your organization before you ask for help with learning application. Time, skill, and culture will all play a part in deciding who should fulfill which role at the application phase.

Managers can also act as coaches, facilitators, or on-the-job trainers. However, our consulting clients have all experienced mixed results when it comes to manager involvement. We have found that when managers are specifically nominated to coach, only around 30 to 50 percent actively become engaged in the required follow-up conversations despite having conversation guides and being briefed fully as to the importance of the role.

Managers can give support and encouragement in a multitude of ways. Note that we emphasize the participant's responsibility to drive behavioral change in this book. While their success isn't solely reliant on manager support, it does make a difference.

Deciding on the Manager's Role

By assessing each manager's skill, appetite, and ability to support learning transfer against the type of behavior change you want to achieve, you will be able to determine whether you'll need to supplement the manager with other options. In addition, you'll want to consider whether it's a technical program with linear changes or a more complex soft skill initiative with more complex changes.

Other options to bolster the manager's role include leveraging peers and other participants, external or internal coaches, technology, or a specifically trained transfer team. Most managers and leaders want to fully support their people through learning. This desire is a great starting point. Giving them the tools, frameworks, and support can help them fulfill this desire and help you create outcomes from your program.

Techniques to Design for Application and Impact

Considering all these factors, the techniques shared in this chapter focus on the application of learning and behavioral change principles to drive organizational impact from learning. Let's get into them.

Technique 32: Follow Up on Action Plans

We discussed action plans in the virtual learning environment in chapter 6. To recap, an action plan involves the learner making decisions about what they're going to take from the learning program and actually putting that into play in their day-to-day role and life. While the act of simply creating an action plan will encourage a degree of learning transfer, following up on the action plan is what turbocharges them. The follow-up is what makes the difference between a static document that signals the close of a program and a guide document that serves as the leaping off point for the learning transfer phase.

There are multiple ways to use an action plan as the starting point, including using it as a basis for following up with technology (discussed in chapter 8), one-on-one, group, or peer initiatives.

Let's consider it in its simplest form: Sharing an action plan with another person—also known as an accountability partner—immediately creates an accountability loop. An accountability partner can be a peer, a manager, technology, or a nominated internal or external coach. It's important, however, that the accountability loop doesn't create a high-pressure environment. A study by Michael Enzle and Sharon Anderson found that a participant's intrinsic motivation decreased if they were being monitored by someone who was there to control their behavior (either to make sure they complied or to evaluate their performance). But if the participant was told that the experimenter was watching them only out of curiosity, there was no observed effect on the participant's intrinsic motivation.[6]

The most powerful way to create accountability through action plans is to support the individual in holding themselves accountable for applying the learning. This creates more sustained outcomes, echoing the work of Daniel Pink in his book *Drive: The Surprising Truth About What Motivates Us*. Helping the learner create intrinsic motivation to change using autonomy, mastery, and purpose can be powerful.[7] Be mindful that, if the learner comes from a hierarchical organization, empowering them to have autonomy may be a leap.

One of the great things about an action plan is that it gives the participant a road map to their success by outlining where they are now, where they want to go, and what they need to do to close the gap based on what they've learned during the training program. The cadence of follow-up conversations will depend on the depth and frequency of the learning; for example, a two-hour virtual module may have two 15-minute follow-up sessions, while longer learning events may have monthly 30-minute conversations. Pairing the follow-up conversations helps ensure accountability and creates a higher level of change, so encourage learners to schedule shorter, more frequent check-ins rather than a single longer conversation.

These action plans can also provide significant data if they are electronic, which helps highlight the themes around what learners are applying in the workplace (bear this in mind as you think about your data collection strategy, which is covered in chapter 10). For example, an organization has launched a leadership program focused on inclusive leadership, but only 10 percent of participants created actions relating to inclusive leadership. By analyzing the action plans, the learning and talent development team could try to understand why and possibly amend the program.

Note, however, that you should use the data only to be informative, not punitive. It should help you make decisions about what to adjust to ensure that future learners are aligning their action plans with the behavioral outcomes you want from the virtual learning program.

Learners can use the questions in Figure 7-2 to support their action plan follow-up conversations and drive accountability.

Figure 7-2. Making the Most of Your Action Plan

Create momentum and turn your learning into action with these tips.
1. Set a specific time at regular intervals to review your action plan over the next 90 days. This is key—make time to reflect deeply.
2. When you are reviewing your plan, get away from distractions and focus—let the action plan drive the agenda. Your conversation may be with someone else or with yourself!
3. Use a calibration score (where you are on a scale of 1–10) to help track progress toward your goal.
4. Celebrate any and all progress. Our brains respond well to positive reinforcement, even in private! Be your own best cheerleader.
5. Get clear on where you want to go next. What number do you want hit to next on your calibration score?
6. What will it take to get there?
7. What barriers may come up? What strategies can you use to overcome them?
8. How will you hold yourself accountable? Set a time to review your progress and stick to it.
9. Remember, focusing on *why* the goal is important to you may be more motivating than the goal itself.
10. And finally, if you ever find yourself simply checking the box on your action plan or in a reflective conversation, pause, take a breath, and refocus. This is an opportunity to go deeper. What is really important to you? What will make a difference in your learning?

Technique 33: One-on-One Coaching After the Program

One-on-one coaching either after the program or as part of it is another way to drive application. A coach can work with the learner to encourage them to reflect and take ownership of making a change. It's important that the learner drives the coaching conversations—the more ownership they have over the process, the better the behavioral change outcomes will be.

The best way to support learning transfer through coaching is to use a coaching methodology specifically designed for transfer and to embed it fully in the program. While many learning programs include a coaching element, many miss the mark because coaching isn't fully integrated to deliver transfer. If the learner establishes an action plan during the program, it can then become a focus of the associated coaching sessions. This ensures the coaching is highly targeted and geared toward applying what they've learned.

The coach—a manager, someone from the learning and talent development team, a peer, or an internal or external coach—helps the learner identify where they are trying to go versus where they are currently, and determine how to bridge the gap between the two. Coaching is a genuine collaboration, which creates accountability for change. Coaching conversations should balance structure and flexibility, provoking excitement and energy in the learner, while keeping them accountable for making changes.[8]

The key for success is to properly equip the coach with the tools to have a reflective conversation. Make sure that the methodology you use has a framework that is replicable, captures outcomes, and uses the principles of reflection and accountability to drive change. The Turning Learning Into Action methodology, for example, focuses on leveraging learning transfer through the use of questions to create ownership, accountability, and behavioral change.[9] In chapter 8, we'll touch on using chatbot technology for follow-up coaching conversations.

Having one-on-one coaching conversations over the phone, particularly without video, is a powerful way to create change. The process of speaking without visual cues really helps us create an internal dialogue. Remember, we really want to focus on helping the individual have a conversation with themselves. The learner is the only one who knows their thoughts, feelings, values, beliefs, fears, and needs, and so can understand the why of their behaviors and create a plan accordingly. In this conversation, the learner can focus on what's working for them and what's not when they're applying what they've learned. It's an efficient way to create long-term behavioral change. The learner also has ownership of coming up with micro-actions to follow through on, so repeated conversations over a period of time, embedded within the program, will help get the best results.

Technique 34: Manager Encouragement and Involvement Using Feedback Loops

The manager can play an important role in the application of learning through encouragement and involvement even if they don't have the capacity or skill for specific one-on-one follow-up coaching. This includes asking the learner about the program and its success, reminding them to ask for help if they need it, and providing any support they request. It basically involves letting the participants know that their manager is expecting them to use their new knowledge and skills and that their use should have an impact.

Here's how this could work in practice: Managers could attend a briefing call to discuss the program's road map of touchpoints and planned outcomes. Additionally, they could be involved in feedback loops to keep the participant accountable. For example, the manager could get a prompt once a participant has had a follow-up coaching conversation reminding them to continue providing support (Figure 7-3).

Figure 7-3. Sample Manager Prompt

Hi [Manager],

Luke had his second learning transfer coaching conversation today with Josephine, his coach. He came away from the call with three actions:
1. Schedule specific, regular times in the calendar to focus on strategy surrounding client services and professional development.
2. Role-model and empower others by making time to do these activities to support the strategy actions.
3. Identify and approach a strategy champion to support the vision for the next quarter.

These actions will help Luke move toward the goals he set for the program. I've attached a copy of his Leadership Essentials action plan for context. Please support Luke in moving forward with his goals by asking him about his goals and progress over the coming weeks.

Thank you,
The Leadership Essentials Team

These prompts can be automated or sent manually. When reaching out to the manager, make sure to strike the balance between confidentiality and transparency and always let the participant know exactly what will be shared.

The success of the manager involvement and encouragement technique will depend on the culture, time, and capabilities within your organization. We discuss at what level to engage with the manager in chapter 9, where we explore which techniques to use and when, but more research is needed in this area. Often, even if managers are thoroughly equipped with question lists and a compelling "why?" they still fail to engage in the process. In fact, among our own studies across multiple organizations, we've seen less than 50 percent of managers engage despite the best preparations. Thus, while manager support is preferred it can't be the sole factor—so combining it with other approaches will bring the best outcomes.

Technique 35: Group Coaching After the Program and Implementation Phase

Group coaching is a useful way to help participants use and apply the learning content. Ideally, group coaching sessions are held regularly at a set time so participants can join when convenient to discuss any issues, barriers, or success stories. Sessions shouldn't be mandatory so that participants can develop buy-in and build accountability.

Historically, organizations have struggled to match the participation rates in the follow-up coaching process to the participation rates of the program itself. Some learners struggle to see the value in the coaching follow-up, particularly if it is part of a group, and so resist attending. They may think "No one will miss me," "This isn't an important part of the program," or "I'm too busy now that I've done the course." This is why it's important to make coaching part of the program, rather than positioning it as follow-up. We need to think carefully about how we position and market the end-to-end process with the learners.

Another challenge is that the benefit of learning from others can be outweighed by the challenge of groupthink—group commitments such as "We must do this" or "We should do that" can feel too vague or broad for individuals to act on. Until these group beliefs become individual commitments, the rate of change within the group can be slow. People learn in groups but change as individuals.

In a study by Marilyn Wood Daudelin, 48 managers from a Fortune 500 company were divided into four groups: individual, helper, peer, and control. Each group was asked to follow the same four-stage reflection process and use the same reflection questions to think about what they had learned. The individual group was asked to reflect on their own. The helper group was asked to reflect with the help of a coach. The peer group was joined by three or four other people from the study and asked to reflect together. And the control group did not engage in any reflection.

As expected, the individual group and helper group achieved more learning than the control group. What was surprising, however, was that the peer group did not show a statistically significant improvement. The reason for this was put down to three things:

- The peer group focused on finding similarities among one another's experiences, which prevented them from personalizing the training and assimilating the learning more fully.
- The need to discuss so many different topics prevented the group from going into useful depth about any one issue, and because there were more people in the group, it was much less structured.
- None of the peer groups followed the reflection process or asked the reflection questions.[10]

In groups, topics are often only discussed superficially (to ensure everyone has a chance to speak), rather than reflecting on the genuine value of the training to each individual. Personalized reflection is key to the transfer of learning, but it is often missing in follow-up discussion groups.

To successfully create behavior change, groups to support learning transfer need to be structured and managed. While they may allow people to exchange views and discuss the material, they can too easily be viewed as a convenient break from work or a forum to vent and complain, rather than a constructive place to solve ongoing implementation issues and resolve challenges. Plus, there is rarely any accountability in a group session. Helping hold people accountable to themselves is easier one-on-one, but if resources are limited, a combination of group and one-on-one coaching can be powerful.

An example where group coaching follow-up worked well was for a large telecommunications company, where we created an 82 percent uplift in goals progress, meaning significant organizational impact was achieved. Managers were attending a program on developing coaching skills. At the end of the program, they created action plans for the practices they would put into place.

Then, they followed up with small group coaching calls of six to eight people facilitated by a trained coach. The calls would start with each person giving a two-minute recap on their action plan and progress toward goals using the calibration scores. Then one person was nominated to "be in the chair" as the participant and another person was nominated to be the coach. This had the dual benefit of keeping people moving forward with action plans and giving them the chance to build their coaching skills and get feedback on their coaching. At the end of the coaching rounds, everyone reflected on what the conversation meant to them and what further actions they would commit to in order to keep their action plan moving forward. Another contribution that can be useful in this format is to have everyone share a win and a lesson learned.

The keys with group coaching follow-up are to ensure that you focus on the application of learning, and that it doesn't fall back into focusing on learning content. The sessions should revolve around participants sharing how they have applied the information they gained in the program. Talking about content is intellectually rewarding for the learner, but by the transfer stage, a lack of content is rarely the reason they aren't moving forward. Getting people connected with thoughts, feelings, values, beliefs, fears, and needs, as well as sharing progress, successes, and barriers, will create more sustained behavior change over a longer period.

Technique 36: Apply Nudging Techniques

Although there are decades of research on nudges within behavioral economics—*Freakonomics,* by Steven Levitt and Stephen Dubner; *Predictable Irrationality,* by Dan Ariely; and *Nudge,* by Richard Thaler and Cass Sunstein—we've only recently thought to apply behavioral nudges to assist with the transfer of learning.[11]

David Halpern's *Inside the Nudge Unit* describes simple techniques that can be used to nudge people to do things and change their behavior. These techniques are based on those used by the UK government to nudge citizens to pay taxes, send in documents, or take important and necessary actions. One example is to remind participants at specific times by saying, "Most successful people in this program are using at least three of the five skills routinely by this time." By indicating that others are using what they've learned, it puts pressure on them to do the same.

Arun Pradhan also captured some great examples of how nudges can make a significant societal impact in his SlideShare presentation "Beyond Training: The Art of Nudging."[12] He highlights the rise of organ donation in the UK: "Organ donors in the UK increased by 100,000 in one year with an opt-in button being added on car insurance renewal forms with a specifically worded nudge: 'If you need an organ transplant would you have one? If so, please help others.'"

We've used nudges with clients to help virtual learners engage in a follow-up process. For example, we've sent a text that says, "Hey John, looking forward to hearing what progress you've made with your action plan today, really keen that we keep up your momentum with the rest of the group. Reply START to begin."

The EAST framework, developed in 2012 by the Behavioural Insights Team, suggests that nudges should be easy, attractive, social, and timely. Let's apply the framework to the text message above:

- Easy—just reply START.
- Attractive—the message is upbeat and positive.
- Social—the team wants to make sure John keeps up with the group.
- Timely—it references John's progress as of today.

Nudge theory can be a powerful guide for structured follow-up that drives behavioral change. Imagine how you can start to use nudging to shift behavior in a set context or increase engagement in your virtual learning.

Technique 37: Observation Sessions With an On-the-Job Trainer

Having an on-the-job trainer is not a new concept. It can be useful to allocate a person in a particular area to follow up with participants and help them if they have questions about the skills they're still developing. This facilitates application and impact.

Subtly shifting the focus from *telling* to *facilitating* through observations and feedback can further influence the outcomes and drive ownership of change. It's imperative that the observation feels like support rather than being watched or judged. We need to ensure that the intrinsic motivation isn't decreased because the learner knows they're being observed and that they still have ownership of change.[13]

For example, a trainer could shadow a medical salesperson out in the field. Once the sales visit is over, the trainer could sit with the participant and debrief. Their focus should be on answering the salesperson's questions and offering advice on what could be done better (rather than acting like an all-knowing oracle in sales techniques). On-the-job trainers should ask the learner questions—not about the content, but about how they observe their own behavior:

- "What three things did you see yourself doing really well in that sales meeting?"
- "What three things do you think, done differently, would have given you a slightly better result?"

The trainer can probe to really understand the participant's point of view and then go into sharing their own observations. This approach builds a lifelong skill that will help the learner learn and change in any situation, rather than only when they're with the on-the-job trainer.

The trainer should also capture notes from the conversation about agreed upon actions for the learner to focus on, which the trainer can use for follow-up next time. This is also a good opportunity to use the learner's action plan. After listening to their initial observations, the trainer could ask the follow-up question "And how do these observations align with the action plan you set yourself at the end of the training?" Each time the participant revisits the action plan and what they learned in the program, they are strengthening the neural pathways for the new content and the behaviors they are looking to put into place.

If an on-the-job trainer isn't available, a peer may be a good substitute, especially if they already work closely with the learner in their day-to-day role. Learners can share feedback on how things are going with their peers and get feedback in return. If participants observe others with the required skill set and are encouraged to support one another by giving positive recognition when they see something has been done properly, they will also provide assistance and support when activities are not done properly. This technique is helpful if the culture permits this type of candid conversation.

Getting Past the Fears of On-the-Job Training

When trainers ask learners questions about their behavior, learners may respond, "I don't know." The temptation can then be for the trainer to jump in and answer the question on the learner's behalf. Unfortunately, this can lead to the learner thinking that they don't actually have to observe themselves because someone else is doing it for them. To avoid this impulse, the trainer should prepare a few different ways to tackle the "I don't know" response in advance, such as:

- "Got it; if you knew you would probably be doing it already. Think a bit deeper though; who would you like to tell you the answer? What do you think they would say?"
- "Got it. Don't think too hard; just go with your gut. What's your gut telling you?"
- "Absolutely fine that you don't know, and of course if you did know, you would take action." Sometimes when we say, "I don't know," it's almost like a trapdoor shutting on our minds. We're also letting ourselves off the hook so we don't have to think about it anymore. Why? Because when we say "I don't know," someone else will usually tell us the answer. So, instead of giving in to the impulse, we have to gently pry open that trapdoor, and think about the question a minute longer. What's underneath the "I don't know"? What's the answer behind the trapdoor?

On-the-job trainers may also worry about what to do if the participant misses something really obvious. What if the participant doesn't see what the trainer sees? In most cases, this is an unfounded fear, especially if the person has been through a training program. Their mind is primed from the training for what good looks like, and they will almost always share what they're thinking if they are in a safe enough space. If, after helping the participant reflect, the trainer wants to add something the participant has missed, they can frame it to indicate what's in it for the participant; for example, "Veronica, I really want to support you in getting the best sales results for your area, and I'm observing something that you might not be seeing. Can I share with you what I'm seeing?" After sharing the observation, the trainer should get the participant's thoughts: "What are you thinking as we talk this through, Veronica?" This shifts the ownership back to the learner, and as we know ownership is key for behavior change.

Technique 38: Host a Lessons-Learned Meeting Once Participants Have Used the Content

This technique has a slightly different focus. Schedule a lessons-learned session to take place after the participants have used the content so they can reflect on what they have learned from actual use. This provides an excellent opportunity for participants to discuss any barriers to success and ways to overcome them. This meeting is also motivational because participants can see the group's progress, which thereby inspires everyone to continue working toward their goals.

During the session, ask each participant to share three successes and three things they wish they had done differently. This is a good way to create richness from the feedback. Sharing the highlights is great, but also getting people to look at the gaps and areas for growth will help continue the momentum for change. It's interesting to note that people don't spend enough time celebrating wins because they find it difficult to vocalize the positives, and they instead tend to focus on where they need to improve. Others may find it hard to identify what they could do differently. Both are important and both have a role to play.

Technique 39: Meaningful Business Projects With Lessons-Learned Graduation

Including meaningful business projects with a lessons-learned graduation could be an important way to drive learning application as part of a training program. This is where an individual would identify, possibly even at the beginning of the program, where they could apply what they've learned directly in the business. One of the challenges of this approach is that the person might try to apply what they've learned only within the context of the project rather than their day-to-day role. It's important to make sure the participant understands how to use what they've learned in other settings with their team, instead of seeing a project only as the place where they use their new frameworks and techniques. This gap needs to be bridged—one option is to have action plans that cover the day-to-day role alongside the project. Ensuring the projects are meaningful and relevant to the organization is key.

Some projects may be experimental in nature, while others may work toward solving a current business challenge, and others may be used to drive innovation. Even if the project doesn't have the intended outcome, participants may find a graduation helpful because people can report back on what has happened and what they've learned along the way. Participants can also reflect on their experience and any advice for the next program, including what they would do differently. This reflection helps people embed the thinking around their behaviors, what they can change, and how they can improve, and continue to build that muscle. So, rather than just giving a presentation on what they did, this presentation actually builds that muscle of learning success by sharing success with other participants. Getting key stakeholders involved alongside peers in these presentations can also be really useful.

Technique 40: Share Success With Other Participants and Key Lessons Learned

Success is a motivator! When specific outcome data is collected, it can be powerful to share that data with other participants. For example, while you are waiting to collect Level 4 data, you could use Level 3 data to propel people forward via the principles of social proof. This demonstrates what their colleagues have achieved and what's possible. Knowing that you'll be sharing data can put subtle pressure on those who have not yet been successful to step up and make progress by the desired time. The results can be communicated verbally, as a virtual focus group, or shared by completing a questionnaire as a group. The high level of involvement in the process enhances the effectiveness of the process.

By including lessons learned within this conversation, it also encourages reflection and insight, which helps build a learning culture and the muscle for moving forward, even if things didn't go as planned or aren't perfect. Learners need to be able to fail in their learning to keep growing, and encouraging sharing lessons learned supports this.[14]

Technique 41: Hold a Contest Based on Achieving Success for Application and Impact

Depending on the culture within your organization, competition can be a motivator to change and apply learning. You could create a contest that incentivizes participants to use the material. The prize can be recognition, or some type of valuable incentive for those doing the best job. The focus is on ensuring that participants follow through, are successful, and report on their success. In other words, you are rewarding those who are doing the best job and hopefully motivating those who are not doing as well to step up and make progress.

Within this contest you can create a leaderboard that focuses not on what someone knows, but on what they've committed to doing and have actually done. The trainer or participants could implement a points system for scoring different activities. A key is to ensure that the activity is not simply a check-the-box exercise, but that it is relevant to each participant's role and long-term growth. Participants can create collaborative score charts and tables, and then tally as people go through what progress they've made.

Competition is a way of making accountability and learning application fun, while sharing what people are achieving and the impact that they're creating in the workplace. And who doesn't love a good contest? In the next chapter, we talk about technology, which can be a useful tool for establishing and running contests.

Next Steps

Challenge yourself to focus on impact. The techniques shared in this chapter are an invitation for you to start experimenting with ways you can drive learning transfer and behavior change as part of your virtual learning initiatives. In turn, this behavior change will drive impact. None of these suggestions requires any face-to-face elements (although the on-the-job trainer role can be difficult to fulfill virtually). Supporting your participants to go beyond knowing what to do and actually doing it is an opportunity to get excited about. Depending on the context of your training program, many of these techniques will help your participants start to shift habitual ways of behaving.

We challenge you as a learning and talent development professional to consider what mindset you need to adopt to become the type of learning leader who is committed to getting impact from your virtual learning initiatives. A tenacious one, a committed one, or a curious one? How will you commit to enabling your learners to apply what they've learned every day (actually change their behavior) and have an impact. And with that mindset in place, you can start embracing different types of technology to support you in getting to impact. While this chapter looks at techniques that do not involve technology, the next chapter focuses on technology-enabled techniques, which is perhaps the fastest-growing area in virtual training.

Technology-Enabled Approaches to Drive Application and Impact

ReMind: Creativity on Prescription—the first program of its kind in Australia—is an evidence-based program that uses creative practices, like drawing, cooking, music, writing, and crafts, to support mental health recovery and well-being. Created by the training organization MakeShift, the program gives people with PTSD, depression, or anxiety diagnoses the tools to shift out of heightened anxiety, numbness, vigilance, or other symptoms and use creative practices as a means of self-care. Many participants are first responders such as police or paramedics.

Before the COVID-19 pandemic, ReMind was delivered exclusively face-to-face. However, the pandemic suddenly made that no longer possible, and the team needed to quickly pivot to deliver the program virtually without sacrificing what made it so successful.

MakeShift, which specializes in education and support for mental health and well-being, knew it needed to develop a powerful virtual learning solution. The team was acutely aware that if the digital program was frustrating for the participant, it would take away from the value of the experience and further burden them.

Simply delivering the content digitally wasn't an option because they needed the experience to be as smooth and easy as possible. The virtual experience also had to be just as engaging and valuable as the face-to-face experience. The approach could not be content based; rather, it needed to be completely centered on the mindset and needs of the learner.

The MakeShift team opted to pivot the program to a virtual and digital delivery combination through how-to videos and live Zoom sessions. Participants received their creative tools (such as paint and paintbrushes or a ukulele) through the mail, allowing them to develop their creative practice at home. When it came to leveraging technology to support application, MakeShift used a conversational intelligence (chatbot) solution.

The chatbot, Coach M, was used to complement the learning delivery, acting as a side-by-side companion throughout the program to prompt action, support learning application, and keep participants on track. Learners could slow down and reflect on their specific learning commitments by initiating two-way coaching conversations with Coach M that were tailored to the individual.

The goal was to create a completely safe space where participants could engage without judgment. Using a chatbot is an excellent way to keep participants accountable without sacrificing psychological safety. The bespoke scripts Coach M used were based on 20,000 human coaching conversations and constantly updated in line with new conversational input from participants.

MakeShift was also able to capture detailed data on participants, while keeping that information private and secure. This was extremely helpful for supporting individual participants as well as informing program delivery going forward.

When the program was delivered face-to-face, participants would often forget to bring their workbooks home so they could complete their reflective exercises. Using Coach M, MakeShift was able to shift that reflective piece to the individual's own mobile device, significantly improving engagement with this process. Based on data collected, 75 percent of participants indicated that Coach M was essential for maintaining a self-care plan and building new habits, and 85 percent of participants found the tools introduced by Coach M to be highly useful. When asked specifically about changing behaviors, participants reported that their follow-through on specific nominated actions and self-care practices was 33 percent higher when working with Coach M, rather than if they had no transfer follow up.

Let's consider what impact these changes in behaviors created. The program was designed to help participants improve mental well-being and emotional regulation through creative practices. While the changes weren't converted to tangible benefits, participants did share their reported impact:

- "I am using those creative outlets to calm my mind and focus on self-care."
- "I'm much better at acknowledging when I'm agitated or anxious. I feel more accepting of my mood changes because I know I have options to try and improve my mood."
- "It [the program] has made some improvement to my mental health."

This program is an excellent example of how using technology in the learning transfer process can prove extremely powerful.

Using technology is an effective, efficient, and convenient way to prompt and support learning application and impact. This chapter explores the many ways software, apps, platforms, AI, and other technology tools can assist in creating and enhancing the application of the knowledge and skills acquired from a virtual learning program.

Role of Technology

As with most aspects of business, many human-based nontechnology solutions have a technology component. In the case of a learning program, that could be an LMS (learning management system), LXP (learning experience system), automated booking system, or online resource for hosting videos or content. Many technology solutions can be used to disperse, share, and deliver learning content. While these platforms are important for the learning program, they are not the type of technology we are covering here. This chapter looks at solutions that predominantly use technology to support and deliver learning transfer specifically, not the learning itself. In other words, which modes of technology can facilitate the *application* of the learning?

Focus on Change—Not Retention

Recall that the focus of this book is on the behavioral change and corresponding impact resulting from learning, which is not to be confused with learning reinforcement or retention. Learning reinforcement leans toward the knowledge end of learning—it reminds people of what they have learned. Retention is about helping people retain knowledge and information. At this point, we want to ensure that what participants have learned is being applied in their day-to-day role. *Embedding*, *sustaining*, and *transferring the learning* can all be used to describe the behavioral change and application phase of a learning program. Application drives impact. Regardless of the definition used, if you want to deliver behavioral change and transfer the learning into sustainable business outcomes, technology can be used very effectively to deliver this.

Benefits of Technology

The benefits of using technology are significant. Technology can enable solutions at scale, which means fewer resources are required to deliver the outcomes. It also means solutions can be easily replicated in other languages, used at any time of day, and consistently delivered. Solutions with a technology focus typically have a higher level of data accompanying them than human-based solutions. Using this data as part of a technology solution can strengthen its delivery by personalizing and contextualizing it for each learner, contributing significantly to your ability to measure and evaluate the program.

Combining Technology Solutions

Different types of technology are often combined within a single solution. As an example, videos and reminders may be embedded into chatbot conversations. You'll need to consider whether the technology should be desktop-enabled or mobile-enabled, which often depends on geographic location, device access (that is, does everyone have access to a mobile phone?), and whether the technology is available on that device.

Let's get into some practical ideas of how you can use technology for learning transfer. This chapter is broken down into two parts:

- Technology that supports ownership, tracking, and driving accountability (focusing on the individual learner)
- Technology that helps learners share their thoughts about the application of learning with others (a social learning focus)

Technology That Supports Ownership, Tracking, and Driving Accountability

These techniques leverage technology that focuses on an individual learner. Technology often focuses on social or group learning, and is used to help people collaborate or complete the program. Given that the individual ultimately decides whether to change behavior, we will focus on technology that supports the individual learner. Let's start by considering chatbots as a tool for behavioral change.

Technique 42: Leverage Chatbots for Learning Transfer

A chatbot is a computer program designed to simulate a conversation. In chapter 7 we outlined the power of a reflective conversation based on an action plan to deliver learning transfer. The action plan, which is created by the learner, contains the decisions regarding what they will apply. Chatbot conversations are spaced over a period of time to enable the learner to reflect on the action plan, review what they have put into place, and explore what strategies they need to move up the scale for implementing an action.

The most familiar chatbots are customer service chatbots, which answer questions about many things, including banking, taxes, and travel. They are often embedded on a webpage, come to your phone via text, or found within a chat function on software such as Microsoft Teams, Slack, WhatsApp, or Webex Teams. Where do people have chat conversations in your organization? This is where learning transfer conversations need to happen—not within your learning software, but where people talk in general about work.

Most chatbots are text-based; in the future, such solutions will likely be voice-activated. However, engaging in a written conversation with a chatbot can inspire deep reflection about learning applications and be likened to a dynamic form of journaling, where we reflect and review our thoughts. This would have similar benefits as having a conversation with ourselves, as discussed in the previous chapter. As such, keeping chatbot conversations in a written form may be more powerful than a voice-based solution.

With a learning transfer chatbot, the tool should be designed not to answer the learner's questions, but to ask the learning questions. Why? Because asking questions creates reflection and answering these questions creates ownership of change. The questions are designed to promote behavior change, drive accountability, and create impact for an organization.

Coach M

Learning technology is a fast-moving area. Solutions using technology are inherently more scalable and repeatable than a people-based approach. When choosing which technology to use for learning transfer, consider, does this technology align with the principles of successful transfer?

Bayer, one of the world's largest pharmaceutical companies, decided to work with Lever–Transfer of Learning and Mobile Coach to implement chatbots to provide learning transfer coaching in support of its sales manager training programs across Bayer Australia. Once the program was implemented, participants on average spent 20 minutes on each conversation with the program's chatbot, Coach M. Participants slowed down and reflected, in conversation with Coach M, on the action plans they'd created, shared progress, and strategized how to overcome barriers that might derail their behavioral change process.

To understand how this type of chatbot works, it helps to forget everything you know about chatbots. These chatbots are not customer service tools designed to help answer your questions. A learning transfer chatbot works in the reverse—it asks the participant questions. The high level of psychological safety that working with a chatbot can offer, because of its inability to pass judgment, can support learners in slowing down, reflecting, and having a powerful conversation with themselves.

Coach M was programed using the nuances of the Turning Learning Into Action methodology, which were based on 20,000 human conversations Lever had over a 12-year period. As a result, the chatbot can simulate a learning transfer conversation to truly leverage what's possible using emerging technology in learning.[1]

To design your chatbot conversation, use a clear conversation methodology and build with either natural language programming or a rules-based program. To test the chatbot's effectiveness, read the scripts or conversations out loud—could you imagine humans having that conversation? This can be a great way to pick up on nuances and changes to be made.

Let's be clear, having a conversation with a chatbot is not as effective as speaking with a human to drive behavioral change. However, some learners still prefer speaking to a chatbot because of the high level of psychological safety that it provides. They find it easier to open up to a chatbot and share more authentically what's happening for them than they would when talking to a person. View chatbots not as replacing a human but as adding to the human-based follow-up process. Chatbots can also create consistency if individual managers have varying levels of coaching ability.

You may be wondering, are chatbots AI? This depends on the background engine you use. When a chatbot is designed thoughtfully, the user often can't tell whether it is AI or not, and as long as it's a sensible and clear conversation, they won't care. When we first started experimenting with learning transfer chatbots, we were genuinely surprised by how much learners would open up to the chatbot and engage with the tool. Setting the expectations accurately for both facilitators and learners is critical.

As with most technologies, you can choose to either build your own chatbot from scratch or purchase an off-the-shelf system with varying levels of customization. If you are using an LMS with an integrated chatbot function, investigate whether it is designed to answer or ask questions—both are useful at different stages of the learning journey.

Chatbots that answer questions can be used to help facilitate a learning conversation as well as serve as a concierge for your program, send out phases of a learning initiative, act as a reminder tool for upcoming sessions, and prompt additional reading or videos.

Technique 43: Augment Your Chatbot With Human Coaching

Humans can also be used to augment learning transfer chatbots. For example, we can create a learning transfer approach where the learner talks with a human transfer specialist (or a manager or an internal coach) as well as a chatbot. The conversational flows are designed so the human is aware of what the learner has shared with the chatbot and is also able, using a simple input form, to share with the chatbot what the learner has told them. This means the chatbot can follow up on the commitments that the learner made when talking to the human and vice versa. When participants follow through on the commitments that they have made, impact is created within the organization.

Technique 44: Use Coaching Videos

Videos have many uses within learning. At the learning transfer stage, video can be used to encourage deep reflection and create ownership. As noted in chapter 7, this book's focus is on non-content-based learning transfer coaching—it's not about adding information or content; it's about using reflection to come up with ideas and create ownership. Because we are driving behavior at the application phase, coaching videos must enable learners to embed or apply what they've learned in the virtual program.

For example, if a learner has identified that they are procrastinating about implementing what they've learned, they might watch a video that's designed to help them get unstuck and move forward with the application by encouraging reflection. Importantly, the focus is no longer on the content; it's about behavior. This video could be relevant to any situation in which the learner is procrastinating implementing the content because it gives them ownership and enables them to come up with the solution for how to move forward.

Videos can also be used to help trigger deep reflective processes. Imagine a learner says "I don't know" in answer to a question from a learning transfer chatbot. Rather than proceeding to tell the learner what to do, the chatbot could build on the principles of self-regulated learning and invite the learner to think about their own experience and frameworks to help answer the question. The chatbot could share a video that would help the learner come up with new ideas even when their initial instinct is that they don't know the answer. You'll find a great example of this type of video at youtu.be/2OMB-gjvN5M.[2]

Before you leap to view the link, take a moment to think about something you've learned that you haven't applied yet in your day-to-day job. Would you know how to answer if someone asked you how you were going to put that knowledge into play? Now, watch the video linked above. Have you changed your answer?

One option for creating video is to use animation software, which can be easy to learn and costs very little (for example, this video was created using Vyond). Make sure that the videos are accessible for all by having subtitles, colors, and characters that are appropriate for the audience. Use of AI-generated video will also become increasingly important in this space. It's relatively quick and easy to generate video using an AI avatar that can read a script you create. Synthesia and Digital Humans are two of the current platforms offering AI-generated video capabilities (visit youtu.be/k9fT38jhuSM to see an example).

While videos can also be used to create just-in-time content, we challenge you to stretch your thinking. Are learners not applying the information because they don't remember it at the transfer stage? Or do you need to think deeper about how to shift behavior to drive impact? The answer likely depends on the context or type of learning. Content-heavy, technical, or product-based programs may just need a quick way to supply information to support learning application, which a video does well. For soft skills or more habitual behaviors, however, it's unlikely that video content will be enough.

Technique 45: Apps and Guided Support Software to Enable Use

Other technologies such as apps or guided support software technology can also be used to assist the learning transfer stage. The scale of the learning experience will influence the implementation of this strategy. It may even be worth investing in a bespoke app or software specifically designed to support a larger program. This could then be used to house real-time information connected with the program.

Such apps can be used to provide encouragement, prompts, and assistance using the program's content. They may bring up the critical information learners need, enable them to review techniques, or watch a video of the task being performed correctly. As an example, you may place a QR code or an AR trigger on a complex piece of machinery on a manufacturing floor, which opens to an embedded video. While the user likely already received training on the machine, in the moment of need it helps to have immediate access to the information.

Depending on the type of learning—but particularly if it's information- or content-heavy technical training—guided support software can be particularly useful for enabling application. This software prompts the learner, assists them, or completes the task for them; it essentially guides the participants to successful use of the process. Studies have shown that using this type of software increases the ROI significantly.[3]

Arguably this type of tool straddles the line between transfer and performance support, depending on whether you focus on the content or the application. Having worked closely with chatbots in the last few years, we've seen a shift away from apps to chatbots. One of the key differences is that learners can converse with chatbots in the same platform that they're already using for chat (such as MS Teams or Slack), and therefore don't need to download another application to their phone. Which tool to use would likely depend on whether you want to generate conversation-based or content-based interactions.

Technique 46: Use Automated Reminders and Nudges for Application and Impact

Learning and talent development teams that embrace automation at different stages and phases within the journey will have a distinct advantage. We've already noted that you can't remind people to make behavior change happen, because that's quickly seen as nagging. But there's a catch—if people feel like they're in control of the reminder process, the prompts will help them. When they choose the schedule, the frequency, and the mode of the reminder, they are taking ownership of the process and so the reminders aren't irritating. The key here is emphasizing autonomy, making it easy for the learner and letting them decide what will best help them.

Reminder systems can be embedded in the learning technology or be stand-alone. Choosing how a person wants to be reminded or what functionality they want to use comes down to several factors: the number of features, popularity, recommendations from others, integrations with other third-party apps, ease of use, and cost. They may include voice activation or integrations within the Google or Microsoft ecosystems. nTask, Wunderlist, Todoist, and Rembo are a few of the more well-known examples today, but the technology is advancing continuously, and new apps appear all the time. Reminders can also be used to help manage the program's flow and serve as a concierge point. This could happen via a chatbot interface in the learner's messaging platform or simply by email.

These messages can be part of the program's communication strategy, as discussed in chapter 5, serving to welcome people to the program, remind them of the virtual module's dates and times, send details about each phase along with early-stage learning requirements, and share logistics and resource links. It could also give options for contacting someone if there is a problem or if they are stuck.

While reminder message tools may not directly influence learning transfer, the administration complexity of a virtual learning program can be really resource attentive, so it's worthwhile to invest the time to create an automated flow for this up front. The added advantage here is that the software or chatbot personality is then ready for use at the learning transfer phase, giving the learner an end-to-end experience. For example, learners in the ReMind case study at the beginning of the chapter met their chatbot, Coach M, before meeting any facilitators. Coach M supplied the link to their intake questionnaires and helped arrange briefing calls with the facilitators. Then it led them through a body scan exercise just before the virtual class began to check in with themselves and how they were feeling. Coach M shared that information with the facilitator, who was able to use it to see if participants were feeling anxious, happy, or low and adjust how they managed the group.

In addition, Coach M sent participants a reminder 10 minutes before each virtual session: "Kettle on time! Here's the zoom link [URL] to the session. You'll have the session open for 3 hours but won't be tied to your computer! And the password is "ReMind." You and I will talk later in the week, but Katy will tell you more about that. Have fun."

A final comment on nudges. As we discussed in detail in chapter 7, different types of nudges can help create behavioral change to drive impact. It's also important to pay attention to this nuance of wording when using technology. For example, a simple way to keep people engaged in a follow-up process when they are falling behind schedule is to inject humor and social accountability using an automated nudge. For example, "Hey Sam—Let's chat soon, I promise it will be painless! And I'm keen that you keep up with the rest of the group. Reply START when you are ready to speak or BOOK if you'd like to schedule a specific time."

The applications for automated nudges and reminders will only grow in the future.

Social Tools to Support Transfer

The second way to leverage technology at the application phase is to integrate with self-reflection and share what has been applied. This creates social proof of application, wins, and challenges, and leverages the social aspect of learning. Let's look at some practical solutions in this category.

Technique 47: Use Selfies to Share

Photos and imagery are such a powerful way to engage people and reflection. Use this technique at the end of the process once someone else is involved. For example, a telecom store's employees participated in a virtual learning program focused on selling a product, which also required access to a database that reflected information about the customer and the product. Later, after one of the learners sold that product in the store, they asked the customer, "Do you mind if I take a selfie with you with my database in the background?" While some customers may not want to do this, many others will. The selfie provided a connection between the program and the sale, showing evidence via the database in the background (application) and the satisfied customer who just made a sale (impact).

The success of this technique will depend on the organization's culture and, to some extent, the specific learning cohort.

Technique 48: Use Social Media Groups or Platforms to Network for Encouragement, Support, and Enablement

Sometimes, it is helpful to create a dedicated group on a social media platform (such as WhatsApp, Facebook, and LinkedIn), or on an organization's specific learning platform, to keep the participant cohort together and in conversation. The group's facilitator can use the platform to encourage learning application, bring up application issues, collect success stories, and facilitate communication, as well as discuss barriers, obstacles, and impediments to success. The sense of community this generates in a virtual cohort can be very powerful and provides a way for learners to stay connected at the application phase and support one another as they begin to apply their learning back in the real world.

This is a low-cost option because many of these platforms are free access tools that people already use in their daily life. However, note that creating and driving conversation may also require energy and commitment from the facilitator. Some cohorts may create this momentum themselves, but others may need someone to help drive engagement in the space.

Specific platforms, such as Adeption, also leverage cohort learning and application. In between virtual sessions, learners using the Adeption platform participate in workouts that inspire reflection and group support. After reflecting on the session and answering questions independently, learners are able to see their colleagues' answers so they can learn from and be inspired by results others are getting from applying the content. The reflections can be shared in the form of word clouds or verbatim comments. This technique not only shows learners how they can apply the learning but also drives them to take action to create impact.

Technique 49: Post-Program Recorded Content Reviews or Application Tips

The rise of social media influencers who create quick, off-the-cuff videos has shown that authentic sharing is just as important as creating an edited, produced message. We can leverage this trend at the learning application stage by allowing learners to share their own videos.

For example, learners could record video clips sharing what they have learned and post it on the company intranet or social platform for others to see. This mirrors the traditional approach of presenting what you have learned in a training program to your colleagues to cement the information. Tools for creating video can be within your organization's LXP; standalone, such as StoryTagger; or open to all, such as YouTube.

Sharing content (in video or otherwise) can drive behavior change if it provokes reflection on learning transfer rather than just sharing the knowledge. So, invite people to share not only what they know, but how they applied that knowledge. Ask them to capture how they put what they've learned into action or how they applied it. What worked, what was challenging, and what will they do differently next time? It's a subtle shift, but a significant one.

Technique 50: Use AI to Gauge the Effectiveness of Communication in Virtual Conversations

Conversation tracking is an area within AI that's constantly evolving in ways that will continue to help drive application and impact. For example, Riff Analytics analyzes conversations between people and tracks not only how much conversation each person is providing, but the tone, quality, and dominance of the conversation. This technology could be used by soft skills program facilitators to see how learners are using and applying the skills on the job. Or, it could be used to gain more insight on team dynamics. On-the-job trainers, coaches, and others could then use those insights to support the learning transfer. There is also an opportunity to share these insights with others to create a collaborative application environment.

Similarly, this type of technology could be applied to help skills acquisition and application. For example, we could leverage AI technology to assess and monitor how learners are using soft skills in practical settings by creating a program that identifies language patterns. This technique could aid transfer through improved skill acquisition and measurement, which may boost the learner's confidence to apply that knowledge. Interflexion and PMOtraining created a role-play game to help learners acquire coaching skills. As learners practiced coaching and giving feedback using the role-play technology, the tool sent feedback and pointers for how to improve. This is an exciting way to deliver soft skills application and feedback in a fully scalable way.[4]

A Personal Story of Technology Reluctance: A Word From Emma

Like many learning professionals, I work in this space because I love people, I believe in their potential, and I want to work with them. However, these feelings also make many of us shy away from technology. My work in the chatbot space was slowed because of my reluctance and my disbelief in what the technology could offer. In fact, I began working with chatbots only because one of my clients saw the potential and insisted we move forward with the tool despite our original claim that chatbots couldn't replace humans in learning transfer. How wrong we ended up being!

Next Steps

Make a decision to experiment. There are many different ways you can use technology in learning transfer and they range in cost and time requirements. Consider what works for your culture and context, but be prepared to stretch your thinking. In the future, we will be thinking about technology and humans not in terms of "either/or" but "and," by leveraging the best of both. Experiment and test for yourselves. Let go of your preconceptions and see what is possible with technology in the space of virtual learning.

Now that we've covered these 50 techniques, you may have questions about how to use them in practice. Which ones will work best for you or be the easiest to implement? How should you even start when creating virtual learning initiatives? In the next chapter we'll briefly review the techniques and then provide some assistance for sorting out which will work best for you.

Selecting the Techniques

Now that you've discovered these 50 techniques to design for application, impact, and ROI, you may be wondering, "Which techniques should I use?"

This chapter provides additional information to help you select the techniques that are right for your project. First, we identify 10 selection criteria to help you make the decision. Then, we provide a rating scale you can use to quantify the advantages and disadvantages of each. We also present a summary of each technique to facilitate your rating process. Finally, in the appendix, we share our ratings of each technique, based on our combined experience, and provide a space for you to enter your own ratings.

The most important ratings will be your own. You know your organization and learners best. Once you use the techniques and become comfortable with them, your perceptions of them will make a significant difference in their use and success.

Selection Criteria

We have developed 10 selection criteria to help you decide which techniques to use:

1. **Cost.** One of the most important issues is how much the technique will cost. While the direct costs are usually considered, indirect costs should be included. A technique may involve purchasing software, implementing processes, or the cost of the time involved to implement the technique. This rating reflects the cost of the technique relative to the cost of other techniques.

2. **Extent of technology.** The use of technology to enable the application of knowledge is growing dramatically. Some may want to invest heavily in technology, while others are skeptical and prefer less technology. Either way, the ratings provide an opportunity to identify the amount of technology needed for each technique. You will also want to consider the security and data privacy provisions. Depending on your organization's requirements, you may want to review your plans with the IT and information security teams.

3. **Effectiveness.** Effectiveness is consistency and impact. The two issues are related. Some techniques seem to work every time and have a huge impact.

Others may not always work, and the impact is very low. There is always a concern about effectiveness, which makes this an important consideration when selecting a technique.

4. **Participant time.** Time is important and scarce. If a technique requires a lot of the participants' time it could be a turnoff if they don't see the value in it. The key is to understand which techniques take less time compared with those that take much more time, and to consider if the time invested is worth the outcomes you will achieve.

5. **Participant's manager involvement.** The most influential individual to enable the use of the program content, beyond the learner's own motivation, is their immediate manager. Some of these techniques do not involve the participant's managers, while others involve them in a significant way. This is important to keep in mind because the manager's time is critical. You want to minimize the amount of time required of a manager while maximizing its effectiveness.

6. **Time of others.** Sometimes other individuals are involved, such as subject matter experts, mentors, coaches, coordinators, support teams, and on-the-job trainers. Involving other people in a program is usually expensive and can be more complicated. To offset the cost, you could get creative and use internal resources—maybe internal coaches or high performers who want to learn how to develop others—rather than having to pay for an outside person. The two issues are to control the time of others and the cost of that time.

7. **Proven.** Some of the techniques presented in this book are time-tested, with hundreds of applications. Others have been used only a few times but show promise. The extent to which the technique is proven is another important consideration.

8. **Ease of implementation.** Some techniques may require a lot of effort for designing and implementing the process, putting things in place, and ensuring that everything is working. Others may take less time for preparation and impact. Some techniques are difficult to implement, and others are easy. The issue is the ease of making it work.

9. **Ease of use.** It's one thing to implement a technique, and it's another thing for others to use it and successfully apply it, particularly the participants. If a technique is complex and cumbersome, it may turn off the users, making it unsuccessful. If it is easy to use, it may work and be successful.

10. **Innovation.** Finally, you need to consider the technique's degree of innovation. In this ever-changing field, there are many possible techniques to use and the list is growing. Some techniques are very innovative in their design and approach,

while others are very simple and time-tested and have been operational for many years. If innovation is important to your organization and your learners, this will need to be considered. Some people like to try new approaches.

The Ratings

Now that we've identified the 10 selection criteria for consideration, let's move to the rating scale. Each criteria will be ranked on a 1 to 5 scale, indicating the degree of intensity for each:

- **Costs:** 1 = very inexpensive; 5 = very expensive
- **Extent of technology:** 1 = very little technology; 5 = very high technology
- **Effectiveness:** 1 = very low level of effectiveness in delivering results; 5 = very high level of effectiveness
- **Participant time:** 1 = small investment of time; 5 = large investment of time
- **Participant's manager involvement:** 1 = low involvement; 5 = very significant involvement
- **Time of others:** 1 = small investment of time; 5 = large investment of time
- **Proven:** 1 = not yet proven; 5 = proven in hundreds of applications
- **Ease of implementation:** 1 = difficult to implement; 5 = very easy to implement
- **Ease of use:** 1 = difficult to use; 5 = very easy to use
- **Innovation:** 1 = very low level of innovation; 5 = very high level of innovation

Brief Description of Techniques

Before we rank the techniques, let's briefly review each one.

1. Define Virtual Learning

Your definition of virtual learning will guide the decisions made about its design, which will in turn affect the learning, application, and impact. This may be as simple as creating a statement like, "Virtual learning brings together 25 (or fewer) remote attendees into an online virtual classroom, with a facilitator, for an interactive learning segment full of collaboration and conversation," or using a statement as detailed as our definition. The point is to come to an agreement among all designers, facilitators, and other stakeholders, so that when a learning and talent development team proposes virtual learning as a solution to a business problem, everyone knows exactly what that means.

2. Design for Interaction, Engagement, and Application

It's an intentional decision to design a virtual learning program for interaction, engagement, and application. To ensure a program is designed for interaction and engagement, many talent development teams create a set of virtual learning standards. These consistent guidelines spell out the expectations for interaction and engagement. Resolving to create an interactive virtual learning program, and then ensuring that all are in agreement about it, creates a pathway to engagement and application.

3. Select the Right Platform

The virtual classroom platform, with its available tools and features, forms the backbone of the online learning experience. Features such as polls, chat, reactions, breakouts, and drawing tools are essential for engagement. But while these tools may seem simple and standard, they are not available everywhere because only some online event platforms were designed with interactive training in mind. Platforms designed for collaborative learning—as opposed to virtual events or meetings—are more likely to include a full set of interaction and collaboration tools. Therefore, it's important to select the best platform for your organization's learning needs.

4. Prepare Facilitators to Support Learning Transfer

Skilled facilitators must be deeply knowledgeable about the anticipated learning outcomes, and familiar with how the participants will be expected to apply the new information. Once a facilitator truly understands how the content will be applied in the workplace, they can support participants in reflecting and finding relevant ways to apply it to their role and context. In preparation for the virtual learning program, the facilitator should immerse themselves in the details that will help them support learning transfer. This research could include interviewing participants, job shadowing, talking with stakeholders, or scanning the organization's business environment.

5. Send More Than a Calendar Invite

Because interactive virtual classes have vastly different participant expectations from a typical meeting, sending a standard calendar invitation won't communicate enough information. Which leads to this simple but effective technique: Send more than a meeting invite. It's not that you should avoid meeting invitations. In fact, they are important because they block out the participants' time on their calendar. It's just that they aren't enough for a learning program that's designed to achieve application and impact.

We recommend sending intentionally scripted, personalized messages to each participant in advance of a virtual learning program. Sending at least one email upon registration, along with reminder messages, is ideal. The exact number depends upon the scope of the virtual learning program.

6. Set Participant Expectations in Advance

Setting expectations in advance helps participants know exactly what to expect when attending a virtual class. It also helps drive the behaviors—engaged, active participants—that you strive for in a virtual learning program designed for application and impact. If participants aren't engaging, then they aren't learning. And if they aren't learning there's no chance of achieving application and impact.

The exact expectations to set in advance will depend upon the learning program. The most obvious option for expectation setting is to send an email, as described in the previous technique. Other methods include updating the program description so it's clear about engagement expectations or sharing a checklist of tasks to complete before the program starts.

7. Clearly Communicate Objectives

Everyone involved—from the stakeholders to the facilitators to the participants—should understand the objectives and how they lead to application and impact. For participants to know why they are in attendance, the objectives need to be clearly communicated multiple times. By knowing the "why?"—the business impact—they will be more likely to engage. When participants are aware of the objectives, they are more likely to achieve them.

8. Create an Evaluation Plan

The evaluation plan should encompass the entire scope of the virtual learning program, including virtual classes combined with other components that support learning transfer. We want to capture behavior change as well as impact. Evaluation plans come in many forms—from a simple one-page task list to a full-blown project plan with multiple swim lanes of stakeholder actions.

9. Create Job Aids and Application Guides

In this technique, designers move beyond the traditional participant workbook to create job aids and application guides. A job aid is a support tool that guides participants through a task. It's a printed or electronic reference document that provides the step-by-step process. Job aids serve to reinforce the learning back on the job, enabling application. Application guides serve a similar purpose but may be more complex in nature. They may be a manual, detailed documentation, or an online website dedicated to support and learning reminders.

10. Create Custom Self-Objectives

When participants can see the specific, personalized benefits of the learning program, they will be more engaged and more likely to want to use their new skills back on the job.

In this technique, designers create a preparation assignment where participants (and their manager, if appropriate) create custom self-objectives after reflecting on the planned learning content and its relevancy to job tasks.

11. Create a Kickoff Event, and Include Managers

A *kickoff event* is like an orientation to the virtual learning program. It sets the stage for participant engagement and ensures everyone's technology works seamlessly. Having a program kickoff also increases participant motivation because they can gain a clearer view of the big picture and desired results. In our experience, they are more likely to complete self-led assignments in a virtual learning series if they have met others in their cohort, recognize the learning expectations, and understand that they play an important role in the learning process. We also encourage the additional step of inviting the participants' managers or direct supervisors to attend the event to gain buy-in and support for the learning process and its application back on the job.

12. Design a Manager Guide to Accompany the Learning Experience

The purpose of the manager guide is to inform managers of the application learning objectives as well as to provide an overview of the learning program. This can be especially useful if the learning journey will take place over an extended period of time because it helps the manager keep track of what the participant is learning and when. The manager guide can also serve as a discussion guide with question prompts and sentence starters.

13. Ensure Easy Access to Application and Impact Data

It's said that what gets measured, gets done. As designers work through the process of creating virtual learning for application and impact, they examine a lot of data to effectively align the program to business needs. Because this data holds the information for measuring impact, it must be easy to access and track. The simpler it is to access the data, the more likely it will be used for application.

14. Use a Commitment Contract With Participants

A commitment contract serves two purposes. First, it encourages motivation throughout a learning journey. This type of commitment contract asks the participant to intentionally agree to complete every learning program component, with the ultimate goal of application and impact on the job. The contract could be kept as a personal commitment for the participant to acknowledge on their own behalf, or it could be shared with the facilitator, a trusted colleague, or the participant's direct supervisor.

The second type of commitment contract goes a step further by asking participants to take specific actions (application) and achieve a consequence (impact). The focus is usually on impact, and the commitment from the participant is to improve the impact by a certain amount by a particular time. This type of contract assumes that both the facilitator and the participant's immediate supervisor will agree and sign off on it. Essentially, this creates a three-way contract for performance improvement that has been agreed to by participants, supported by their manager, and given additional efforts on the part of the facilitator, administrator, or program owner.

15. Use the Platform's Welcome Message to Reinforce Purpose
Many virtual classroom platforms have a lobby or waiting room that can be used to set the tone for the program. It's an opportunity to display an onscreen reminder of expectations and objectives so they're at the forefront of participants' minds. The welcome message could be text, visual, or even video, as long as it's used to establish or remind participants of expectations. Going into a virtual learning program with the right mindset—to engage and learn—will help participants apply the content.

16. Create a Warm Welcome
Participants should be promptly acknowledged and warmly greeted when they enter the virtual classroom. When the online atmosphere feels welcoming and inviting, participants will feel encouraged to get involved. Instead of stark silence, have conversation. Have a soft opening that invites participants into the experience. Be intentional about what's displayed onscreen when they join. Use the time before the program starts to set the tone, teach participants how to use the interactive platform tools, and preview the training topic. Generate excitement and capture their attention.

17. Create Immediate Interaction
Immediately—within the first two minutes of the start time—give participants the opportunity to interact. It can be a simple interaction, such as a poll question or a chat prompt; the goal is to get the participants clicking, typing, or talking right away. The majority of a program's housekeeping content can either wait a few minutes or be converted to an engaging exercise. Participants need to quickly interact with the tools and with one another or you will lose a prime opportunity to set the stage for an interactive learning experience.

18. Include WIIFM at the Start
Sharing the WIIFM (What's in it for me?) near the start of each virtual class reminds participants of the program's importance. WIIFM can be shared in multiple ways, from a

static visual aid to a small group or breakout discussion. This also helps participants focus on the virtual class rather than any other distractions surrounding them, because it reminds them of the priorities.

19. Make It Social

The social aspect of virtual learning is a critical ingredient of engagement. A design that emphasizes social connections makes for a better overall learning experience. Participants learn from one another through robust conversation and collaboration. Remote participants also feel less isolated when they realize they're part of a group. By designing conversation and teamwork into virtual learning, participants become part of a community. When they feel connected to others, they are more likely to get involved. On the other hand, if a participant stays anonymous, they are more likely to tune out and multitask. We want connected participants who learn and apply that information.

20. Select Activities for Maximum Involvement

When planning class activities, the designer should intentionally create interactions to include everyone. In a cohort of 20 participants, all 20 participants need to apply the information. Stakeholders expect it, their managers expect it, and the facilitator should expect it as well. Facilitators should minimize times when only one person gets to talk, and make the most of breakouts, whiteboards, and other collaboration exercises.

21. Ask Questions With Intent and Inclusion

Virtual facilitators can generate dialogue by asking an initial discussion question that's both *precise* and *prescriptive*. In other words, it's a specific question that includes directions on how to respond. This technique avoids the dreaded silence by first gaining input and then expanding upon it for conversation, which not only jump-starts conversation, but also intentionally includes all participants.

For example, if a facilitator asks, "Who else has a comment about this topic?" only a few may respond. But if a facilitator says, "Raise your hand if you have a comment, otherwise click on the 'no' button," this phrasing implies that everyone is expected to give input. Skilled facilitators who adopt this technique can keep all participants immersed in the learning, which will then enable application and impact.

22. Use the Tools Creatively

Virtual classroom platforms provide an abundance of tools to involve participants. Using these tools creatively keeps participants involved and, more important, leads to better results. It's not about using the platform tools just to use them. It's about using them to further the learning results. For example, you can use polls for input, chat for dialogue, webcams for conversation, and whiteboards for team collaboration. It's also important to maintain interest by not using the same activity over and over again. Participants will get bored quickly if they're only asked to "type your response in chat." Designers should get creative with the available tool set in ways that keep the content fresh and exciting.

23. Use Visuals to Keep Attention

Most virtual classroom platforms emphasize screen sharing or document sharing, which means slides take center stage. Therefore, instructional designers need to intentionally create slides that fit an interactive virtual class. The longer a slide stays on the screen, the more likely a participant is to check out. When participants grow visually tired and look away, it increases the possibility they'll lose interest and attention. Remember, passive participants usually aren't learning, which negatively affects their ability to apply new skills. During periods of short presentation times, keep the screen moving for visual interest.

24. Use Realistic Scenarios

Our design process emphasizes application and impact. It's not enough for learning to take place during a virtual class; it then needs to be applied so that it has business impact. One aspect of this learning transfer incorporates using realistic scenarios. Participants should be able to easily recognize themselves in proposed situations without having to reach too far to make a connection. Stories, case studies, role plays, and scenarios should make sense in the context of the participants' workplace and the organization's realities.

25. Incorporate formative feedback

Virtual platform tools make it easy to collect participant feedback. Polls allow for multiple-choice and short answer responses. Chat opens up the ability to type and provide open-ended input. Whiteboards let participants freely write and draw. And reactions can be used to quickly gauge participant sentiment. These tools can and should be used to gather formative feedback during a program. Designers can build in knowledge checks throughout the event to assess understanding and comprehension, which will help the facilitator know if more application practice is required or if it's time to move to the next topic.

26. Include Self-Reflection Time

All learning programs should include self-reflection time. The challenge in a virtual class is to design the self-reflection activity in a way that doesn't encourage participants to multitask. In addition, the activity should encourage participants to go beyond just recalling new information they have learned and to also consider application of the content.

27. Teach to Application and Impact

When application and impact objectives are developed and provided to all stakeholders, it clearly shows what they should do after the program (Level 3) and why they are in the program in the first place (Level 4). This instructs the facilitator and producer to teach toward the objectives.

When the instructional designer ensures the content, exercises, activities, and materials speak to actual use and the impact, it redefines the program's measure of success as not what participants learn, but what they do with what they learn. Now the stakeholders will focus on that definition of success—impact and not learning.

28. Integrate Application Activities

When sequencing a virtual learning program, application activities should be in the forefront of everyone's mind. Learning isn't enough. Application activities must be integrated into the learning experience. Common examples of application activities include case studies, role plays, and realistic scenarios. These exercises allow participants to practice and explore their new skills in real-world environments.

29. Connect Content Between Sessions

A key benefit of virtual learning is its ability to provide practice and application exercises throughout a blended journey. When these application activities are placed between virtual classes, the facilitator can link the content from one session to another and give time for participants to practice their new skills in real-word scenarios between the sessions. Participants get the benefit of immediate application. They're also able to discuss these activities with others and receive expert guidance from the facilitator as needed.

30. Have Action Plan Presentations

The action plan starts with the impact measure that the participant wants to improve and lists the actions they will take to improve the impact measures. This not only serves as a way to organize and plan the action steps, but it also increases motivation because the participant gains ownership over the action plan. In addition, when action plans are presented to the group, they further serve to increase commitment. More important, the action plan serves as a data collection tool, because the evaluation team receives the completed plans to show the successes for application and impact. Action planning is the preparation step in great learning transfer. It's essential that this is captured during the learning experience, ideally about three-quarters of the way through the program.

31. Finish With a Call to Action

The close of a virtual class is just as important as its opening. The closing call to action activity leaves a parting impression and is the springboard to the next step. Participants should leave the virtual class knowing exactly what to do next. If there's an application assignment to complete before the next gathering, or it's time to finish the formal program and move into the next phase, everyone should be aware of the next steps. Beyond recognizing what to do, participants should also know why they need to do it. Therefore, finish each virtual class with a specific call to action. It could build on the action plans or be a way to review and amend. It will help participants feel energized, excited, and eager to apply their new knowledge and skills.

32. Follow Up on Action Plans

Action plans created as part of a learning program will enable participants to make decisions and commitments as to what and how they will apply what they've learned in their day-to-day roles. The completed action plan shows a road map of their success, which becomes a jumping-off point for change. Reviewing how the action plans are aligned with organizational outcomes for a program can be very beneficial for the learning team, and the information can be used to make program improvements. A buddy, a manager, or even a chatbot can follow up on the action plan, which helps create accountability for change.

33. One-on-One Coaching After the Program

One of the most powerful ways to deliver behavioral change is to combine the learning program with a coaching-based approach. The coaching support (in the form of creating space for reflection, ownership, and accountability) can be provided by a manager, a buddy, an internal coach, an external coach, or even a chatbot if people are open to technology. The best outcomes occur when conversations are focused on the participant's action plan and take place over several weeks or months, depending on the program structure.

34. Manager Encouragement and Involvement Using Feedback Loops

This technique is a follow-up on the preprogram expectation and involves what the manager would say to the participant as soon as they've completed the program. For example, the manager could ask the participant about the program, remind them to ask for help if they need it, and provide any necessary support. What's important is that the manager is letting the participant know they are expecting them to use the knowledge and skills from the program, and that the use should have an impact.

Feedback loops can also be powerful because they keep the manager informed of what a participant has achieved or what goals they are working toward. The manager has a high level of influence and the learning design team can include them in the virtual learning program by providing conversation summaries and prompts to help facilitate manager/participant interactions.

35. Group Coaching After the Program and Implementation Phase

If positioned as an integral part of a virtual program, group coaching sessions can be engaging and beneficial. For best outcomes use an external facilitator and a conversation methodology that emphasizes accountability and reflection. These can be weekly sessions or monthly, occurring at a set time for participants to tune in and discuss their issues or concerns. This is a great technique for uncovering and confronting barriers. It's also a great way to share success stories.

36. Apply Nudging Techniques

Nudges are techniques used to change a person's behavior and fall under the umbrella of behavioral economics. For example, facilitators could highlight milestones to participants at specific times by saying something like, "Most successful people in this program are using at least three of the five skills routinely by this time." Indicating that people are using these skills puts subtle pressure on others to do it too.

37. Observation Sessions With an On-the-Job Trainer

Having an on-the-job trainer follow up with participants, check on participants, and help if they have questions is a tried-and-true technique. When the trainer shifts the emphasis toward accountability, it puts the responsibility back on the participant for driving ownership of change. By asking questions and facilitating solutions, rather than giving advice and direction, the on-the-job trainer can help the participant create long-term change and facilitate application and impact.

38. Host a Lessons-Learned Meeting Once Participants Have Used the Content

Hold a lessons-learned session after the participants have used the content, at a predetermined follow-up time, to allow them to reflect on what they learned from the actual use. This also provides an excellent opportunity to bring up impediments and barriers to success so that the participants can help one another overcome them. This meeting is motivational because when participants see how others have made progress, they will be inspired to do the same.

39. Meaningful Business Projects With Lessons-Learned Graduation

As a part of leadership programs, participants are encouraged to deliver a capstone project and present their findings to senior stakeholders at graduation. A focus on lessons learned in addition to outcomes can help promote reflection and a learning culture.

40. Share Success With Other Participants and Key Lessons Learned

Sharing success can be a motivator for change if participants are inspired by others' actions. For example, if data has been collected at Level 3, but you are still waiting to collect Level 4 data, you can share the Level 3 data to show how successful others have been. This may put subtle pressure on those who have not yet been successful to step up. To make the process more reflective, you could encourage participants to focus on lessons learned as well as outcomes to promote a learning mindset.

41. Hold a Contest Based on Achieving Success for Application and Impact

The contest is an incentive for participants to use the material. The prize could be recognition or some type of valuable reward for those doing the best job. The focus is on ensuring that participants follow through, are successful, and report their success. By rewarding those doing the best job, you'll also motivate everyone else to step up and make progress.

42. Leverage Chatbots for Learning Transfer

A chatbot is a computer program designed to simulate a conversation. Chatbots created specifically for learning transfer can be used to help hold individual participants accountable for change and applying their learning. A participant would speak to the chatbot via text or a chat platform such as Microsoft Teams, sharing the progress they have made toward their learning application goals and brainstorming ideas for next steps. The conversations would happen over a period of time and generate rich data to show the participant's progress and the program's impact.

43. Augment Your Chatbot With Human Coaching

Augmenting a chatbot solution with a human coach can leverage the best of both worlds—one-on-one support and technology. The human coach could be a manager, an internal coach, or an external coach. The participant would have some human conversations and some chatbot reflective conversations, and both the coach and the chatbot would always be informed of what the participant is sharing.

44. Use Coaching Videos

Video can be used in many ways throughout the virtual learning journey. For example, video is great for sharing additional content and giving specific tips. It can also be a powerful tool for driving behavioral change by increasing reflection and accountability. Carefully timed video as part of a reflective conversation or an application phase follow-up can be used to ask questions and encourage participants to reflect further and brainstorm ways to move forward.

45. Apps and Guided Support Software to Enable Use

Sometimes, if the program involves many participants, it may be helpful to create an app that participants can use to access real-time information. The app could provide encouragement, prompts, and assistance using the program's content. It may bring up the critical information participants need or allow them to review the techniques or a video of performing the task correctly. The goal is to help participants use what they have learned.

In larger-scale systems, it can be helpful to create software that guides participants through the application and use. This software prompts them, assists them, or completes the task for them, providing feedback as they use what they have learned.

46. Use Automated Reminders and Nudges for Application and Impact

Learning teams can leverage automation and routine messaging to stay connected with participants. Messages can be used to send reminders, which ideally participants have scheduled, to encourage ownership of the follow-up process. Automation ensures the messages are helpful and timely.

47. Use Selfies to Share

This technique is designed for individuals in the sales area, although it can work in other settings. This action is taken at the end of the process, when another person is involved, such as in a sales scenario when a satisfied customer has just purchased an item. By taking a selfie with the customer and product they've sold, the participants create physical proof of the connection between the program and the sale. This technique can also be used to share wins.

48. Use Social Media Groups or Platforms to Network for Encouragement, Support, and Enablement

Create a group for participants using WhatsApp, Facebook, LinkedIn, or other social media platforms to keep the group together and in conversation. The group's facilitator can encourage application, bring up application issues, collect success stories, and facilitate communication, as well as discuss barriers, obstacles, and impediments to success.

49. Post-Program Recorded Content Reviews or Application Tips

Participants could use their smartphones to create a video featuring a summary of the topic or content covered. Or they could share how they have applied the learning, what results they have achieved, and tips for others. Future and current participants can use these videos as tools and inspiration for what's possible.

50. Use AI to Gauge the Effectiveness of Communication in Virtual Conversations

AI technology can identify language patterns, including tone, quality, and dominance in real-time scenarios. This can be used to support the application of learning to give feedback on real or role-played, language-based scenarios, such as those for coaching or sales.

Ratings

Now that we've reviewed the techniques, it's time to apply ratings. We've created a worksheet to help with this process, capturing all 50 techniques and providing space for your ratings of all 10 criteria (Figure 9-1).

As you experience using these techniques, you will gain new perspectives. You'll likely rate the techniques differently than others and that's expected. As you build expertise and better understand your organization's culture and your participants, you may want to return to these ratings and update your answers. If you're curious how we rate each technique, we've put our composite ratings in the appendix.

Figure 9-1. Technique Selection Criteria Worksheet: Selecting Techniques to Deliver Impact and ROI

Each technique you are considering implementing is in the left column below. Each technique is ranked for each criterion.

Criteria and Ranking Scale

Technique	Costs	Extent of Technology	Effectiveness	Participant Time	Participant's Manager Involvement	Time of Others	Proven	Ease of Implementation	Ease of Use	Innovation
1. Define virtual learning										
2. Design for interaction, engagement, and application										
3. Select the right platform										
4. Prepare facilitators to support learning transfer										
5. Send more than a calendar invite										
6. Set participant expectations in advance										
7. Clearly communicate objectives										
8. Create an evaluation plan										
9. Create job aids and application guides										
10. Create custom self-objectives										
11. Create a kickoff event, and include managers										
12. Design a manager guide to accompany the learning experience										
13. Ensure easy access to application and impact data										
14. Use a commitment contract with participants										
15. Use the platform's welcome message to reinforce purpose										
16. Create a warm welcome										
17. Create immediate interaction										
18. Include WIIFM at the start										
19. Make it social										
20. Select activities for maximum involvement										
21. Ask questions with intent and inclusion										

Figure 9.1 *(cont.)*

Technique	Costs	Extent of Technology	Effectiveness	Participant Time	Participant's Manager Involvement	Time of Others	Proven	Ease of Implementation	Ease of Use	Innovation
22. Use the tools creatively										
23. Use visuals to keep attention										
24. Use realistic scenarios										
25. Incorporate formative feedback										
26. Include self-reflection time										
27. Teach to application and impact										
28. Integrate application activities										
29. Connect content between sessions										
30. Have action plan presentations										
31. Finish with a call to action										
32. Follow up on action plans										
33. One-on-one coaching after the program										
34. Manager encouragement and involvement using feedback loops										
35. Group coaching after the program and implementation phase										
36. Apply nudging techniques										
37. Observation sessions with an on-the-job trainer										
38. Host a lessons-learned meeting once participants have used the content										
39. Meaningful business projects with lessons-learned graduation										
40. Share success with other participants and key lessons learned										
41. Hold a contest based on achieving success for application and impact										
42. Leverage chatbots for learning transfer										
43. Augment your chatbot with human coaching										

Figure 9.1 *(cont.)*

Technique	Costs	Extent of Technology	Effectiveness	Participant Time	Participant's Manager Involvement	Time of Others	Proven	Ease of Implementation	Ease of Use	Innovation
44. Use coaching videos										
45. Apps and guided support software to enable use										
46. Use automated reminders and nudges for application and impact										
47. Use selfies to share										
48. Use social media groups or platforms to network for encouragement, support, and enablement										
49. Post-program recorded content reviews or application tips										
50. Use AI to gauge the effectiveness of communication in virtual conversations										

Criteria and Ranking Scale

Next Steps

This chapter provides a tool to guide you through using the various techniques. It's not meant to be complicated or cumbersome, but a helpful job aid you can quickly reference when considering whether to use a particular technique. You read about the technique, and you think it looks feasible. You want to see how it stacks up against the 10 criteria. You can also look to the appendix to see how the authors view it. And remember, your perception of the technique may change as you use it.

The previous chapters focused on ensuring that your program is connected to the business, that you have the right solution, and that you have designed it to deliver reaction, learning, application, and impact. Now you are ready to implement the program. Once the program is implemented, you have to collect the data. This is covered in chapter 10.

PART 3

Evaluating Impact and ROI

Data Collection for Application and Impact

Discount Casual Shop has more than 2,000 stores in the United States, Canada, and Europe. The fashion chain focuses on casual clothing at discounted prices. During the COVID-19 pandemic, stores were initially closed but then reopened to minimal traffic flow. Although the chain had an online operation and was able to pivot much of the business to a virtual format, there was a desire to get the retail stores back to normal as quickly as possible.

There were several challenges facing the store managers. First was managing the staff through this difficult period. Second was managing the customer interactions and traffic in the stores, maintaining social distancing, and dealing with the societal issues of the pandemic. The third issue involved getting customers to return to in-store shopping and making them comfortable in this setting.

To meet these challenges, the learning and development team created a workshop called Managing for Turbulent Times, which addressed the following skills:
- Addressing challenges and roadblocks
- Setting clear goals and expectations
- Identifying opportunities for improvements
- Fostering open and clear communications
- Providing feedback and support
- Listening with empathy
- Managing conflicts and differences
- Building trust and confidence
- Recognizing and rewarding team members
- Action planning for improvement

Figure 10-1 shows the program design for the workshop, which featured five 30-minute e-learning sessions followed by a 15-hour virtual session, which was broken into small chunks with plenty of break time built in. On-the-job coaching, use of tools, and documenting the results were done after the workshop ended.

Figure 10-1. Program Design: Managing in Turbulent Times

	Awareness and Alignment	Learning, Engagement, and Practice	Application, Impact, and Reporting
	Technology-Based	Virtual Design	On the Job
30-min e-learning module	• Awareness of situation • Need to improve	• Expectations and commitment • 360-degree feedback	• Connect with the manager and coach
30-min e-learning module	• Program design • Process flow • Responsibilities	• 10 skills to manage in turbulent times • Skills videos	• Implement actions • Make adjustments
30-min e-learning module	• Possibilities • Tips • Tactics	• Virtual practice • Engagement and reflection	• Review videos • Use tools • Use a learning portal
30-min e-learning module and survey	• 360-degree feedback • Use • Rules	• Skill-impact linkage • Planning » Business impact » Behaviors and actions	• Impact capture • Analysis • Documentation
30-min e-learning module	• Alignment • Business impact measures • Making the connections		• Reporting • Sharing

To understand whether this program worked, there would need to be a tremendous amount of data collection involving different methods, timing, and data sources. First, to see how well the e-learning modules were working, then to measure the success of the virtual session in terms of reaction and learning, and finally to follow up to make sure the program made a difference. There was an action plan built into the process that required collecting the action plans to assess the success of the coach and the enablement pieces. The evaluation also included a review of the videos and use of the learning portal.

A Review of Data Collection

Now that the virtual learning program has been designed to deliver reaction, learning, application, and impact, it's helpful to review data collection methods that measure the success of the virtual learning program. Data collection has relevance throughout the program cycle, both for reaction and learning data during the program and to confirm the effectiveness of the program via application and impact data in the follow-up. This chapter explores data collection methods, principles, and timing, with emphasis on application and impact, where the issue of making it stick is a concern. Data collection also reveals areas where the virtual program isn't working and opportunities for improvement.

Questionnaires and Surveys

The questionnaire is the most common method of data collection, especially in virtual learning. Ranging from short reaction queries to detailed follow-up tools, questionnaires are used to obtain subjective information about the participants as well as objective data to measure business results and ROI analysis. With its versatility and popularity, the questionnaire is an optimal method for capturing levels of data (reaction, learning, application, and business impact).

Surveys are a specific type of questionnaire that captures attitudes, beliefs, and opinions. The principles of survey construction and design are similar to questionnaire design.[1] A questionnaire may include:

- Multiple-choice questions, which ask the respondent to select the most applicable response.
- Checklist (multianswer) questions, which provide a list of items for respondents to review and select those that apply in the situation.
- Two-way questions, which have alternate responses (such as yes or no, agree or disagree, or two other possible responses).
- Ranking scales, which require the respondent to rank a list of items.
- Open-ended questions, which have no "correct" answer and provide ample blank space for the participant to write their response.

Virtual classroom platform tools make it simple and easy to ask these types of questions. Almost all platforms include built-in polling for multiple-choice, multiple-answer, and short answer responses. And many platforms have recently added advanced polling options such as ranking, word clouds, and unlimited text. Two-way questions can be asked in many ways, either via traditional polling or by using reactions (yes or no, agree or disagree). Finally, the facilitator can also post the link to an external survey tool in chat or another easily accessible area, and some platforms may even open that link automatically on the participants' computer.

The areas of feedback used on reaction questionnaires depend on the purpose of the evaluation. Some forms are simple, while others are detailed and require considerable time to complete. Specific to a virtual program, questions should ask about participant's perception of the software used, and if they had any trouble getting or staying connected. When a comprehensive evaluation is planned, and impact and ROI are being measured, a comprehensive list of questions is necessary. For example, questions might target the following areas:

- Use of materials, guides, and technology
- Application of knowledge and skills
- Frequency of use of knowledge and skills
- Success with use of knowledge and skills
- Change in work or work behavior
- Improvements and accomplishments
- Monetary impact of improvements
- Improvements linked to the program
- Confidence level of data supplied
- Perceived value of the investment
- Linkage with output measures
- Barriers to implementation
- Enablers to implementation
- Management support for implementation
- Target audience recommendations

This feedback can be useful in making adjustments to a program and documenting performance after the program.

Interviews

Another helpful data collection method is the interview. The instructional designer or someone on the learning and talent development team usually conducts the interview, which can secure data not available in business or organization databases or data that may be difficult to obtain through questionnaires or observations. Interviews may also uncover success stories that can be useful in communicating evaluation results. Participants may be reluctant to describe their results in a questionnaire, but may be willing to volunteer the information to a skillful interviewer using probing techniques. The interview is particularly useful for collecting application or performance data. However, one major disadvantage is that it is time-consuming, because it requires interviewer preparation to ensure the process is consistent.

Interviews are categorized into two basic types: structured and unstructured. A structured interview is much like a questionnaire. The interviewer asks specific questions that allow the interviewee little room to deviate from the menu of expected responses. The structured interview offers several advantages over the questionnaire. For example, an interviewer can ensure that the questions are answered and that the responses supplied by the interviewee are correctly interpreted.

An unstructured interview has built-in flexibility, allowing the interviewer to probe for additional information. It uses a small number of core questions that can lead to more detailed information as important data is uncovered. At Levels 3 and 4, the interviewer must be skilled in interviewing a variety of individuals and using the probing process to uncover barriers and enablers and to explore success stories. The steps to design and implement an interview are similar to those of the questionnaire.

Focus Groups

Much like interviews, focus groups are helpful when in-depth feedback is needed. A focus group involves a small group discussion conducted by an experienced facilitator, who solicits qualitative feedback on a planned topic. Group members are invited to provide their thoughts, because individual input builds on group input.

Focus groups have several advantages over questionnaires, surveys, or interviews. The basic premise of using focus groups is that when quality perspectives are subjective, several individual perspectives are better than one. The group process, where group members stimulate ideas in others, is an effective method for generating qualitative data. Focus groups are less expensive than individual interviews and can be quickly planned and conducted. They should be small (eight to 12 individuals) and consist of a representative sample of the target population. Group facilitators should have expertise in conducting focus groups with a wide range of individuals. The flexibility of this data collection method makes it possible to explore organizational matters before the training initiative as well as to collect unexpected outcomes or application after the program. Barriers to implementation can also be explored through focus groups, while examples and real concerns can be collected from those involved in the initiative.

Focus groups are particularly helpful when there is a need for qualitative information about the success of a program. For example, focus groups can be used to:
- Collect information contributing to diagnosis and the proposed solution.
- Gauge the overall effectiveness of program application.
- Identify the barriers to and enablers of a successful implementation.
- Isolate the impact from other influences.

Focus groups are helpful when evaluation information is needed but cannot be collected adequately with questionnaires, interviews, or quantitative methods. However, for a complete evaluation, focus group information should be combined with data from other instruments.

Observations

Another potentially useful data collection method is observation. The observer may be an immediate manager, a member of a peer group, or an external party. However, the most common observer, and probably the most practical, is a member of the learning and talent development team. A unique consideration for observations after virtual learning programs is the location. Because all participants were remote, on-site visits and/or travel may be necessary to complete an observation. Or, coordination of local team members could be preferable.

To be effective, observations need to be systematic and well developed, minimizing the observer's influence and subjectivity. Observers should be carefully selected, fully prepared, and understand how to interpret, score (if relevant), and report what they see.

This method is helpful for collecting data on soft skills programs, such as employee engagement, leadership development, management training, coaching, and executive education. For example, 360-degree feedback surveys include observation, because behavior changes are solicited from direct reports, colleagues, internal customers, immediate managers, and even self-input. This is considered a delayed report method of observation. This feedback process can be part of the actual program, or it could be used before participating in another development initiative.

For observation to be successful, it must be invisible or unnoticeable. Invisible means that the person under observation is not aware that it is taking place. For instance, Starbucks uses secret shoppers to observe their employees. The secret shopper takes note of how long orders take to process, the demeanor of the server, whether the store and bathrooms are clean, and whether the server is familiar with new drink offerings. The observation continues immediately following the visit, when the secret shopper checks the temperature of their drink order. This observation activity is invisible to the server.

Unnoticeable observations are situations in which the person under observation may be aware that it is taking place but doesn't notice, because it occurs randomly or over a longer period of time. Examples of unnoticeable observations include listening in on customer service calls ("This call may be monitored for quality assurance purposes") or a 360-degree feedback process.

Action Plans

The concept of action plans was introduced in chapters 6 and 7. They are a great tool for transferring learning to the job and also a great data collection tool. Action plans are connected to Level 4 and are a tool to drive application and impact, meaning that the starting point for the program is the Level 4 measure. They follow the process outlined in this book, starting with the end in mind with a clear, specific need. Each participant in the program will identify an impact measure (or maybe two or three) they want to improve with a very specific objective and a list of the actions they will take to improve the business measure. Essentially, the plan contains data for Level 3, which is the actions that are being taken, and data for Level 4, the impact.

To be efficient and comprehensive, action plans can not only capture the Level 4 data but also serve to document the improvement's monetary value and isolate the program's effects on the data. It is helpful to understand how an action plan is developed to realize the power of the action planning process in making the evaluation for impact and ROI much more manageable. (Figure 10-2 shows an example of an action plan with measures.)

First, the requirement of the action plan is introduced along with the program description. It is not a surprise to participants. They know that the plan will support the program and that time is allocated in the program to develop the plans. In this example of a virtual management development program, the participant attending this program, Ginger Sanford, has identified a measure that she wants to improve. The follow-up date for collecting impact data has been decided as part of the design process. It's in November, and the program begins in May, creating a six-month follow-up. Ginger brings to the program a precise impact objective for improving the number of service complaints from 21 per month to 15 per month in six months. She knows this impact objective in advance, and when time is allowed in the session to complete the plan, she can transfer that specific objective onto the plan, as indicated in this figure.

As Ginger learns the program content, she identifies specific actions that she could take to improve the impact measure. She keeps these potential actions as notes until she completes the plan. At that point, she lists the steps she wants to follow with specific follow-up times. When completed, the left side of the plan contains the Level 3 data showing the specific actions to be taken by a particular time.

Next, Ginger moves to the right side and lists the unit of measure. It is best to think about a unit of measurement, such as one complaint. With the cost of one complaint, you can multiply this number by the improvement in complaints to arrive at the total monetary value. On line B, she enters the value of the complaint, in this case, $600. Where did she obtain this amount? It depends; she may already know the value, and in that case, it's a standard value, as described later in this book. Or Ginger may obtain the amount from someone in the department that investigates these complaints. That is what she did in this example. Ginger went to a person in the customer service department who could provide the cost of the complaints. That technique is called expert input. There are even more techniques that could be used, explored in the next chapter. If you don't know it as a standard value and there is no one to provide it, a third option involves asking the participants to estimate the value. This technique is called participant estimation. While

Figure 10-2. Action Plan From a Virtual Management Development Program

Name: Ginger Sanford **Facilitator Signature:** _____ **Objective:** Reduce service complaints by at least 25%

Evaluation Period: May to November **Follow-Up Date:** November 30 **Improvement Measure:** Service complaints

Current Performance: 21 per month **Target Performance:** 15 per month

Action Steps		Analysis	
1. Review reasons for complaints; sort out items under our control	May 30	A.	What is the unit of measure? 1 service complaint
2. Change protocol with customers based on step 1	June 10	B.	What is the value (cost) of one unit? $600
3. Have a team sharing session each week to focus on complaints	June 11	C.	How did you arrive at this value? Provided by John M. in the customer services dept.
4. Provide team feedback when necessary for members who need help	June 15	D.	How much did the measure change during the evaluation period? (Monthly value) 8 per month
5. When a team member prevents a complaint, establish a complaint prevention award	June 20	E.	List the other factors that have influenced this change: Service delivery process enhancement, product quality improved, supplier changed
6. Celebrate monthly successes	July 1	F.	What percent of this change was actually caused by this program? 30%
7. Have three-month review and adjust as necessary	August 15	G.	What level of confidence do you place on the above information? (100% = Certainty and 0% = No confidence) 80%
Intangible Benefits			
Comments: Program helped us focus			

line B shows the unit value, line C explains how you obtained the value, which is necessary for credibility.

Line D is completed six months after the program is conducted. How much did that measure actually change? In Ginger's case, the actual change is a reduction of eight complaints per month, which means she is down to 13, which is a little better than her target.

Usually, measures in a system are influenced by other factors, so Ginger is asked what other factors influenced this change. She identifies three things: service delivery enhancement, product quality improvement, and a different supplier. Then she is asked what percent of the change was caused by this program. Ginger allocates 30 percent, which means 70 percent went to those three other factors.

This issue is covered more in the analysis discussed in the next chapter. While there are other techniques, in this example, the technique for isolating the effects of the program is participant estimate. The participant should be very credible, and the most credible person in this case is Ginger, who knows all the other factors and is in the best position to estimate how much goes to each factor.

Still, this is an estimate, so the next step is to adjust for the error in the estimate. That is the confidence question on line G. How confident are you in the above information? If Ginger is certain, she would put 100 percent. With other factors, she cannot be that certain, so it will be less than 100 percent. As she reports that number, she is essentially reflecting the error. If she is 80 percent confident, as indicated in this example, there is a 20 percent chance of error. Therefore, we want to remove 20 percent from the 30 percent. This is achieved by multiplying the 80 percent by 30 percent. This is credible because she's the most credible person to provide this data, it's collected in a nonthreatening and unbiased way, and it's adjusted for error. The results are acceptable to the management team because the process is conservative and credible.

So there you have it. In Ginger's case, the value delivered by this program is:

$$\underset{\text{(complaints)}}{\text{8 per month}} \times \underset{\text{(a year)}}{\text{12 months}} \times \underset{\text{(allocation)}}{\text{30\%}} \times \underset{\text{(confidence)}}{\text{80\%}} \times \underset{\text{(unit value)}}{\text{\$600}} = \text{\$13,824}$$

The monetary values of all the action plans of the participants are calculated and totaled to arrive at the total monetary benefits for the program you are evaluating.

The advantage of using an action plan for data collection is that the three challenging parts of conducting an ROI study are built into the document:

- The post-program data is collected for Levels 3 and 4.
- The monetary value is derived.
- The impact of the program is isolated in the data.

This is very credible and not very difficult. In this virtual management development program example, the total monetary benefits for the program can then be compared with the cost of the program to develop the actual ROI.

In summary, the action plan process is very powerful not only to transfer learning to the job but to provide a method of data collection that is powerful for the evaluation team, the organization, and the participant, as Ginger sees the value she has delivered.

Monitoring Performance

One of the more important methods of data collection is monitoring the organization's records. Performance data is available in every organization to report on impact measures, such as output, quality, cost, time, job engagement, and customer satisfaction. As emphasized in chapter 2, the key is to start with a business impact measure connected to the virtual learning program.

Performance measures should be reviewed to identify how they're related to the proposed program. Sometimes, an organization has several performance measures related to the same objective. For example, a new talent development program may be designed to increase productivity from the team, which could be measured in a variety of ways, including:

- Team or individual output (products, services, projects)
- Output per unit of time
- Gross productivity (revenue per person)
- Time savings (when the saved time is used on other productive work)
- Fewer team members or hours worked (with the same output)

Each of these measures gauges the efficiency or effectiveness of the team. All related measures should be reviewed to determine those most relevant to the program.

Improving the Response Rate for Data Collection

One of the greatest challenges in data collection is achieving an acceptable response rate, which is unlikely if you require too much information. Getting the maximum response rate is critical when the primary data collection method hinges on input obtained through questionnaires, surveys, and action plans. Here are a few ways to boost response rates through optimal data collection design and administration techniques:

- Provide advance notice about the questionnaire.
- Clearly communicate the reason for the questionnaire.
- Indicate who will see the results of the questionnaire.
- Show how the data will be integrated with other data.

- Keep the questionnaire as simple as possible.
- Keep questionnaire responses anonymous—or at least confidential.
- Make it easy to respond with email.
- Use two follow-up reminders.
- Ask a top executive to sign the introduction letter.
- Send a summary of results to the target audience.
- Have a third party collect and analyze the data.
- Communicate a time limit for submitting responses.
- Design the questionnaire with a professional format to attract attention.
- Provide options to respond (such as electronically or on paper).
- Review the questionnaire in a formal session at the end of the program.

Built-In Data Collection Tools

As emphasized in chapters 6 and 7, building application and data collection tools into the virtual learning program is an area where designing for results works extremely well. This is particularly helpful for programs where data collection can easily be incorporated into the program. Ranging from action plans to job aids, these tools come in a variety of types and designs discussed earlier. The success of action plans depends on whether they've been built into the process. Figure 10-3 shows the steps to follow to ensure the action plan presented in Figure 10-2 is incorporated into the process and becomes an integral part of achieving business success.

Figure 10-3. Sequence of Activities for Action Planning

Before	1. Communicate the action plan requirement early.
	2. Require one or more impact measures to be identified by participants.
During	1. Describe the action planning process.
	2. Allow time to develop the plan.
	3. Teach the action planning process.
	4. Have the facilitator approve the action plan.
	5. Require participants to assign a monetary value for each proposed improvement.
	6. If possible, require action plans to be presented to the group.
	7. Explain the follow-up mechanism.
After	1. Support the participant in actioning the plan through reflective conversations with a coach, buddy, manager, or chatbot.
	2. Require participants to provide improvement data.
	3. Ask participants to isolate the effects of the program.
	4. Ask participants to provide a level of confidence for estimates.
	5. Collect action plans at a predetermined follow-up time.
	6. Summarize the data and calculate the ROI (optional).
	7. Report results to sponsor and participants.
	8. Use results to drive improvement.

Improvement Plans and Guides

Sometimes, the phrase *action plan* is not appropriate, particularly if the organization has previously used it to refer to other projects and programs, creating an unsavory impression. In this case, other terms can be used. Some prefer the concept of *improvement plans*, recognizing that a business measure has been identified and improvement is needed. The improvement may involve the entire team or just an individual. *Application guide* is another good term; it can include a completed example as well as what is expected from the participant and tips and techniques to make it work.

As discussed in chapter 6, selecting the right wording for describing the action plan's goals is important; *commitments* and *experiments* are popular alternatives to *goals*.

Application Tools and Templates

Moving beyond action and improvement plans brings a variety of application tools, such as simple forms, technology support to enhance an application, and guides to track and monitor business improvement. All types of templates and tools can be used to keep the process on track, provide data for those who need it, and remind a participant of where they are going. See the authors' website for examples and refer to chapter 8 for ideas on how to use technology to support behavioral change.

Performance Contract

Perhaps the most powerful built-in tool is the performance contract, which is much like an action plan and serves as a contract for performance improvement between the participant and their immediate manager. The participant meets with the manager before the program, and they agree on specific measures to improve and the amount of improvement. This contract can be enhanced if a third party enters the arrangement (for example, the virtual program facilitator or a project coordinator for other types of projects).

Performance contracts are powerful because the person is pledging to change their performance using the content, information, and materials from the virtual learning program, and they have the added support from their immediate manager and the facilitator or project manager. When programs are implemented using a performance contract, they deliver very significant changes in the business measure.

The performance contract is designed to collect data and support behavior change and learning transfer. Figure 10-4 shows a performance contract for a sales representative involved in sales-enabling processes, including a combination of formal learning sessions, online tools, and coaching. The goal is to increase sales with existing clients. The sales manager approves the contract, along with the participant and program facilitator.

Figure 10-4. Example of a Performance Contract

Name: Laura Gibson		**Manager:** Cathy Wieser		**Facilitator:** Tim Ockers

Objective: Increase sales with existing clients by 20%

Evaluation Period: January to March

Improvement Measure: Monthly sales

Current Performance: $56,000 per month   **Target Performance:** $67,000 per month

Action Steps		**Analysis**
1.	Meet with key clients to discuss issues, concerns, and other opportunities.	January 31	A. What is the unit of measure? Monthly sales for existing clients
2.	Review customer feedback data—look for trends and patterns.	-	B. What is the value (cost) of one unit? 25% profit margin
3.	Counsel with "at risk" clients to correct problems and explore opportunities for improvement.	February 2	C. How did you arrive at this value? Standard value
4.	Develop business plan for high-potential clients.	February 5	D. How much did the measure change during the evaluation period? (Monthly value) $11,000
5.	Provide recognition to clients with long tenure.	Routinely	E. What other factors have influenced this change: Changes in market, new promotion
6.	Schedule appreciation dinner for key clients.	February 15	F. What percent of this change was actually caused by this program? - 60%
7.	Encourage marketing to delegate more responsibilities.	February 20	G. What level of confidence do you place on the above information? (100% = Certainty and 0% = No confidence) 90%
8.	Follow up with each discussion and discuss improvement and plan other actions.	Routinely	
9.	Monitor improvement and provide support when appropriate.	March 15	
Intangible Benefits: Client satisfaction, loyalty		**Comments:** Excellent, hard-hitting program

Selecting the Appropriate Method for Each Level

This chapter presented several methods to capture data. Collectively, these methods represent a wide range of opportunities for collecting data in a variety of situations. Eight specific issues should be considered when deciding which method is appropriate for a situation or evaluation level.

Type of Data

An important issue to consider when selecting the method is the type of data to be collected. Some methods are more appropriate for Level 4, for example, while others are best for Levels 3, 2, or 1. Figure 10-5 shows the most appropriate methods of data collection for each of the four levels. For example, follow-up surveys, observations, interviews, and focus groups are best suited for Level 3 data, sometimes exclusively. Performance monitoring, action planning, and questionnaires, on the other hand, can readily capture Level 4 data.

Figure 10-5. Collecting Application and Impact Data

Method	Level			
	1	**2**	**3**	**4**
Surveys	✓	✓	✓	
Questionnaires	✓	✓	✓	✓
Observations		✓	✓	
Interviews	✓	✓	✓	
Focus groups		✓	✓	
Tests		✓		
Simulations		✓		
Action planning			✓	✓
Performance contracting			✓	✓
Performance monitoring			✓	✓

Participants' Time for Data Input

Another important factor is the amount of time participants must spend with data collection and evaluation systems. Time requirements should always be minimized, and the method should be positioned so that it is a value-added activity (that is, if the participants understand that the activity is valuable, they will not resist). This often means using sampling, which keeps the total participant time to a minimum. Some methods, such as performance monitoring, don't require any participant time, while others, such as interviews and focus groups, require a significant investment of time.

Manager Time for Data Input

Always minimize the amount of time required for a participant's direct manager to allocate to data collection. Some methods, such as performance contracting, may require significant involvement from the supervisor, before and after the training initiative. Other methods, such as questionnaires administered directly to participants, may not require any supervisor time.

Cost of Method

Cost is always a consideration. Some data collection methods are more expensive than others. For example, interviews and observations are very expensive. Surveys, questionnaires, and performance monitoring are usually inexpensive.

Disruption of Normal Work Activities

An issue that may generate the most concern among managers and administrators is the amount of disruption the data collection will create. Try to disrupt routine work processes as little as possible. Some data collection techniques, such as performance monitoring, require very little time and distraction from normal activities. Questionnaires generally do not disrupt the work environment, and can often be completed in only a few minutes, or even after normal work hours. On the other extreme, some items, such as observations and interviews, may be too disruptive to the work unit.

Accuracy of Method

Some data collection methods are more accurate than others. For example, performance monitoring is usually very accurate, whereas questionnaires can be distorted and unreliable. If actual on-the-job behavior must be captured, observation is one of the most accurate methods of doing so.

Utility of an Additional Method

Because there is such a wide variety, it is tempting to use too many different data collection methods. The more data collection methods used, the higher the time and costs of the evaluation, but little additional value may be gained. Utility refers to the added value of the use of an additional data collection method. If more than one method is used, this question should be addressed: Does the value obtained from the additional data warrant the extra time and expense of the method? If the answer is no, the additional method should not be implemented.

Cultural Bias for Data Collection Method

The culture or philosophy of the organization can dictate which data collection methods are used. For example, some organizations are accustomed to using questionnaires and find that the process fits in well with their culture. Other organizations will not use observation because their culture does not support the potential invasion of privacy that's often associated with it.

Timing of Data Collection

Reaction and learning data are usually captured at the end of a module, session, learning asset or program. For application and impact, it depends on several issues. One of the advantages of the ROI Methodology is that it provides very specific guidelines for when to collect data for application and impact. This helps prevent evaluators from waiting too long to collect the data or collecting it too soon. If data is collected too late, participants may not be able to make the connections between the program and its application and impact. If data is collected too soon, it will have to be collected again. Let's review a few basic guidelines.

Collecting Application Data

The issue for application is identifying the time needed for participants to be routinely using what they are supposed to be using or doing what they should be doing. Sometimes, the required action is just a one-time process, such as completing a conflict of interest questionnaire. At other times, the action might be following systematic behaviors or procedures, such as a diabetic patient who's learning to manage the effects of diabetes through the proper control of insulin.

First, document what a successful application looks like, usually through application objectives (for example, the routine use of information, skills, knowledge, or contacts). Next identify at least two different subject matter experts (SMEs). The first SME should know the content of the programs and what participants are expected to do. The second SME should know the participant's situation; for example, where they are located, their stressors, their environment, and the barriers that will naturally exist while trying to make this project successful.

Ask the SMEs to indicate how long it will take a participant to be successful with application, considering two issues: the complexity of what the participant is being asked to do and their opportunity to do it. If it is a simple process that the participant will do every day, then they will likely be using it routinely in a matter of days. However, if it is a very complex task, it will take longer. Or, if the participant will do the task only once a month, it is also going to take longer to become successful. Complexity and opportunity for use are thus the two factors for determining the timing of Level 3 data collection.

In some situations, application data can become apparent relatively quickly. For example, if the program was focused on automating a new disability claim process, Level 3 data would focus on how long it took learners to automate their routine. In another example, it could take a large amount of time for participant behavior in an online youth unemployment program to become routine and systematic in the interviewing, searching, and relationship building process.

The good news is that Level 3 application usually occurs quickly. However, if application data collection occurs too quickly, the participant may not know how to do what they've learned, and if it occurs too late, participants may have forgotten it. Learning retention is an important issue.

Collecting Impact Data

Impact is a consequence of the application. This is the data that is recorded in the system, such as productivity, mistakes, and errors. Impact represents the why for implementing the virtual program. The amount of time required to capture impact is represented by the length of time between the routine use of the process and the impact. Sometimes, this length of time is short, and other times it is much longer.

For example, when learners use new technology to process disability claims, the impact is shown when claims are processed more quickly (time), with fewer mistakes (quality), and with less cost. And, that impact will occur quickly, most likely within two to three weeks after routine use is in place. However, for youth unemployment, it may take several months to find a job that fits the participant's career interests and income requirements, depending on the job market.

The same two SMEs consulted for application data would then be asked to indicate how long it should take for the impact to occur. Sometimes, the ultimate impact may take much longer to manifest. For example, a virtual diabetes education program should demonstrate impact by preventing serious adverse health outcomes from diabetes, such as hospitalization, surgeries, emergency room visits, and even amputations or death. While those consequences can be prevented, it generally takes a long time before that impact occurs. In these cases, it is possible to use surrogate measures to determine impact. For example, having certain behaviors in place might correlate with preventing these adverse outcomes, suggesting, "Doing this will save the healthcare system this much money."

Most long-term impact outcomes have early indicators, predictors, or surrogate measures. This allows you to evaluate whether a program will have long-term impact early in the process. Adjustments can then be made at that time, instead of waiting for a long-term impact that may not be seen for five or 10 years.

Next Steps

Data collection is often considered one of the top three challenges of evaluating virtual learning at the impact and ROI levels. This chapter covers collecting data at the reaction, learning, application, and impact levels. The methods include some well-known and well-used techniques for collecting data and a few that might not be as familiar. Collectively, they will enable you to capture the data you need. After the data is collected, you will need to follow a series of steps to analyze the data. The first and perhaps one of the most important is to isolate the effects of virtual learning from other influences. Then you convert the data to money, capture the program's costs, and calculate the ROI. These analysis steps are not challenging and follow the systematic and logical processes described in the next chapter.

Make It Credible: Measuring Results and Calculating ROI

In healthcare, clinicians and administrative professionals are often promoted based on their technical skills and ability. However, clinicians receive minimal leadership training in their formal medical education. To address this gap in knowledge and performance, Carilion Clinic's Institute for Leadership Effectiveness (ILE) designed the virtual PEAKS Leadership Development Process based on a needs analysis and best practice research.

Carilion Clinic is a leading healthcare provider with core values of collaboration, commitment, compassion, courage, and curiosity. Opened in 1899, Carilion Clinic has transformed from a small, regional hospital to an enterprise healthcare system that employs roughly 14,000 individuals and serves a span of approximately 20 regions within Southwest Virginia.

For phase one of the process (six months), leaders focused on self-leadership concepts including a 360-data review, self-discovery, internal and external self-awareness, trust and authenticity, risk, missing the target, and vulnerability. Each module reflected the same format and included prework, a facilitated discussion, post-work, and group coaching. In phase two, which follows the same virtual format as phase one, leaders will receive content related to 360-degree people leadership, operations, and strategy.

During the rollout of phase one, top executives asked for impact and ROI data. Data was collected for phase one through Level 4 (impact). Findings indicated that there was a 90 percent agreement with all items at Level 1 (reaction). At Level 2 (learning), the most significant areas of knowledge growth were social and emotional intelligence and authenticity. Level 3 (application) data revealed changes in performance related to social and emotional intelligence and prudence. Level 4 (impact) data revealed that PEAKS participants scored higher on employee engagement items and had higher retention when compared with non-PEAKS participants. Additional impact and ROI data will be calculated at the conclusion of the program.

For most evaluation studies, impact data are factual, measured, or monitored from the data systems in the organization. In the Carilion Clinic case, phase one was initially focused on behavior change, rather than impact. Fortunately, the team was able to make an adjustment for phase two to allow for the collection of targeted organizational metrics that can be used to calculate ROI. The challenge is showing how much of the change in impact data can be attributed to the program. In addition, some executives want to see the monetary value of the improvement as well as the monetary benefits compared with the cost of the program (ROI). These issues are addressed in this chapter.

This level of measurement must be planned, systematic, and implemented in a sensible way. It can be accomplished with a minimum of additional budget, and can make a drastic difference. The challenge is to design your virtual learning programs for results and then make them happen. However, data analysis and interpretation are often thought of as the most challenging tasks of measurement and evaluation. And this challenge is compounded by a misunderstanding of the techniques as well as a fear of math and statistics. This chapter offers a simple explanation of this process in five key steps:

1. Isolate the impact of the virtual learning program from other influences. These factors must be taken into account because other variables often affect the impact of programs.
2. Convert data to monetary values by locating or calculating a monetary value.
3. Tabulate the costs of the program using direct and indirect costs.
4. Determine the ROI, a common approach to calculate value that can be used in comparison with other types of investment.
5. Discuss intangibles—the impact measures that are not converted to money.

These steps are not unique to virtual learning. However, there are several nuances specific to virtual learning that must be considered. These issues will be addressed throughout the descriptions and highlighted for awareness.

Isolating the Effects of the Program

Here's a common situation: Following the implementation of a major leadership development program, an organization experiences an improvement in retention. The two events appear to be related, and an executive wants to know how much of the improvement was due to the leadership development program. Unfortunately, the learning and talent development team is rarely able to answer that question with any degree of certainty. The change in performance may be related to the leadership program, but other factors may also have contributed to the improvement.

This section explores several techniques that can be used to answer the question "What impact did the program have on performance?" with a much greater degree of certainty. Taking the time to carry out this step creates additional credibility by focusing attention on other variables that may have influenced performance.

Use of Comparison Groups

The most credible approach for isolating the impact of a virtual learning program is to use comparison groups, similar to the design of a scientific experiment. This approach involves observing an experimental group that has the benefit of the program and a control group that does not. Both groups should have similar characteristics and, if feasible, be selected randomly. When both groups are subjected to the same environmental influences, the difference in each group's performance can be attributed to the virtual program.

When participants are joining a virtual learning program remotely, ensuring similar environmental influences may be extra challenging. The nature of virtual learning and remote work means that no two participant workspaces are the same. Some participants may be joining from a noisy, crowded cubicle space, while others are working from home. Distractions can be overcome through intentional design and engaging facilitation, but this requires extra effort and attention. As we've mentioned before, participants must be engaged to learn, and without learning there will be no impact. Therefore, when selecting comparison groups for virtual learning programs, consider the characteristics and composition of the remote participants. Figure 11-1 illustrates how a typical control group is set up.

Figure 11-1. Use of Control Groups

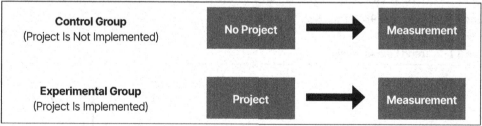

One major disadvantage of this method is that the program is withheld from one group. For example, take a situation in which the group that participated in a sales training program had $6 million more in revenue than the control group. Is the data gained from withholding the program from the control group worth it? There always needs to be a solid business reason for using a control group.

Trend Line Analysis

Another useful technique for approximating the impact of a virtual program is the trend line analysis. In this approach, a trend line is projected from a series of points that represents the initial performance level of the target audience, and it extends to a point that represents the anticipated performance level without the program. Upon completion of the program, this trend line is used to compare the actual performance against the predicted performance level. Any improvement in performance above what was predicted can be reasonably attributed to the virtual learning program. However, this requires that two conditions exist:

- The trend that was established before the program would have continued into the post-program period.
- No other new influences were introduced after the program was conducted.

Participants can usually validate these assumptions. While this is not an exact process, it does provide a reasonable estimation of the program's impact.

Figure 11-2 shows an example of a trend line analysis taken from a logistics company. The figure displays the percentage of on-time shipments before and after a virtual learning program that was conducted in June. Prior to conducting the program, the company was seeing an established downward trend in the shipment rate. The trend line shows that while this downward trend would have continued (according to the participants), the program had a dramatic effect on the on-time shipments. The participants and others involved in the program could not identify any other factors that could have influenced this measure.

It is tempting to measure the improvement by comparing the average six-month shipping rates prior to the program with the average of the six months after the program. However, it is more accurate to compare the rate in month six after the virtual program with the predicted trend line value of the same month. In this example, the difference is 28 percent (95 versus 68).

Figure 11-2. Trend Line Analysis

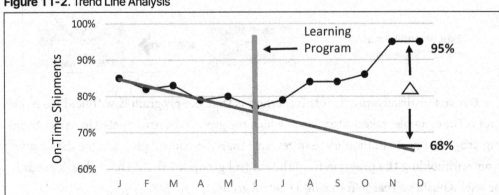

The main disadvantage of this approach is that it may not always be accurate, although it may not be any more or less accurate than other methods. In addition, this approach requires that the events influencing the performance variable prior to the program are still in place after the program.

The primary advantages of this approach is that it is simple and inexpensive, and takes very little effort. If historical data is available, a trend line can be projected quickly.

Analytical Modeling

The forecasting model provides a more analytical approach to trend line analysis, which is necessary if there are other influences in the post-program period. This approach is used to predict the future level of performance if the learning program had not been implemented and compares that with the actual value. The difference is attributed to the virtual learning program. Forecasting represents a mathematical relationship, which uses an equation to forecast the value of the anticipated performance improvement. This mathematical modeling is usually developed by others in the organization.

The primary advantage of this process is that it can be an accurate predictor of the performance variables that would occur without implementing the program, if appropriate data and models are available. The method is simple for linear relationships.

However, a major disadvantage occurs when considering many variables because it makes the process more complex and requires a more sophisticated statistical analysis. Even then, the data may not fit the model. Additionally, many organizations have not developed mathematical relationships for output variables as a function of one or more inputs and without them, this method is impossible to use. If the numbers are available, they could provide valuable evidence of the impact of a virtual learning program. However, the presentation of specific methods is beyond the scope of this book and is contained in other works. (See the additional resources section for more information.)[1]

Participant Estimation

An easy method to isolate the impact of a program is to secure information directly from participants. This approach assumes that participants are capable of estimating what portion of their performance improvement was related to the virtual learning program. Although their input is an estimate, it usually has considerable credibility, because participants have produced the improvement resulting from the program. To make it even more credible, the amount is adjusted by the potential error of the estimate expressed as a confidence in the estimate. As an added enhancement, management may be asked to approve the participants' estimates.

Figure 11-3 shows a sample of these estimates for one program. Participants estimated their percent improvement and the confidence levels. Then their managers reviewed and approved the estimates. In essence, this means that the managers confirmed participants' estimates.

Figure 11-3. Example of a Team Member's Estimates

Factor That Influenced Improvement	% of Improvement	Confidence Expressed as a %	Adjusted % of Improvement
Learning Program	60%	80%	48%
Six Sigma	15%	70%	10.5%
Environmental Change	5%	60%	3%
System Change	20%	80%	16%
Other	___ %	___ %	___ %
Total	**100%**		

The process has some disadvantages. Because it is an estimate, it does not have the accuracy desired by some professionals. In addition, if participants are uncomfortable providing this type of estimate, the input data may be limited.

However, the approach also has several advantages. It is a simple process that is easily understood by participants and others who review evaluation data. There is also an extensive body of research that suggests these estimates are accurate. This approach is also inexpensive, takes little time and analysis, and contributes an efficient addition to the evaluation process. Finally, despite being an estimate, it originates from a credible source.

Expert Estimation

Another approach is to rely on external or internal experts to estimate what portion of results can be attributed to a virtual learning program. For this process to be credible, however, the experts must be carefully selected based on their knowledge of the process, initiative, and situation. For example, a company could ask an expert in quality to estimate how much quality improvement could be attributed to a Six Sigma program.

Using expert estimations is most effective if the expert has been involved in similar programs and is able to estimate the impact of those factors based on previous experience or historical data.

Converting Data to Monetary Units

Chapter 2 presented the types of data necessary for evaluating a virtual learning and talent development program. However, before the data can be used to compare benefits with costs, it must be converted to monetary values. This section provides additional insight into practical ways to perform this conversion.

Converting Increased Output

Many programs are designed to change output, and the value of that increased output is typically easy to calculate. For example, when implementing a virtual learning program to increase sales, the change in output (sales) can be measured by calculating the sales improvement after the program and multiplying it by the average profit per sale, a standard value.

In another example, consider machine operators in a pharmaceutical plant who package drugs for shipment. Production managers participate in an virtual program to learn how to increase production through better use of equipment and work procedures. The value of the increased output is the operating profit margin of the added output. Fortunately, most of these conversions exist as standard values.

Converting Time Savings

Some virtual programs are aimed at reducing the time it takes to perform a task, deliver a service, or respond to a request. Time savings are important because employee time is money, as reflected by wages, salaries, and paid benefits. The most common result is reduced costs of effort for program participants. The monetary savings are reflected in multiplying the hours saved by the effort cost per hour. This is appropriate for the portion of time saved that is used on other productive work. When an online program drives time savings, participants should estimate the percent of time that was used on other productive work and then provide examples of that other work. This is the only way for the results to be credible.

Converting Improved Quality

Quality improvement is an important and frequent target of employee engagement programs. The cost of poor quality to an organization can be astounding. According to quality expert Phillip Crosby (1979), an organization could increase its profits by 5 to 10 percent if it concentrated on improving quality.[2] To calculate the return on the program, the value of the quality improvement must be calculated.

The most obvious cost of poor quality is the scrap or waste generated by mistakes; for example, defective products, spoiled raw materials, and discarded paperwork. The cost of a defective product can be easily calculated in a production environment—it is the total cost incurred at the point the mistake is identified minus the salvage value. The costs of paper and computer entry errors can also be significant; for example, an error on a purchase order can be enormous, if the wrong items are ordered.

Many mistakes and errors result in costly rework, especially if a product is delivered to a customer but must be returned for correction or an expensive program is implemented with serious errors. When determining the cost of rework, labor and direct cost are both significant. Maintaining a staff to perform rework is an additional overhead cost for the organization. In a manufacturing plant, for example, the cost of rework is in the range of 15 to 70 percent of a plant's productivity. In banks, an estimated 35 percent of operating costs could be blamed on correcting errors.

Calculating the Value

Occasionally an organization will develop and accumulate cost for specific data items. For example, some organizations monitor the cost of grievances. Although it's extremely variable, establishing an average cost per grievance provides a basis for estimating the cost savings for a reduction in grievances. Because of their relative accuracy, historical costs should be used to estimate the value of data items, unless this data is unavailable or requires too many resources to obtain.

Using Expert Input

Internal and external expert input can also be used to estimate the value of data. Internal experts are those employees who are proficient and knowledgeable in their fields. For example, a purchasing expert could estimate the salvage value of defective parts, an industrial engineer could estimate the time it takes to complete a task or perform a function, and a marketing analyst could estimate the cost of a customer complaint. Using internal experts also provides an excellent opportunity to recognize individuals in the organization. Their expert analysis should not be challenged, because others in the organization have no better basis to make the estimate.

External experts may also provide estimates, depending on their expertise in a given field. For example, an external consultant could estimate the cost of a grievance and then give that figure to several organizations.

External Studies

Extensive analyses of similar data in other organizations may be extrapolated to fit an internal situation. For example, many experts have attempted to calculate the cost of absenteeism. Although these estimates can vary considerably, they may still serve as a rough value for other calculations after making some adjustments for a specific organization. There are hundreds of studies covering the cost of variables such as absenteeism, turnover, tardiness, grievances, complaints, and lost time due to accidents. Typical sources to pursue may include the Corporate Leadership Council, *Academy of Management Journal*,

Journal of Applied Psychology, Human Resources Management, OD Practitioner, Human Resource Development Quarterly, and *Workforce Management.*

Participant Estimation of Value

As noted earlier in this chapter, employees who are directly involved in a virtual learning program may be capable of estimating the value of an improvement. Either during the program or in a follow-up, participants should be asked to estimate the value of their improvements. To provide further insight, they should also be asked to furnish the basis for their estimate and their level of confidence in it. Estimations by participants are credible and may be more realistic than other sources, because participants are usually directly involved with the improvement and are knowledgeable of the issues. If given encouragement and examples, participants are often creative at estimating these values—for example, asking managers to estimate the value of reducing the time to process a loan after participating in a special program. Although their responses won't be precise, they may provide a credible estimate of the value.

Management Estimation

A final strategy for converting soft data to monetary values is to ask managers who are concerned about the virtual learning program evaluation to estimate the value of an improvement. Several management groups may be targets for this estimation, including the supervisors of program participants, middle management, or even members of the C-suite.

These strategies are effective for converting soft data to monetary values when calculating the return on a program. However, a word of caution: Whenever a monetary value is assigned to subjective information, it needs to be fully explained. And, if there is a range of possible values, the most conservative one should be used to ensure credibility for the process.[3]

Tabulating the Costs of the Program

After an analysis yields a need, the learning and talent development team designs and develops a solution or acquires and implements one. The team routinely reports to the client or sponsor throughout the process and then undertakes an evaluation to show the program's success. A group of costs also supports the process (such as administrative support and overhead costs). For these costs to be fully understood, the project needs to be analyzed in several different categories.

The most important task is to define which specific costs to include in the tabulation of program costs. This step involves decisions that will be made by the learning and talent development team and, in most cases, approved by management. Finance and accounting staff may also need to approve the list. Figure 11-4 shows the recommended cost categories for a fully loaded, conservative approach to estimating costs.

Figure 11-4. Program Cost Categories

Cost Item	Prorated	Expensed
1. Needs assessment	✓	
2. Design and development	✓	
3. Acquisition costs	✓	
4. Technology costs	✓	
5. Implementation costs		
Salaries and benefits for coordination time		✓
Salaries and benefits for participant time		✓
Materials and supplies		✓
6. Maintenance and monitoring		✓
7. Administrative support and overhead	✓	
8. Evaluation and reporting		✓

Needs Assessment Costs

One of the most overlooked items is the cost of conducting the initial assessment or diagnosis of the need for the program. In some projects, this cost is zero, because the program is implemented without an initial assessment of need. However, as organizations focus increased attention on needs assessment, this cost item becomes more significant.

While it's best to collect data to the fullest extent possible on all costs associated with the needs assessment, estimates are appropriate. These costs include the time it takes team members to conduct the assessment, direct fees, expenses for external consultants who conduct the diagnosis, and internal services and supplies used in the analysis. The total costs are usually prorated over the life of the project. Depending on the type and nature of the project, the life cycle should be kept to a reasonable number, somewhere in the one-to-two-year timeframe. The exception would be for expensive projects for which the needs are not expected to change significantly for several years.

Design and Development Costs

One of the most significant items is the cost of developing the program. This cost includes internal staff and consultant time for the development of software, job aids, and other support material directly related to the project. As with diagnostics costs, development costs are usually prorated, perhaps using the same timeframe. Three to five years is recommended, unless the project is expected to remain unchanged for many years and the development costs are significant.

Acquisition Costs

In lieu of development costs, many organizations purchase off-the-shelf software or programs to use or modify to fit their needs. The acquisition costs for these programs include the purchase price and other costs associated with the rights to implement the program. These costs should be prorated, typically over three to five years, using the same rationale described previously. If the organization needs to modify or further develop the program, those costs should be included as development costs. In practice, many programs have both acquisition and development costs.

Technology Costs

Effective virtual learning requires an investment in technology. Organizations that are new to virtual learning will need to factor in initial setup fees, and all organizations will need to include costs for ongoing software licenses. Some platforms are more extensive than others and therefore require upskilling for both designers and facilitators. Hardware costs include dual monitors for facilitators, webcams for facilitators and participants, high-quality noise-canceling headsets, and in some cases green screens or other tech accessories. Some organizations already include these items in their equipment or IT budgets, while other organizations need to upgrade and invest. Organizations may even invest in dedicated virtual training rooms within their buildings, in which a facilitator and producer team can use built-in equipment to create professional quality broadcasts.

Implementation Costs

Perhaps the most important segment of learning program costs is the implementation. There are five major cost categories:

- **Salaries of coordinators and organizers.** Include the salaries of all individuals involved in coordination and direct support of the program. If a coordinator is involved in more than one program, their time should be allocated to the specific program under review. The key point is to account for all the direct time of internal employees or external consultants who worked on the program. In addition, make sure to include the employee benefits factor each time direct labor costs are involved.

- **Materials and supplies.** Many virtual learning programs still require materials and supplies. In some cases, workbooks and job aids are shipped to participant locations. In other cases, an electronic repository is used for document sharing. An organization may save on printing costs, but should replace that line item with online storage fees or increased internet bandwidth needs.
- **Participants' salaries and benefits.** Include the salaries plus employee benefits for the people participating in the virtual program for their time away from work. Estimates are appropriate in this analysis.

Maintenance and Monitoring

This item includes all costs related to a program's routine operation. It encompasses all costs in the same categories listed under implementation, as well as additional equipment and services as needed.

Overhead

Another charge is the cost of overhead, which is the additional costs incurred by the learning and talent development function that are not directly charged to a particular program. The overhead category represents any fixed cost not considered in the previous calculations, such as the cost of administrative support, administrative expenses, and the salaries of program managers. A rough estimate developed through some type of allocation plan is usually sufficient.

Evaluation

The evaluation cost is included in the virtual program costs to compute the fully loaded cost. For an ROI evaluation, these costs include developing the evaluation strategy and plans, designing instruments, collecting data, analyzing data, and preparing and presenting results. Cost categories include time, purchased services, materials, purchased instruments, and surveys.

Calculating the ROI

ROI is a figure that must be used with caution, because it can be interpreted or misinterpreted in many ways. This section presents some general guidelines to help calculate the ROI and interpret its meaning.

The monetary benefits are derived using the impact measures after they are converted to money. A group of employees is often involved in a virtual learning program, so the investment figure should be the total costs of analysis, development, implementation, operating, and evaluation totaled together in the bottom part of the equation.

With these considerations for calculating the ROI, the following formula is used:

$$\text{ROI (\%)} = \frac{\text{Net Benefits}}{\text{Costs}} \times 100$$

The net benefits are the benefits minus the costs. The formula is multiplied by 100 to convert it to a percent.

To illustrate this calculation, consider a virtual learning program designed to reduce error rates. The average daily error rate per employee dropped from 20 to 15 because of the program. Before the program, an employee spent an average of 30 minutes correcting errors. If employees average $20 per hour and 20 employees completed the program, the weekly operational savings for this program using base pay savings is $1,000 (or 5 × 0.5 × $20 × 20). The annual savings is $52,000. This means that the time saved can be used on other productive work. If the program costs $40,000, the ROI after the first year is calculated as follows:

$$\text{ROI} = \frac{\$52,000 - \$40,000}{\$40,000} \times 100 = 30\%$$

This suggests that for every dollar invested in the program, the dollar is recovered plus another 30 cents is returned. These figures may be more meaningful to managers who use ROI calculations for capital expenditures. ROI may be calculated prior to a virtual learning program to forecast the potential cost effectiveness or after a program to measure the results achieved. The methods of calculation are the same.

Similar to ROI, the BCR is calculated by dividing the total of the benefits derived from the program by the total cost of the program. A BCR greater than one indicates a positive return, while a ratio of less than one indicates a negative ROI. The benefits portion of the ratio is a tabulation of all the benefits derived from the program converted to monetary values, and the total costs include all the cost categories, as described earlier in this chapter.

Using the previous example, the BCR is calculated as:

$$\text{BCR} = \frac{\$52,000}{\$40,000} = 1.3$$

This suggests that for every dollar invested, $1.30 was received in benefits.

Identifying the Intangibles

Perhaps the first step to understanding intangibles is to clearly define the difference between tangible and intangible assets in a business organization. Tangible assets are required for business operations; they are readily visible, rigorously quantified, and routinely represented as line items on balance sheets.

Intangible assets are the key to competitive advantage. They are invisible, difficult to quantify, and not tracked through traditional accounting practices. With this distinction, it is easy to understand why intangible measures are more challenging to convert to money. In the ROI Methodology, intangibles are defined as impact measures not converted to money because the conversion would require too many resources or the result would not be credible, for example:

- Job satisfaction
- Organizational commitment
- Climate
- Engagement
- Employee complaints
- Recruiting image
- Brand awareness
- Stress
- Leadership effectiveness
- Resilience
- Caring
- Career-mindedness
- Customer satisfaction
- Customer complaints
- Customer response time
- Teamwork
- Cooperation
- Conflict
- Decisiveness
- Communication

To connect the intangibles to the virtual learning program, a simple question is asked about the list of intangibles: To what extent did this program influence each of these measures? A five-point scale is provided for response. The program participant is usually the one to provide the data.

Next Steps

This chapter discussed key issues in calculating the business contribution. One of the first issues is the concept of isolating the effects of the program from other influences, which determines the extent to which the virtual learning program caused the improvement. The second issue involves converting data to monetary values. The third issue is the cost of the program, and calculating the ROI is the fourth issue of data analysis.

Data collection and analysis have little use without conveying the results to the right audience in the right way. The next chapter will highlight how to communicate the results to key stakeholders and leverage the results to increase commitment, support, influence, process improvement, and funding. Sometimes, using the results creatively to make things better going forward is just as important as delivering them.

12

Telling the Story: Communicating the Results and Using the Data

The call center of a major insurance company was experiencing problems with call resolution for customers with claims issues. The net promoter score was decreasing, call escalations were increasing, and first call resolution was much lower than desired. As a result, the company implemented a four-hour virtual learning program for all call center employees. This interactive program explored the key issues of dealing with customers, listening to customers, clearly understanding customer issues, and knowing the full range of potential solutions. Additionally, the program presented a variety of skills to provide good service to keep the customer calm and conclude the call with a good feeling.

The virtual program had a very positive reaction. There was significant knowledge gain, and participants used their new skills with the customers. Call escalations were reduced, first call resolutions increased, and net promoter scores increased. More important for some, the program yielded an ROI of more than 100 percent.

Next came the task of communicating the data to the right people. The organization wanted to report the data to program participants and their immediate managers as well as all call center managers and several senior executive groups. The intent was to ensure that all stakeholders saw the program's value and understood the importance of learning as a way to drive significant business results.

When program results are measured—particularly at Levels 3, 4, or 5—the data is typically provided only to the key client, supporter, or major sponsor. Beyond that, other stakeholders are often omitted from any formal communication plan. To maximize the value, however, all key stakeholders—from participants to top executives—need to know the results. This is the seventh step in the eight-step process. The challenge is to identify the key stakeholders, craft the message, determine the method of communication, and share results in a timely manner. The eighth step is to use the results to optimize the investment in virtual learning programs. Both steps are covered in this chapter.

Before you share evaluation results, you need to be able to answer several questions:

- What is the best way to convey results?
- When is the best time to convey results?
- What is the purpose of the communication?
- Who is the intended audience?

This chapter will address these questions and more. It highlights the dos and don'ts of communicating evaluation results, describes a best practice report formula that can be used to sustain momentum and change, and outlines key ingredients for a communication plan. We also discuss the use of storytelling in sharing the data.

Communication Basics

Communicating results effectively is a systematic process with specific rules and steps. Let's look closer at this process.

Make Communication Timely

Program results should be communicated as soon as they are known and packaged for presentation. The timing of communication is a critical factor in the program. Not sharing the results in a timely fashion can lead to a missed opportunity for well-timed improvement. Several questions about timing must be addressed:

- Is the audience prepared for the information when considering the content and other events?
- Are they expecting it?
- When is the best time to have the maximum impact on the audience?

Customize Your Communication to a Specific Audience

The communication will be more efficient if it is designed for each specific group's interests, needs, and expectations. The length, content, detail, and slant will vary with the audience. Figure 12-1 shows some specific audience groups, with the most common reasons for communicating results.

Communicating with a participant's immediate manager is important because they may need to support and allow employees to be involved in the program. An adequate ROI improves their commitment to employee learning while enhancing the learning team's credibility.

Participants also need feedback on the overall success of their efforts. However, this target audience is often overlooked, because it is assumed that they don't need to know.

Figure 12-1. Common Target Audiences

Primary Target Audience	Reason for Communication
Client or sponsor	To secure approval of results
All managers	To gain support for learning and talent development
Participants	To secure agreement with the issues, create the desire to be involved, and improve the results and quality of data
Top executives	To enhance the credibility of the learning and talent development team
Immediate managers of participants	To reinforce the application and impact and build support for the program
Talent development team	To drive action for improvement
Facilitators	To see the results of their work
HR executive	To show the complete results of the program
Evaluation team	To underscore the importance of measuring results
All employees	To demonstrate accountability for expenditures
Prospective participants	To market future programs

The learning and development team members should also receive information about virtual learning program results. And, depending on reporting relationships, HR may also be included. For small teams, the individual conducting the evaluation may be the same person who coordinated the effort. For larger departments, the evaluation may be implemented by a separate function. In either case, the team needs detailed information about the program's effectiveness so that they can make adjustments if the program is repeated.

Select the Mode of Communication Carefully

Depending on the group, one medium may be more effective than another, so it is important to select the appropriate medium to communicate the results. Figure 12-2 illustrates the most common options for communicating results.

For example, some groups may appreciate in-person meetings over special reports, whereas sending a brief summary to senior management will likely be more effective than a full-blown evaluation report. The increased use of video and visual communications may mean certain audiences expect to receive results using this medium. Infographics highlighting key data or smartly styled e-books that share the data story are examples of sharing data visually. Short-form reels that point to the most important results, longer-form prerecorded video overviews, or live-streaming video with real-time Q&A are ways to use video to share results.

Figure 12-2. Options for Communicating Results

Detailed Reports	Brief Reports	Online Reporting	Mass Publications	Live Presentations (online or in-person)
• Impact study • Case study (internal) • Case study (external) • Major article • Whitepaper	• Executive summary • Slide overview • One-page summary • Brochure • Infographic	• Website • Email • Blog • Video (prerecorded) • Social media	• Announcement • Bulletin • Newsletter • Brief article • E-book	• Executive briefing • Management meeting • Staff town hall • Team gathering

Keep Communication Neutral

It's important for the evaluator to remain neutral and unbiased when sharing the information. Let the results inform as to whether the program hit the mark. Separate fact from fiction and replace opinions with data-driven statements. Audiences that view communications from the learning and talent development team with skepticism may be on the lookout for biased information and opinions. If boastful statements turn off individuals, the content of the communication will be lost. Observable, believable facts carry more weight than extreme claims.

Include Testimonials

Testimonials are more effective if they come from individuals with audience credibility. Perceptions are strongly influenced by others, particularly by those who are admired or respected. Testimonials about virtual learning program results, when solicited from people who are generally respected in the organization, can have a strong impact on the effectiveness of the message. They can usually be collected from participants at each evaluation level: reaction, learning, application, and impact. It's easy to quickly capture these testimonials via chat, whiteboard, or a short-answer poll question during the course of the virtual program.

Be Flexible

Look for ways to include evaluation reporting through the timing and forums of other organizational reports; a special communication sent at an unusual time may create more work than it's worth. The content should also be consistent with organizational practices.

Even if the results aren't as expected, make sure to continue sending information to any group, such as senior management, that regularly receives communication. If results (such as a negative ROI) are omitted, it might leave the impression that the team is reporting only good results, which will harm credibility.

Use Visuals

Whether you capture results using an infographic or a dashboard, visuals can be a good way to create interest in what you share. A visual document can be distributed before a meeting or presentation or as a handout for afterward. It could also be included as part of a more detailed report, as described further along in this chapter. Figure 12-3 shows a dashboard covering a combination of data from Levels 1 and 3, as well as Level 4.[1]

Figure 12-3. Example of a Virtual Learning Dashboard Report

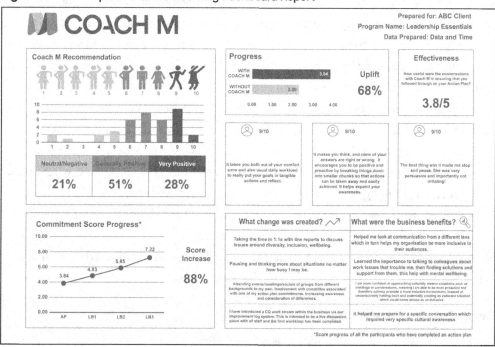

Use Communication to Drive Improvement

Because information is collected at different points during the process, providing feedback enables groups to take action and make adjustments if needed. As a result, the quality and timeliness of communication is critical. Even after the evaluation is completed, communication is necessary to make sure the target audience fully understands the results achieved as well as how the results may be enhanced in future programs or in the current program, if it is still operational. This is the key to making important adjustments at all phases of the project.

Use Storytelling

Unlike more traditional commentaries on business results, design thinking presumes that numbers cannot tell the whole story and that other means of communication are required to define and articulate the results. The design thinking approach believes that stories are uniquely useful in their ability to bring people onto the same page, organize information, and present it in an efficient and accessible manner.

Stories foster empathy and connectedness, because they prioritize information and objectives by providing a clear beginning, middle, and end. The narrative structure of a story is a teaching tool that can make complex data or relationships more accessible to an audience. Because the important ideas are set in a metaphor that people can easily understand, both storytellers and listeners can move past arcane details and focus on the problem at hand. The immediacy of the story helps people track the important relationships while empathizing with the subject. This allows for a richer experience and fosters greater insight into the nature of the program, its place in the organization, and how the choices of the participants contribute to its success.[2]

Why tell stories? The simple reason is that they work. According to author and trainer Paul Smith, there are 10 compelling reasons to tell stories; here are eight of them:

- Storytelling is simple.
- Storytelling is timeless.
- Stories are contagious.
- Stories are easier to remember.
- Stories inspire.
- Stories appeal to all types of learners.
- Stories fit in the workplace, where most of the learning happens.
- Storytelling shows respect for the audience.[3]

It's important to use a logical structure to develop stories. Although the structure can vary, Figure 12-4 presents an efficient checklist that is appropriate for most stories.

Figure 12-4. Story Structure Checklist

Hook	❑ Why should I listen to this story?
Content	❑ Where and when did it happen? ❑ Who is the hero? (Are they relatable?) ❑ What do they want? (Is that worthy?)
Challenge	❑ What is the problem or opportunity? (Relevant?)
Conflict	❑ What did the hero do about it? (Honest struggle?)
Resolution	❑ How did it turn out in the end?
Lesson	❑ What did you learn?
Recommended Action	❑ What do you want me to do?

Adapted from Smith (2012)

The Cautions of Communicating Results

Communications can go astray or miss the mark. Several cautions should be observed early and often in the process. Here are four critical ones.

Don't Hide the Results

The least desired communication action is doing nothing. Communicating results is almost as important as producing results. Getting results without communicating them is like planting a flower and not watering it. By not sharing the findings from your virtual learning program, you can cause the organization to miss out on a key opportunity to make adjustments and bring about the desired change.

Don't Overlook the Political Aspects of Communication

Communication is one of those issues that can cause major problems. Because the results of a virtual program may be closely linked to political issues within an organization, communicating them may upset some while pleasing others. If certain individuals do not receive the information, or if it is delivered inconsistently between groups, problems can quickly surface. The information must not only be understood; issues relating to fairness, quality, and political correctness make it crucial that the communication be constructed and delivered effectively to all key individuals.

Don't Skimp on the Recommendations

Recommendations are probably one of the most critical issues—they are the main conduit to change. However, sometimes recommendations are simply given as an afterthought or skipped altogether. The best recommendations include specific, action-oriented steps based on conclusions drawn from the evaluation study, which are then discussed with key stakeholders for buy-in and ownership. The point is to collaborate with stakeholders so they can internalize the results and necessary actions.

Don't Ignore the Audience's Bias

Opinions are difficult to change, and a negative opinion toward a program or team may not be swayed simply by presenting the facts. However, facts may strengthen the opinions held by those who already support the virtual learning program because they reinforce their position and provide a defense they can use in discussions with others. A project team with a high level of credibility and respect may have a relatively easy time communicating results. Low credibility, on the other hand, can create problems when a team is trying to be persuasive.

The Complete Report

The type of report a learning and talent development team issues should depend on the degree of detail and information presented to the various target audiences. Brief summaries of program results with appropriate charts may be sufficient for some communication efforts. In other situations, particularly those involving major programs requiring extensive funding, a detailed evaluation report may be best. A complete and comprehensive impact study report is usually necessary at least in the early uses of the approach in this book. This report can then be used as the basis for sharing more streamlined information with specific audiences. Figure 12-5 offers a formula for creating a report that effectively conveys program results. It has all the necessary ingredients to communicate outcomes in the best possible way.

Figure 12-5. Results Report Format

General Information • Background: What were the needs that precipitated the virtual learning program? • Why was this program selected? • Objectives of study: What are the goals and targets for this program? • What are the intended results? • Opening story
Methodology for Impact Study • Levels of evaluation: Describe the evaluation framework to set the stage for showing the results. • ROI process: Briefly describe the process that was used. • Collecting data: Which methods were used to collect data, and why? Also, when was data collected? • Isolating the effects of the program: Which methods were used to isolate the effects of the intervention, and why? • Converting data to monetary values: Which methods were used to convert data to money, and why?
Data Analysis How was data analyzed?
Results General Information
Response Profile Include demographics of the population that responded or participated in the evaluation.
Results: Reaction and Planned Action • Data sources • Data summary • Key issues
Results: Learning • Data sources • Data summary • Key issues

Figure 12-5. *(cont.)*

Results: Application and Implementation • Data sources • Data summary • Key issues
Results: Impact • Data sources • Data summary • Key issues
Costs of the Virtual Learning Program—Direct and Indirect
Results: ROI Calculation and What It Means
Results: Intangible Measures
Relevant Story, If Feasible
Barriers and Enablers This section of the report can be a powerful mechanism to lead into conclusions and recommendations. What obstacles were experienced that kept the organization from experiencing the kind of results it wanted? If barriers were noted, action items should be developed to minimize them in the future for the organization.
Conclusions Summarize key findings from the data.
Recommendations Based on the conclusions, what changes are needed? What are stakeholders willing to do?

While the impact study report is an effective, thorough way to present ROI data, several cautions are in order. Because this report documents the success of a virtual learning program involving other individuals, credit for the success must go completely to those involved—the program's participants and their immediate managers. Their performance generated the success.

The methodology should be quickly explained, along with the assumptions made in the analysis. The reader should easily see how the values were developed and the specific steps followed to make the process more conservative, credible, and accurate. Detailed statistical analyses, if used, should be placed in an appendix. This report can be condensed into an executive summary of three to five pages or even a one-page summary with infographics (as shown in Figure 12-3).

Using Meetings

Meetings can provide a fertile ground for telling the virtual learning program's story and communicating the results. Along the chain of command, staff meetings are held to review progress, discuss current problems, and distribute information. These meetings can provide an excellent forum for discussing the results achieved in a program relating to the group's activities. Program results can also be sent to executives for use in a staff meeting, or a member of the evaluation team can attend and present the information.

Regular meetings with management groups are a common practice. Typically, discussions focus on items that might help work units, so a discussion of the program and its results would be easily integrated into the regular meeting format. A few organizations have also initiated the use of periodic meetings for all key stakeholders, where a project leader reviews progress and discusses the next steps. Including a few highlights from interim program results in these meetings can be helpful in building interest, commitment, and support for the program.

Presentation of Results to Senior Management

Perhaps one of the most challenging and stressful types of communication is presenting an impact study to the senior management team, which also serves as the client for a project. The challenge is convincing this highly skeptical and critical group that outstanding results have been achieved (assuming they have) in a reasonable timeframe, while also addressing salient points and making sure the managers understand the process.

Two potential reactions can create problems. First, if the results are very impressive (high ROI), it may be difficult to convince the managers to accept the data as credible. On the other extreme, if the data is negative, it's important to ensure that managers don't overreact and look for someone to blame. Figure 12-6 presents several guidelines to help ensure this process is planned and executed properly.

Figure 12-6. Guidelines for the Executive Briefing

Purpose of the Meeting:	
• Create awareness and understanding of ROI.	• Drive improvement from results.
• Build support for the ROI Methodology.	• Cultivate effective use of the ROI Methodology.
• Communicate results of study.	
Use These Ground Rules:	
• Do not distribute the impact study until the end of the meeting.	• Spend less time on the lower levels of evaluation data.
• Be precise and to the point.	• Present the data with a strategy in mind.
• Avoid jargon and unfamiliar terms.	
Follow This Presentation Sequence:	
1. Describe the program, and explain why it is being evaluated.	7. Show the costs.
2. Present the methodology process.	8. Present the ROI.
3. Present the reaction and learning data.	9. Show the intangibles.
4. Present the application data.	10. Review the credibility of the data.
5. List the barriers to and enablers of success.	11. Summarize the conclusions.
6. Address the business impact.	12. Present the recommendations.

Routine Communication Tools

An internal, routine publication—such as a newsletter, a magazine, a newspaper, or an electronic message—is one way to share program results with all employees or stakeholders. The content can have a significant impact if it is communicated appropriately; however, the scope should be limited to general-interest articles, announcements, and interviews.

Results communicated this way must be important enough to arouse general interest. For example, a story with the headline "New Employee Onboarding Program Decreases Costs" will likely catch the attention of many readers, because they know about the program and can appreciate the relevance of the results. On the other hand, reports highlighting the accomplishments of a small group may not generate interest if the audience cannot relate to the results. Because results may not be achieved until weeks or even months after the program is completed, communicating results is a way to keep people interested in the program. This may keep them motivated to continue the virtual learning program or introduce similar ones in the future.

Stories about those involved in a virtual program and the results they have achieved can help create a favorable image. Employees see that the organization is investing resources to improve performance and prepare for the future. This type of story also provides information about a program that people may not know about and generates desire for others to participate. Public recognition of program participants who deliver exceptional performances can enhance employee engagement and drive them to excel.

Optimize Results: Using Black Box Thinking to Increase Funding

An instructional designer, along with the entire learning and talent development team, must use business evaluation for maximum value. This means using results to make improvements. If a virtual program is not as successful as it needs to be, the data collected usually indicates what must change to make it better. If it is successful, the data also shows what can be changed to make it more successful. Optimizing results is the goal, particularly when they include business impact and ROI data. Optimization increases the ROI, which helps funders and decision makers decide where to invest in the future, such as allocating more budget to a particular area. The challenge is making continuous improvements that lead to optimization that leads to allocation. This is the eighth and final step in the evaluation process.

Process Improvement Is the Key

With the intense competition for resources, especially those related to technology, it is important to show the value of virtual learning projects to key funders and supporters.

Very credible and unmistakable results make a great case for maintaining or increasing funding. However, it starts with the issue of process improvement, as data is collected and used to make changes to improve the program. Whether the virtual program is delivering the desired results or not, the challenge is to make it even better, using the results and increasing the ROI. Even with competitive funding situations, you can keep or improve your budget. Figure 12-7 shows this connection between the evaluation and allocation of funds.

Figure 12-7. Evaluation, Optimization, and Allocation

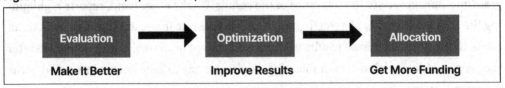

Learning From Failure: Black Box Thinking

If a virtual learning program fails to deliver the desired results, the reason for the failure must be uncovered and adjustments must be made. We can learn a lot from black box thinking—which is derived from the idea of the black box on an airplane—and Matthew Syed's book *Black Box Thinking: Why Most People Never Learn From Their Mistakes—but Some Do* brings into focus the power and payoff of learning from failure.[4]

Failure is something we all have to endure from time to time, whether it is missing a deadline, flunking an exam, or even the local football team losing a match. Sometimes, failure can be far more serious—for doctors and others working in safety-critical industries, getting it wrong can have deadly consequences.

As mentioned in the beginning of this book, in learning and talent development programs, we know that:

1. 60 to 90 percent of job-related learning is wasted (not used on the job, although we want it to be used). The culprit: failure in the system.
2. Most learning and talent development functions do not measure success at the levels desired by top executives (Levels 4 and 5). The culprit: fear of results (perceived failure).

The failure of learning programs (or the fear of failure) is serious, although it may seem trivial. After all, what will it hurt if participants:

- Attend a program when they are not in a role to use the skills and knowledge?
- Are not interested in the content and are not motivated to use it?
- Choose not to learn the content?
- Fail to use what they learned on the job?

This is not so important unless you examine the numbers for the entire organization. We have a dozen clients with more than $1 billion each in their learning and talent development budgets. If 50 percent of participants do not use what they learn, this is a waste of more than $6 billion in these 12 organizations alone. Now, that's important.

We cover up mistakes, not only to protect ourselves from others but to protect us from ourselves. Studies have demonstrated that humans have a sophisticated ability to delete failures from our memory. Far from learning from mistakes, we edit them out of the official autobiographies we keep in our own heads.

We offer a different perspective—we need to redefine our relationship with failure, as individuals and as organizations. This is the most important step on the road to a high-performance learning organization. Only by redefining failure will we unleash progress, creativity, and resilience.

Making Adjustments in Virtual Learning Programs

The good news is that the causes of failure (or disappointing results) can be identified, and adjustments can be made at different points in the cycle. These adjustments are all aimed at making the virtual program more successful—moving it from mediocre or negative results to delivering very positive results. Even if the results are positive, adjustments can still make improvements. This helps us with the prospects of improved funding, but will also address other important issues.

Stakeholders may be concerned that disappointing results will reflect unfavorably on them and their individual performance. Some fear this outcome will lead to budget cuts or the decision to discontinue the program. This is not necessarily the case. The principal issue is the reason for the ROI evaluation. If you wait for the funder, sponsor, or top executive to ask for the results, then you are at a disadvantage, with a short timeline. And if the virtual learning program was not properly designed to achieve the desired results, you will have missed the opportunity to make the needed adjustments.

In addition, the request for results could place you on the defensive if you're not already prepared to share them, and that's not a good place to be. You always want to be on the offensive, be proactive, and drive accountability. This positions you in a much better situation for sponsors to react to negative data. In this scenario, you are initiating the evaluation of the virtual program to ensure that it is delivering results. If it's not, adjustments are made. The continuous process of evaluating and improving virtual learning programs is the best way to overcome the fear of negative results.

It's also possible that the virtual learning program will need to be discontinued. (Although, this shouldn't happen if the steps described in this book are followed properly.) Perhaps the wrong audience was involved, the wrong solution was implemented, or the program was not aligned to business measures. If there is no way to adjust or modify the program to deliver positive results, then it is best to eliminate it.

Influencing Budget Allocation

An important goal of evaluation is to influence funding for virtual learning programs. Whether the objective is to minimize budget reductions, maintain the current budget, or increase the budget, this is probably the most important outcome of a results-based approach. We witnessed some organizations increase the learning and talent development budget during the COVID-19 pandemic, even as budgets were being cut in other places. This is moving beyond avoiding budget cuts or maintaining existing budgets to increasing budgets in the face of reductions in other areas. This is powerful, and it is a culmination of designing for value through the process.

At this point, it's helpful to revisit the concept of cost and investments. An organization has many activities that represent costs, and the perception executives have about these costs becomes critical. If executives see the activity as an investment with a positive ROI, then they may be reluctant to minimize or reduce it. If the program has no apparent impact, or there is no credible data to show its effects, then executives may be tempted to reduce, minimize, control, or even eliminate it. Figure 12-8 summarizes the cost versus investment issue. It's a simple but powerful concept.

Figure 12-8. Cost vs. Investment Perception

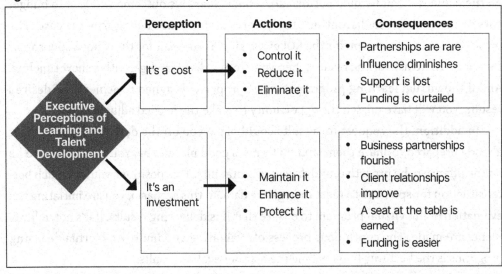

Exercise

How do top executives who provide funding for learning and talent development see these virtual learning programs in your organization? Do they see learning as an investment or an expense?

If learning is not perceived as an investment, you could easily see ups and downs in funding, where budgets are cut during tough times and increased during lean times, often wreaking havoc with programs that are aimed at delivering value. To convince executives that learning is an investment, you must show an ROI calculation for a few of the major programs.

Competition for Funding

The competition for funds is fierce. The money in the learning and talent development budget is often desired by other departments in the organization. If talent development funding is significant, with facilities and many staff members, then it really becomes a target for operations, marketing, and support executives. Although they may already have significant budgets, marketing and IT, for example, might still want to claim part of the learning budget. This causes a dilemma from the perspective of the top executive. IT and marketing typically show the ROI of major projects, whereas HR and learning and talent development rarely show the value of what they are doing. As a popular *Harvard Business Review* article suggested, "Few HR departments have felt compelled to make the case that any of their practices could drive profits. Many don't calculate ROI, even though other functions have been expected to do so for at least a generation. That just feeds into business leaders' view of HR as a cost center where the goal is always to cut, cut, cut."[5]

The chief talent development officer (CTDO) or chief learning officer (CLO) must make sure there is a mechanism in place to convince executives that the current budget is a good investment, and this is accomplished with data. And this requires impact and ROI data, not data from Levels 3, 2, or 1, and certainly not from Level 0.

A retired CLO from IBM once told us that when he was promoted to head of learning, he was warned that he needed to bring data to the budget meeting to get his budget approved because everybody brings data. You must have convincing data showing that you are making a difference and that your proposed budget contributes to that. The more credible and specific the data, in terms of impact and finance, the more convincing your story and the more likely your budget is approved.

Anxiety and Downturns Translate Into Cost Reduction

When there is a downturn in the economy, executives look for budgets that they can easily cut. If they see it as an expense or a cost, it's easy to cut. If they see it as an investment, they may not cut it. You want them to resist the temptation to cut learning budgets. Also, as we have noticed in the global economy, when there is uncertainty, anxiety, or volatility with pandemics, wars, politics, and terrorism, there is a tendency to prepare for the unknown by having a tighter ship and leaner budget. This translates into significant budget controls and sometimes budget cuts. We even have witnessed companies with record profits still cutting budgets because of the uncertain future. They are trimming the parts that don't add value—those items that are "nice to do" instead of "absolute must-dos." Without data showing that HR and learning and development make a difference, it is difficult even to argue to keep the budget.

The COVID-19 pandemic has had a lasting effect on many organizations, not only in terms of keeping budgets in check but in demanding up-front accountability before new projects are implemented. The concept of forecasting ROI is now common in many organizations, even for learning and talent development. We have had several learning and development managers say that they cannot implement a major project unless they provide an ROI forecast. This is a tremendous change from what we have experienced previously.

Shifting the Budget

When virtual learning programs across the learning and talent development function are evaluated to ROI, some interesting results can materialize. For example, online soft skills programs often deliver a much higher ROI. Soft skills—such as leadership development, management development, team leader onboarding, communications, coaching, and team building—can have high impact and high ROI, because they influence individuals who have a team of people reporting to them. If one person learns to improve the performance of a team of 20 people, there is a multiplicative effect. Training one person affects 20 individuals, and improves their productivity, quality, and time measures. If an executive or a CFO sees this, they may not understand it quickly, but they'll get it after an explanation.

Armed with this data, it is easier to make a case that organizations need virtual soft skills programs as well as online technical and hard skills training. And this may alter the allocation of budgets for soft skills training. After all, soft skills are what create sustainable companies, the most admired organizations, the most innovative organizations, and the greatest places to work. Great organizations are built by people working with other people using soft skills. This shift can have an important consequence, but only if you have the data to show it.

Next Steps

Telling the story of your virtual learning program evaluation is crucial. If it is not executed adequately, the full impact of the results will not be recognized, and the study may be a waste of time. The first part of this chapter began with sharing the basics and general dos and don'ts for communicating results, which can serve as a guide for any significant communication effort. We discussed the target audiences, along with the most commonly used media for communicating program results. The communication process must be planned and properly executed to produce the desired outcomes.

Additionally, this chapter covered the last two steps in the ROI Methodology, which involve using the results of an evaluation and improving the virtual learning program to optimize the ROI. With this increased ROI, the allocation of funds can be influenced. Ultimately, you can influence the funding for learning and talent development, but only if you have credible data to show you made a difference and are delivering a positive ROI for major virtual learning programs.

This chapter is also the capstone of the philosophy of the book. It details why a serious approach to evaluating your virtual learning programs is needed. You have serious budgets, serious challenges, and serious consequences. You must show the value of your programs. The approach is not to measure your way to a positive ROI for your virtual learning programs but to design the entire process to deliver ROI. Remember, from an organizational perspective, if application and impact do not occur, the virtual program is a waste. The definition of the success of learning has shifted—it's not when learning has occurred, but when virtual learning is used and has an impact. This new definition of success represents a mind shift for many stakeholders.

The learning design and evaluation approach presented in this book requires ongoing investment and funding to continually upgrade technology needs and upskill facilitators and designers to stay on top of the changes. By effectively designing virtual learning programs that lead to application and impact, and telling the story of that impact, we can create an ongoing, sustainable, successful virtual learning environment.

When it comes to delivering results from virtual learning, hope is not a strategy, luck is not a factor, and doing nothing is not an option. The importance of accountability for virtual learning programs has shifted. Change is inevitable; progress is optional. It's up to each of us to make sure virtual learning delivers the desired results. For more details on any of the 50 techniques, please visit the authors' website or contact us directly. We wish you much success!

Acknowledgments

From Cindy

Partnering with the incredible team of global experts—Jack, Patti, and Emma—has been an amazing learning experience. Our collaborative approach and fruitful discussions were inspiring on many levels. It was a true team effort, and for that I am grateful. A special thank you goes to Hope Nicholas with ROI Institute, who kept us moving along when we needed it most. Her organizational skills are top-notch!

In addition, thanks to everyone on the ATD Press team who believed in our team and this project, especially Justin Brusino and Alexandria Clapp, who helped us solidify our original thoughts, and Melissa Jones, who helped us find a consistent voice through her editing expertise. I appreciated their encouragement and support along the way.

Finally, a special thank you to my ever-patient husband, Bobby, who read through every draft, and my young son, Jonathan, who learned about the book writing process as he asked a million questions along the way. I'm forever grateful for them both.

From Emma

It's been such a pleasure to be involved in this publication working with a talented team of authors. Heartfelt thanks to Cindy, Jack, and Patti for being wonderful to collaborate with; it's been so rewarding to learn from you and craft this book together. Special thank you also to Hope Nicholas at ROI Institute who shepherded us so calmly and efficiently throughout the writing and editing process. Thank you Hope. You are a marvel.

And thank you to the dedicated team at ATD Press, led by Melissa Jones who has been steering the project with exceptional editing and an eye for detail. The team made the whole process a joy.

I couldn't have done this without the support of my amazing team, and most importantly Cherry who keeps the business running so I can spend time writing. Thank you, Cherry.

And a final thank you to my clients who inspire me to keep experimenting and pushing the boundaries of what's possible with learning transfer.

From Patti and Jack

We would like to acknowledge the great work of our editor, Hope Nicholas, director of publications at ROI Institute, who kept all four authors on track. Additionally, we are always supported by our entire outstanding team at ROI Institute. The success that we've had, and the new techniques that we have uncovered, all came from our wonderful clients who invited us into their organizations and worked with us, as we explored and experimented with all types of approaches to make things work. Fortunately, they did! Finally, we appreciate the ongoing support from the ATD Press team. Melissa Jones made this a much better book. Thanks, Melissa.

From Patti: It is always exciting to create content worthy of publication—and this content certainly is. Investing in virtual learning is at an all-time high. Yet, the satisfaction with and the impact of that investment is marginal at best. Working with and leveraging the expertise of Cindy and Emma to help organizations design and deliver virtual training that delivers real results has been a joy. They are amazing collaborators, and I have learned much from them. In addition, as always, working with Jack gives me my energy. He encourages me and challenges me to be my best. More than that, however, he makes me laugh every single day, as he did throughout this project. Thank you for your ongoing love and friendship, Jack.

From Jack: I would like to acknowledge the tremendous influence and impact that Patti has had in our organization, work, and evaluation system. In terms of the evaluation and measurement methodology, she is an outstanding consultant, a top-notch facilitator, a sought-after keynote speaker, an amazing writer, and a tenacious researcher. Most of all, she is my best friend and loving spouse.

Appendix: Technique Selection Criteria Worksheet

The Technique Selection Criteria Worksheet is intended to be a helpful job aid you can quickly reference when considering whether to use a particular technique. If you're curious about how we rate each technique, we've compiled our composite ratings here.

Technique	Costs	Extent of Technology	Effectiveness	Participant Time	Participant's Manager Involvement	Time of Others	Proven	Ease of Implementation	Ease of Use	Innovation
1. Define virtual learning	1	1	5	1	2	4	5	3	5	1
2. Design for interaction, engagement, and application	2	4	5	1	1	3	5	3	4	4
3. Select the right platform	2	2	4	1	1	3	5	4	4	1
4. Prepare facilitators to support learning transfer	2	1	5	2	2	3	4	3	3	2
5. Send more than a calendar invite	1	3	5	2	1	2	5	5	4	2
6. Set participant expectations in advance	1	1	5	3	1	2	5	5	4	2
7. Clearly communicate objectives	1	1	4	2	1	3	4	5	4	2
8. Create an evaluation plan	1	2	4	1	1	1	5	2	4	2
9. Create job aids and application guides	2	3	4	1	1	1	4	3	3	2
10. Create custom self-objectives	1	2	4	4	2	2	4	2	3	2
11. Create a kickoff event and include managers	2	2	4	4	4	4	4	3	3	3
12. Design a manager guide to accompany the learning experience	2	1	4	1	4	4	3	4	4	3
13. Ensure easy access to application and impact data	3	3	4	1	1	1	4	3	4	3

Criteria and Ranking Scale

Criteria and Ranking Scale

Technique	Costs	Extent of Technology	Effectiveness	Participant Time	Participant's Manager Involvement	Time of Others	Proven	Ease of Implementation	Ease of Use	Innovation
14. Use a commitment contract with participants	1	1	3	4	3	2	3	3	4	1
15. Use the platform's welcome message to reinforce the program's purpose	1	3	3	2	1	1	5	5	4	3
16. Create a warm welcome	1	2	4	2	1	1	5	4	5	3
17. Create immediate interaction	1	3	4	1	1	1	5	5	5	4
18. Include WIIFM at the start	1	1	4	1	1	1	4	5	5	2
19. Make it social	1	2	4	1	1	1	5	4	5	4
20. Select activities for maximum involvement	1	2	4	1	1	1	5	5	5	3
21. Ask questions with intent and inclusion	1	1	5	1	1	1	5	5	5	4
22. Use the tools creatively	1	4	4	1	1	1	5	4	4	4
23. Use visuals to keep attention	1	3	4	1	1	1	5	4	4	3
24. Use realistic scenarios	2	3	4	1	1	1	5	4	4	2
25. Incorporate formative feedback	1	3	4	1	1	1	4	4	4	2
26. Include self-reflection time	2	1	4	4	1	1	4	4	4	3
27. Teach to application and impact	1	2	5	4	1	1	5	5	4	2
28. Integrate application activities	2	2	5	4	1	1	5	4	4	3
29. Connect content between sessions	2	2	4	4	1	1	5	4	4	3
30. Have action plan presentations	2	1	5	5	2	1	4	4	4	3
31. Finish with a call to action	1	1	5	4	1	1	4	4	4	2
32. Follow up on action plans	2	2	3	2	5* 1†	1	3	4	4	2
	*If the manager is following up †If the buddy is another resource									
33. One-on-one coaching after the program	4	1	5	2	5* 1†	5‡ 1§	5	2	4	2
	*If manager is the coach †If the coach is another resource ‡If an external coach is used §If technology is used									
34. Manager encouragement and involvement using feedback loops	1	1	3	2	5	1	3	*	2	1
	*Depends on culture									

Criteria and Ranking Scale

Technique	Costs	Extent of Technology	Effectiveness	Participant Time	Participant's Manager Involvement	Time of Others	Proven	Ease of Implementation	Ease of Use	Innovation
35. Group coaching after the program and implementation phase	1	1	3	2	5* 1†	2	2	3	4	2
*If manager is the coach † If the coach is another resource										
36. Apply nudging techniques	2	3	2	1	1	1	2	3	2	3
37. Observation sessions with an on-the-job trainer	2	1	3	2	5* 1†	3	3	3	3	2
*If manager is the observer † If the observer is another resource										
38. Host a lessons-learned meeting once participants have used the content	1	1	2	1	1	2	3	4	4	1
39. Meaningful business projects with lessons-learned graduation	1	1	2	3	2	1	3	3	4	1
40. Share success with other participants and key lessons learned	1	1	1	2	1	2	3	4	4	1
41. Hold a contest based on achieving success for application and impact	1	1	3	4	2	1	2	4	4	1
42. Leverage chatbots for learning transfer	3	5	4	4	1	1	4	4	4	5
43. Augment your chatbot with human coaching	4	4	5	4	2	3	4	4	4	5
44. Use coaching videos	1	3	3	3	1	1	3	4	4	2
45. Apps and guided support software to enable use	4	4	4	2	1	1	3	1	3	2
46. Use automated reminders and nudges for application and impact	3	3	2	1	1	1	2	2	3	3
47. Use selfies to share	1	2	1	1	1	1	2	5	5	1
48. Use social media groups or platforms to network for encouragement, support, and enablement	1	2	3	2	1	1	3	5	5	2
49. Post-program recorded content reviews or application tips	1	2	2	3	1	1	3	4	3	2
50. Use AI to gauge the effectiveness of communication in virtual conversations	4	5	4	4	1	1	3	1	2	5

Notes

Chapter 1

1. Association for Talent Development (ATD), *2022 State of the Industry* (Alexandria, VA: ATD Press, 2022).

2. Adapted from C. Udell, *Learning Everywhere: How Mobile Content Strategies are Transforming Training* (Nashville, TN: Rockbench Publishing and Alexandria, VA: ATD Press, 2012).

3. J.J. Phillips, *Handbook of Training Evaluation and Measurement Methods*, 1st ed. (Houston, TX: Gulf Publishing, 1983).

4. P. Ketter, "Celebrating 70 years of TD Magazine," *TD*, July 1, 2016, td.org/magazines/td -magazine/celebrating-70-years-of-td-magazine.

5. C. Huggett, "The State of Virtual Training 2022," Cindy Huggett, December 7, 2021, cindyhuggett.com/blog/2022sovt.

6. D. Zack, *Singletasking: Get More Done—One Thing at a Time* (Oakland, CA: Berrett-Koehler Publishers, 2015).

7. T. Brown, *Change By Design: How Design Thinking Transforms Organizations and Inspires Innovation* (New York: Harper Business, 2009).

8. I. Mootee, *Design Thinking for Strategic Innovation: What They Can't Teach You at Business or Design School* (Hoboken, NJ: Wiley, 2013).

9. Mootee, *Design Thinking for Strategic Innovation.*

10. P.P. Phillips and J.J. Phillips, *Business Case For Learning: Using Design Thinking to Deliver Business Results and Increase the Investment in Talent Development* (Alexandria, VA: ATD Press; West Chester, PA: HRDQ, 2017).

Chapter 2

1. L. Freifeld, "Training Top 100 Best Practice: Edward Jones' Branch Office Administrator Onboarding," *Training*, October 26, 2021, trainingmag.com/training-top-100-best -practice-edward-jones-branch-office-administrator-onboarding.

2. J.J. Phillips and P.P. Phillips, *Measuring for Success: What CEOs Really Think About Learning Investments* (Alexandria, VA: ATD Press, 2009).

3. J.J. Phillips and P.P. Phillips, *The Consultant's Guide to Results-Driven Business Proposals: How to Write Proposals That Forecast Impact and ROI* (New York: McGraw-Hill, 2010).

Chapter 3

1. D.G. Robinson, J.C. Robinson, J.J. Phillips, P.P. Phillips, and D. Handshaw, *Performance Consulting*, 3rd ed. (Oakland, CA: Berrett-Koehler, 2015).

2. W. Rothwell, C.K. Hohne, and S.B. King, *Performance Improvement*, 3rd ed. (New York: Routledge, 2017).

3. R. Kaufman and I. Guerra-Lopez, *Needs Assessment for Organizational Success* (Alexandria, VA: ATD Press, 2013).

4. R.A. Defelice, "How Long Does It Take to Develop Training? New Question, New Answers," ATD blog, January 13, 2021, td.org/insights/how-long-does-it-take-to-develop-training-new-question-new-answers.

5. C. Huggett, *Virtual Training Tools and Templates: An Action Guide to Live Online Learning* (Alexandria, VA: ATD Press, 2017).

Chapter 4

1. C. Huggett, *The Virtual Training Guidebook: How to Design, Deliver, and Implement LIve Online Learning* (Alexandria, VA: ATD Press, 2014).

2. Phillips and Phillips, *Business Case for Learning.*

Chapter 5

1. V. Combs, "Do You Spend 30% of Your Week in Meetings? Survey Says Many People Do," TechRepublic, January 14, 2022, techrepublic.com/article/do-you-spend-30-of-your-week-in-meetings-survey-says-many-people-do.

2. G. Mineo, "How to Get More People to Open Your Emails," HubSpot blog, June 11, 2021, blog.hubspot.com/marketing/get-more-email-opens-video.

3. Huggett, *Virtual Training Tools and Templates.*

Chapter 6

1. Huggett, "The State of Virtual Training 2022."

2. Microsoft, "Research Proves Your Brain Needs Breaks," Microsoft Work Trend Index Special Report, April 20, 2021, microsoft.com/en-us/worklab/work-trend-index/brain-research.

3. Huggett, "The State of Virtual Training 2022."

4. Adapted from Huggett, *Virtual Training Tools and Templates.*

5. S. Likens and D.L. Eckert, "How Virtual Reality Is Redefining Soft Skills Training," PwC, June 4, 2021, pwc.com/us/en/tech-effect/emerging-tech/virtual-reality-study.html.

6. D.A. Kolb, *Experiential Learning: Experience as the Source of Learning and Development* (Englewood Cliffs, NJ: Prentice Hall, 1984).

7. P.P. Phillips and J.J. Phillips, *Thirty Techniques to Design Virtual Learning to Deliver Impact and a Positive ROI* (Birmingham, AL: ROI Institute, 2020).

Chapter 7

1. E. Weber, *Turning Learning into Action: A Proven Methodology for Effective Transfer of Learning* (London: Kogan Page, 2014).

2. Weber, *Turning Learning into Action.*

3. E. Panadero, "A Review of Self-Regulated Learning: Six Models and Four Directions for Research," *Frontiers in Psychology* 8(2017), frontiersin.org/articles/10.3389/fpsyg.2017.00422.

4. D. Kahneman, *Thinking Fast and Slow* (New York: Farrar, Straus and Giroux, 2011).

5. N. Doige, *The Brain that Changes Itself* (New York: Viking Press, 2007).

6. M. Enzle and S. Anderson, "Surveillant Intentions and Intrinsic Motivations," *Journal of Personality and Social Psychology* 64(2): 257–263.

7. D. Pink, *Drive: The Surprising Truth About What Motivates Us* (New York: Riverhead Books, 2009).

8. Weber, *Turning Learning into Action.*

9. Weber, *Turning Learning into Action.*

10. M.W. Daudelin, "Learning From Experience Through Reflection," *Organizational Dynamics* 24(3), sciencedirect.com/science/article/abs/pii/S0090261696900042.

11. S. Levitt and S. Dubner, *Freakonomics: A Rogue Economist Explores the Hidden Side of Everything* (New York: William Morrow, 2009); D. Ariely, *Predictably Irrational: The Hidden Forces That Shape Our Decisions* (Toronto: HarperCollins, 2008); R. Thaler and C. Sunstein, *Nudge: Improving Decisions About Health, Wealth, and Happiness* (New Haven, CT: Yale University Press, 2008).

12. A. Pradhan, "Beyond Training: The Art of Nudging," Slideshare, AITD, June 6, 2019, slideshare.net/arunpradhan4/beyond-training-the-art-of-nudging.

13. M. Enzle and S. Anderson, "Surveillant Intentions and Intrinsic Motivations," *Journal of Personality and Social Psychology* 64(2): 257–263.

14. A. Edmondson, "Strategies for Learning From Failure," *Harvard Business Review*, April 2011, hbr.org/2011/04/strategies-for-learning-from-failure.

Chapter 8

1. To learn more, read the Bayer case study. ATD Case Study Team, "Bayer: Chatbot Coaching for Learning Transfer," ATD 10-Minute Case Studies, 2019, casebycase.td.org/bayer-chatbot-coaching-for-learning-transfer.

2. View an example video at youtu.be/2OMB-gjvN5M. E. Weber, "Thinking Creatively—Coach M," YouTube, November 26, 2017, youtu.be/2OMB-gjvN5M.

3. Phillips and Phillips, *Thirty Techniques.*

4. P.P. Phillips, J.J. Phillips, R. Ray, and H. Nicholas, *Proving the Value of Leadership Development: Real Studies from Top Leadership Development Providers.* (West Chester, PA: HRDQ, 2022).

Chapter 10

1. P.P. Phillips, J.J. Phillips, and B.C. Aaron, *Survey Basics* (Alexandria, VA: ATD Press, 2013).

Chapter 11

1. P.P. Phillips and J.J. Phillips, *Making Human Capital Analytics Work: Measuring the ROI of Human Capital Processes and Outcomes* (New York: McGraw-Hill, 2015).

2. P.B. Crosby, *Quality Is Free: The Art of Making Quality Certain: How to Manage Quality—So That It Becomes a Source of Profit for Your Business* (New York: McGraw-Hill, 1979).

3. J.J. Phillips, W. Brantley, and P.P. Phillips, *Project Management ROI: A Step-by-Step Guide for Measuring the Impact and ROI for Projects* (Hoboken, NJ: John Wiley and Sons, 2012).

Chapter 12

1. For a deeper explanation of the dashboard see TransferOfLearning.com/insights.

2. Mootee, *Design Thinking for Strategic Innovation*.

3. P. Smith, *Lead With a Story: A Guide to Crafting Business Narratives That Captivate, Convince, and Inspire* (New York: AMACOM, 2012). Used with permission.

4. M. Syed, *Black Box Thinking: Why Most People Never Learn from Their Mistakes—But Some Do* (New York: Portfolio, 2015).

5. P. Cappelli, "Why We Love to Hate HR . . . and What HR Can Do About It," *Harvard Business Review*, July 1, 2015.

Index

Page numbers followed by *f* and *t* refer to figures and tables respectively.

About the Authors

 **Cindy Huggett** is a pioneer in the field of online learning with more than 20 years of experience in providing virtual training solutions and more than 30 years in the world of talent development. She's a leading industry expert known for teaching thousands of training professionals how to design and deliver practical, engaging interactive online classes to today's global workforce through workshops, speaking, coaching, and consulting. Cindy partners with organizations to upskill facilitators, maximize online learning design, and facilitate actionable learning solutions that meet today's needs and leverage tomorrow's technologies.

Cindy has written several acclaimed books on virtual training, including *The Facilitator's Guide to Immersive, Blended, and Hybrid Learning*; *Virtual Training Tools and Templates: An Action Guide to Live Online Learning*; *The Virtual Training Guidebook: How to Design, Deliver, and Implement Live Online Learning*; and *Virtual Training Basics*. She's the co-author of two *Infoline* issues and a contributor to many other industry publications, including *TD* magazine and the third edition of *ATD's Handbook for Training and Talent Development*.

A sought-after conference speaker, Cindy has presented at the ATD International Conference & EXPO, TechKnowledge, Training, DevLearn, TechLearn, Learning, and the annual SHRM Conference. She also delivers ATD's Master Trainer and Master Instructional Designer Programs.

Cindy holds a master's degree in public and international affairs from the University of Pittsburgh and a bachelor's degree from James Madison University. She also has a Certified Professional in Learning and Performance (CPLP, now CPTD) designation. Cindy is a past member of the global ATD Board of Directors, was recognized by the *Triangle Business Journal* as a 40-Under-40 Award recipient, and co-founded a nonprofit organization to promote volunteering and community service in her local area. She's also a yoga teacher with a special focus on mobility for aging seniors.

You can reach Cindy at cindy@cindyhuggett.com.

Jack J. Phillips, PhD, is chair of the ROI Institute and a world-renowned expert on accountability, measurement, and evaluation. Jack provides consulting services for Fortune 500 companies and major global organizations. The author or editor of more than 100 books, he conducts workshops and presents at conferences around the world.

Jack has received several awards. In 2005, the Association for Talent Development awarded him its highest award, Distinguished Contribution to Workplace Learning and Development for his work on ROI. For three years, *Meeting News* recognized Jack as one of the 25 most influential leaders in the meetings and events industry based on his work on ROI. His work has been featured in the *Wall Street Journal*, *BusinessWeek*, and *Fortune* magazine, as well as several television programs and on CNN.

Jack's expertise in measurement and evaluation is based on more than 27 years of corporate experience in the aerospace, textile, metals, construction materials, and banking industries. He has served as training and development manager at two Fortune 500 firms, as senior human resource officer at two firms, as president of a regional bank, and as management professor at a major state university. Jack regularly consults with clients in manufacturing, service, and government organizations in more than 70 countries in North and South America, Europe, the Middle East, Africa, Australia, and Asia.

Jack has undergraduate degrees in electrical engineering, physics, and mathematics; a master's degree in decision sciences from Georgia State University; and a PhD in human resource management from the University of Alabama. He has served on the boards of several businesses, nonprofits, and associations, and served as a president of the International Society for Performance Improvement.

You can reach Jack at jack@roiinstitute.net.

Patti P. Phillips, PhD, is the CEO of ROI Institute, the leading source of ROI competency building, implementation support, networking, and research. As an author, researcher, consultant, and coach, Patti has helped organizations implement the ROI Methodology and measurement and evaluation to drive organizational change. Her work spans private, public, nonprofit, and nongovernmental organizations.

Patti serves as vice-chair of the board of trustees of the United Nations Institute for Training and Research. She is chair of the Institute for Corporate Productivity's People Analytics Board; senior advisor, human capital, for the Conference Board; and board member of the International Federation for Training and Development Organizations. Additionally, she serves as board chair for the Center for Talent Reporting (CTR) and is a fellow of the Association for Talent Development (ATD) Certification Institute. Patti is also on the UN System Staff College faculty in Turin, Italy. Her work has been reported on by CNBC and Euronews and published in more than a dozen business journals.

Patti's academic accomplishments include a bachelor's degree in education from Auburn University; a master's degree in public and private management from Birmingham Southern College, and a PhD in international development from the University of Southern Mississippi.

Patti, along with her husband, Jack Phillips, contributes to various journals and has authored books about measurement, evaluation, analytics, and ROI. In 2019, she and Jack received the Distinguished Contributor Award from the Center for Talent Reporting for their contribution to the measurement and management of human capital. In November 2019, Patti and Jack were named two of the top 50 coaches globally by the Thinkers 50 organization, and were finalists for the Marshall Goldsmith Distinguished Achievement Award for Coaching. Additionally, in May 2022, Patti and Jack received the Association for Talent Development's highest honor, the Thought Leader Award. Recipients of this award have contributed significant thought leadership to the talent development profession, which has had sustained impact over several years.

You can reach Patti at patti@roiinstitute.net.

 **Emma Weber** is CEO and founder of Lever–Transfer of Learning. Emma's firm belief is that the key aim of learning in the workplace is to create tangible business benefits. This is also the platform on which she has built her successful global business. Emma established Lever–Transfer of Learning to help organizations and their employees convert learning into effective action on the job. Under her guidance, Lever now delivers Turning Learning into Action (TLA) programs throughout 20 countries and in 12 languages.

Emma trains and mentors the Lever TLA team and has been coaching leaders and managers within Fortune 500 organizations for the last 20 years. Prior to starting her own business, Emma's first career was in retail buying and merchandising where she led teams in the UK and Middle East.

Emma is the author of *Turning Learning into Action: A Proven Methodology for Effective Transfer of Learning* (Kogan Page, 2014) and a co-author of *Making Change Work: How to Create Behavioral Change in Organizations to Drive Impact and ROI* (Kogan Page, 2016).

About ATD

The Association for Talent Development (ATD) is the world's largest association dedicated to those who develop talent in organizations. Serving a global community of members, customers, and international business partners in more than 100 countries, ATD champions the importance of learning and training by setting standards for the talent development profession.

Our customers and members work in public and private organizations in every industry sector. Since ATD was founded in 1943, the talent development field has expanded significantly to meet the needs of global businesses and emerging industries. Through the Talent Development Capability Model, education courses, certifications and credentials, memberships, industry-leading events, research, and publications, we help talent development professionals build their personal, professional, and organizational capabilities to meet new business demands with maximum impact and effectiveness.

One of the cornerstones of ATD's intellectual foundation, ATD Press offers insightful and practical information on talent development, training, and professional growth. ATD Press publications are written by industry thought leaders and offer anyone who works with adult learners the best practices, academic theory, and guidance necessary to move the profession forward.

We invite you to join our community. Learn more at td.org.